C-3945   CAREER EXAMINATION SERIES

This is your
PASSBOOK for...

Environmental Police Officer

Test Preparation Study Guide
Questions & Answers

COPYRIGHT NOTICE

This book is SOLELY intended for, is sold ONLY to, and its use is RESTRICTED to individual, bona fide applicants or candidates who qualify by virtue of having seriously filed applications for appropriate license, certificate, professional and/or promotional advancement, higher school matriculation, scholarship, or other legitimate requirements of education and/or governmental authorities.

This book is NOT intended for use, class instruction, tutoring, training, duplication, copying, reprinting, excerption, or adaptation, etc., by:

1) Other publishers
2) Proprietors and/or Instructors of "Coaching" and/or Preparatory Courses
3) Personnel and/or Training Divisions of commercial, industrial, and governmental organizations
4) Schools, colleges, or universities and/or their departments and staffs, including teachers and other personnel
5) Testing Agencies or Bureaus
6) Study groups which seek by the purchase of a single volume to copy and/or duplicate and/or adapt this material for use by the group as a whole without having purchased individual volumes for each of the members of the group
7) Et al.

Such persons would be in violation of appropriate Federal and State statutes.

PROVISION OF LICENSING AGREEMENTS – Recognized educational, commercial, industrial, and governmental institutions and organizations, and others legitimately engaged in educational pursuits, including training, testing, and measurement activities, may address request for a licensing agreement to the copyright owners, who will determine whether, and under what conditions, including fees and charges, the materials in this book may be used them. In other words, a licensing facility exists for the legitimate use of the material in this book on other than an individual basis. However, it is asseverated and affirmed here that the material in this book CANNOT be used without the receipt of the express permission of such a licensing agreement from the Publishers. Inquiries re licensing should be addressed to the company, attention rights and permissions department.

All rights reserved, including the right of reproduction in whole or in part, in any form or by any means, electronic or mechanical, including photocopying, recording, or by any information storage and retrieval system, without permission in writing from the Publisher.

Copyright © 2025 by
National Learning Corporation

212 Michael Drive, Syosset, NY 11791
(516) 921-8888 • www.passbooks.com
E-mail: info@passbooks.com

PASSBOOK® SERIES

THE *PASSBOOK® SERIES* has been created to prepare applicants and candidates for the ultimate academic battlefield – the examination room.

At some time in our lives, each and every one of us may be required to take an examination – for validation, matriculation, admission, qualification, registration, certification, or licensure.

Based on the assumption that every applicant or candidate has met the basic formal educational standards, has taken the required number of courses, and read the necessary texts, the *PASSBOOK® SERIES* furnishes the one special preparation which may assure passing with confidence, instead of failing with insecurity. Examination questions – together with answers – are furnished as the basic vehicle for study so that the mysteries of the examination and its compounding difficulties may be eliminated or diminished by a sure method.

This book is meant to help you pass your examination provided that you qualify and are serious in your objective.

The entire field is reviewed through the huge store of content information which is succinctly presented through a provocative and challenging approach – the question-and-answer method.

A climate of success is established by furnishing the correct answers at the end of each test.

You soon learn to recognize types of questions, forms of questions, and patterns of questioning. You may even begin to anticipate expected outcomes.

You perceive that many questions are repeated or adapted so that you can gain acute insights, which may enable you to score many sure points.

You learn how to confront new questions, or types of questions, and to attack them confidently and work out the correct answers.

You note objectives and emphases, and recognize pitfalls and dangers, so that you may make positive educational adjustments.

Moreover, you are kept fully informed in relation to new concepts, methods, practices, and directions in the field.

You discover that you are actually taking the examination all the time: you are preparing for the examination by "taking" an examination, not by reading extraneous and/or supererogatory textbooks.

In short, this PASSBOOK®, used directedly, should be an important factor in helping you to pass your test.

ENVIRONMENTAL POLICE OFFICER

WHAT THE JOB INVOLVES
Environmental Police Officers perform and supervise staff performing duties involved in protecting the watershed areas, water supply systems and installations maintained by the Department of Environmental Protection of the City of New York; enforce the City's Watershed Rules and Regulations and other laws; and perform special duties or assignments as may be directed by superior officers. Environmental Police Officers may perform aerial reconnaissance. All personnel perform related work.

At <u>Assignment Level I,</u> under supervision, an Environmental Police Officer patrols and secures water supply facilities and lands, and monitors the environmental integrity of watershed areas. Environmental Police Officers patrol the watershed area, reservoir areas, installations and other sites maintained by the Department of Environmental Protection for the purpose of safeguarding life and property; maintain order by preventing breaches of the peace, despoilage and theft, and by arresting offenders; investigate suspicious persons and occurrences and make lawful arrests when probable cause exists; collect evidence and consult with superior officers about the preparation thereof for court presentation; testify at trials and note dispositions made of these cases by the court; submit reports on all unusual incidents, including accidents, occurring during the officer's tour of duty; may administer first aid when an accident occurs on the officer's post; direct traffic as needed; investigate and report instances of contamination of water courses or violation of Watershed Rules and Regulations; and may provide technical training and participate in public education programs.

THE TEST: You will be given a multiple-choice test. Your score on this test will be used to determine your place on an eligible list. The multiple-choice test may include questions which may require the use of any of the following abilities:

Written Comprehension - understanding written sentences and paragraphs.

Written Expression - using English words or sentences in writing so that others will understand.

Memorization - remembering information, such as words, numbers, pictures and procedures. Pieces of information can be remembered by themselves or with other pieces of information.

Problem Sensitivity - being able to tell when something is wrong or is likely to go wrong. It includes being able to identify the whole problem as well as elements of the problem.

Number Facility - adding, subtracting, multiplying and dividing quickly and correctly

Deductive Reasoning - applying general rules to specific problems and coming up with logical answers. It involves deciding if an answer makes sense

Inductive Reasoning - combining separate pieces of information, or specific answers to problems, to form general rules or conclusions. Involves ability to think of possible reasons why things go together.

Information Ordering - following correctly a rule or set of rules or actions in a certain order. The rule or set of rules used must be given. The things or actions to be put in order can include numbers, letters, words, pictures, procedures, sentences, and mathematical or logical operations.

Spatial Orientation - determining where you are in relation to the location of some object or to tell where the object is in relation to you.

Visualization - imagining how something would look when it is moved around or when its parts are moved or rearranged. It requires the forming of mental images of how patterns or objects would look after certain changes, such as unfolding or rotation. One has to predict how an object, set of objects, or pattern will appear after the changes have been carried out.

HOW TO TAKE A TEST

I. YOU MUST PASS AN EXAMINATION

A. WHAT EVERY CANDIDATE SHOULD KNOW

Examination applicants often ask us for help in preparing for the written test. What can I study in advance? What kinds of questions will be asked? How will the test be given? How will the papers be graded?

As an applicant for a civil service examination, you may be wondering about some of these things. Our purpose here is to suggest effective methods of advance study and to describe civil service examinations.

Your chances for success on this examination can be increased if you know how to prepare. Those "pre-examination jitters" can be reduced if you know what to expect. You can even experience an adventure in good citizenship if you know why civil service exams are given.

B. WHY ARE CIVIL SERVICE EXAMINATIONS GIVEN?

Civil service examinations are important to you in two ways. As a citizen, you want public jobs filled by employees who know how to do their work. As a job seeker, you want a fair chance to compete for that job on an equal footing with other candidates. The best-known means of accomplishing this two-fold goal is the competitive examination.

Exams are widely publicized throughout the nation. They may be administered for jobs in federal, state, city, municipal, town or village governments or agencies.

Any citizen may apply, with some limitations, such as the age or residence of applicants. Your experience and education may be reviewed to see whether you meet the requirements for the particular examination. When these requirements exist, they are reasonable and applied consistently to all applicants. Thus, a competitive examination may cause you some uneasiness now, but it is your privilege and safeguard.

C. HOW ARE CIVIL SERVICE EXAMS DEVELOPED?

Examinations are carefully written by trained technicians who are specialists in the field known as "psychological measurement," in consultation with recognized authorities in the field of work that the test will cover. These experts recommend the subject matter areas or skills to be tested; only those knowledges or skills important to your success on the job are included. The most reliable books and source materials available are used as references. Together, the experts and technicians judge the difficulty level of the questions.

Test technicians know how to phrase questions so that the problem is clearly stated. Their ethics do not permit "trick" or "catch" questions. Questions may have been tried out on sample groups, or subjected to statistical analysis, to determine their usefulness.

Written tests are often used in combination with performance tests, ratings of training and experience, and oral interviews. All of these measures combine to form the best-known means of finding the right person for the right job.

II. HOW TO PASS THE WRITTEN TEST

A. NATURE OF THE EXAMINATION

To prepare intelligently for civil service examinations, you should know how they differ from school examinations you have taken. In school you were assigned certain definite pages to read or subjects to cover. The examination questions were quite detailed and usually emphasized memory. Civil service exams, on the other hand, try to discover your present ability to perform the duties of a position, plus your potentiality to learn these duties. In other words, a civil service exam attempts to predict how successful you will be. Questions cover such a broad area that they cannot be as minute and detailed as school exam questions.

In the public service similar kinds of work, or positions, are grouped together in one "class." This process is known as *position-classification*. All the positions in a class are paid according to the salary range for that class. One class title covers all of these positions, and they are all tested by the same examination.

B. FOUR BASIC STEPS

1) Study the announcement

How, then, can you know what subjects to study? Our best answer is: "Learn as much as possible about the class of positions for which you've applied." The exam will test the knowledge, skills and abilities needed to do the work.

Your most valuable source of information about the position you want is the official exam announcement. This announcement lists the training and experience qualifications. Check these standards and apply only if you come reasonably close to meeting them.

The brief description of the position in the examination announcement offers some clues to the subjects which will be tested. Think about the job itself. Review the duties in your mind. Can you perform them, or are there some in which you are rusty? Fill in the blank spots in your preparation.

Many jurisdictions preview the written test in the exam announcement by including a section called "Knowledge and Abilities Required," "Scope of the Examination," or some similar heading. Here you will find out specifically what fields will be tested.

2) Review your own background

Once you learn in general what the position is all about, and what you need to know to do the work, ask yourself which subjects you already know fairly well and which need improvement. You may wonder whether to concentrate on improving your strong areas or on building some background in your fields of weakness. When the announcement has specified "some knowledge" or "considerable knowledge," or has used adjectives like "beginning principles of..." or "advanced ... methods," you can get a clue as to the number and difficulty of questions to be asked in any given field. More questions, and hence broader coverage, would be included for those subjects which are more important in the work. Now weigh your strengths and weaknesses against the job requirements and prepare accordingly.

3) Determine the level of the position

Another way to tell how intensively you should prepare is to understand the level of the job for which you are applying. Is it the entering level? In other words, is this the position in which beginners in a field of work are hired? Or is it an intermediate or advanced level? Sometimes this is indicated by such words as "Junior" or "Senior" in the class title. Other jurisdictions use Roman numerals to designate the level – Clerk I, Clerk II, for example. The word "Supervisor" sometimes appears in the title. If the level is not indicated by the title, check the description of duties. Will you be working under very close supervision, or will you have responsibility for independent decisions in this work?

4) Choose appropriate study materials

Now that you know the subjects to be examined and the relative amount of each subject to be covered, you can choose suitable study materials. For beginning level jobs, or even advanced ones, if you have a pronounced weakness in some aspect of your training, read a modern, standard textbook in that field. Be sure it is up to date and has general coverage. Such books are normally available at your library, and the librarian will be glad to help you locate one. For entry-level positions, questions of appropriate difficulty are chosen – neither highly advanced questions, nor those too simple. Such questions require careful thought but not advanced training.

If the position for which you are applying is technical or advanced, you will read more advanced, specialized material. If you are already familiar with the basic principles of your field, elementary textbooks would waste your time. Concentrate on advanced textbooks and technical periodicals. Think through the concepts and review difficult problems in your field.

These are all general sources. You can get more ideas on your own initiative, following these leads. For example, training manuals and publications of the government agency which employs workers in your field can be useful, particularly for technical and professional positions. A letter or visit to the government department involved may result in more specific study suggestions, and certainly will provide you with a more definite idea of the exact nature of the position you are seeking.

III. KINDS OF TESTS

Tests are used for purposes other than measuring knowledge and ability to perform specified duties. For some positions, it is equally important to test ability to make adjustments to new situations or to profit from training. In others, basic mental abilities not dependent on information are essential. Questions which test these things may not appear as pertinent to the duties of the position as those which test for knowledge and information. Yet they are often highly important parts of a fair examination. For very general questions, it is almost impossible to help you direct your study efforts. What we can do is to point out some of the more common of these general abilities needed in public service positions and describe some typical questions.

1) General information

Broad, general information has been found useful for predicting job success in some kinds of work. This is tested in a variety of ways, from vocabulary lists to questions about current events. Basic background in some field of work, such as sociology or economics, may be sampled in a group of questions. Often these are principles which have become familiar to most persons through exposure rather than through formal training. It is difficult to advise you how to study for these questions; being alert to the world around you is our best suggestion.

2) Verbal ability

An example of an ability needed in many positions is verbal or language ability. Verbal ability is, in brief, the ability to use and understand words. Vocabulary and grammar tests are typical measures of this ability. Reading comprehension or paragraph interpretation questions are common in many kinds of civil service tests. You are given a paragraph of written material and asked to find its central meaning.

3) Numerical ability

Number skills can be tested by the familiar arithmetic problem, by checking paired lists of numbers to see which are alike and which are different, or by interpreting charts and graphs. In the latter test, a graph may be printed in the test booklet which you are asked to use as the basis for answering questions.

4) Observation

A popular test for law-enforcement positions is the observation test. A picture is shown to you for several minutes, then taken away. Questions about the picture test your ability to observe both details and larger elements.

5) Following directions

In many positions in the public service, the employee must be able to carry out written instructions dependably and accurately. You may be given a chart with several columns, each column listing a variety of information. The questions require you to carry out directions involving the information given in the chart.

6) Skills and aptitudes

Performance tests effectively measure some manual skills and aptitudes. When the skill is one in which you are trained, such as typing or shorthand, you can practice. These tests are often very much like those given in business school or high school courses. For many of the other skills and aptitudes, however, no short-time preparation can be made. Skills and abilities natural to you or that you have developed throughout your lifetime are being tested.

Many of the general questions just described provide all the data needed to answer the questions and ask you to use your reasoning ability to find the answers. Your best preparation for these tests, as well as for tests of facts and ideas, is to be at your physical and mental best. You, no doubt, have your own methods of getting into an exam-taking mood and keeping "in shape." The next section lists some ideas on this subject.

IV. KINDS OF QUESTIONS

Only rarely is the "essay" question, which you answer in narrative form, used in civil service tests. Civil service tests are usually of the short-answer type. Full instructions for answering these questions will be given to you at the examination. But in case this is your first experience with short-answer questions and separate answer sheets, here is what you need to know:

1) Multiple-choice Questions

Most popular of the short-answer questions is the "multiple choice" or "best answer" question. It can be used, for example, to test for factual knowledge, ability to solve problems or judgment in meeting situations found at work.

A multiple-choice question is normally one of three types—
- It can begin with an incomplete statement followed by several possible endings. You are to find the one ending which *best* completes the statement, although some of the others may not be entirely wrong.
- It can also be a complete statement in the form of a question which is answered by choosing one of the statements listed.

- It can be in the form of a problem – again you select the best answer.

Here is an example of a multiple-choice question with a discussion which should give you some clues as to the method for choosing the right answer:

When an employee has a complaint about his assignment, the action which will *best* help him overcome his difficulty is to
- A. discuss his difficulty with his coworkers
- B. take the problem to the head of the organization
- C. take the problem to the person who gave him the assignment
- D. say nothing to anyone about his complaint

In answering this question, you should study each of the choices to find which is best. Consider choice "A" – Certainly an employee may discuss his complaint with fellow employees, but no change or improvement can result, and the complaint remains unresolved. Choice "B" is a poor choice since the head of the organization probably does not know what assignment you have been given, and taking your problem to him is known as "going over the head" of the supervisor. The supervisor, or person who made the assignment, is the person who can clarify it or correct any injustice. Choice "C" is, therefore, correct. To say nothing, as in choice "D," is unwise. Supervisors have and interest in knowing the problems employees are facing, and the employee is seeking a solution to his problem.

2) True/False Questions

The "true/false" or "right/wrong" form of question is sometimes used. Here a complete statement is given. Your job is to decide whether the statement is right or wrong.

SAMPLE: A roaming cell-phone call to a nearby city costs less than a non-roaming call to a distant city.

This statement is wrong, or false, since roaming calls are more expensive.

This is not a complete list of all possible question forms, although most of the others are variations of these common types. You will always get complete directions for answering questions. Be sure you understand *how* to mark your answers – ask questions until you do.

V. RECORDING YOUR ANSWERS

Computer terminals are used more and more today for many different kinds of exams.
For an examination with very few applicants, you may be told to record your answers in the test booklet itself. Separate answer sheets are much more common. If this separate answer sheet is to be scored by machine – and this is often the case – it is highly important that you mark your answers correctly in order to get credit.
An electronic scoring machine is often used in civil service offices because of the speed with which papers can be scored. Machine-scored answer sheets must be marked with a pencil, which will be given to you. This pencil has a high graphite content which responds to the electronic scoring machine. As a matter of fact, stray dots may register as answers, so do not let your pencil rest on the answer sheet while you are pondering the correct answer. Also, if your pencil lead breaks or is otherwise defective, ask for another.

Since the answer sheet will be dropped in a slot in the scoring machine, be careful not to bend the corners or get the paper crumpled.

The answer sheet normally has five vertical columns of numbers, with 30 numbers to a column. These numbers correspond to the question numbers in your test booklet. After each number, going across the page are four or five pairs of dotted lines. These short dotted lines have small letters or numbers above them. The first two pairs may also have a "T" or "F" above the letters. This indicates that the first two pairs only are to be used if the questions are of the true-false type. If the questions are multiple choice, disregard the "T" and "F" and pay attention only to the small letters or numbers.

Answer your questions in the manner of the sample that follows:

32. The largest city in the United States is
    A. Washington, D.C.
    B. New York City
    C. Chicago
    D. Detroit
    E. San Francisco

1) Choose the answer you think is best. (New York City is the largest, so "B" is correct.)
2) Find the row of dotted lines numbered the same as the question you are answering. (Find row number 32)
3) Find the pair of dotted lines corresponding to the answer. (Find the pair of lines under the mark "B.")
4) Make a solid black mark between the dotted lines.

VI. BEFORE THE TEST

Common sense will help you find procedures to follow to get ready for an examination. Too many of us, however, overlook these sensible measures. Indeed, nervousness and fatigue have been found to be the most serious reasons why applicants fail to do their best on civil service tests. Here is a list of reminders:

- Begin your preparation early – Don't wait until the last minute to go scurrying around for books and materials or to find out what the position is all about.
- Prepare continuously – An hour a night for a week is better than an all-night cram session. This has been definitely established. What is more, a night a week for a month will return better dividends than crowding your study into a shorter period of time.
- Locate the place of the exam – You have been sent a notice telling you when and where to report for the examination. If the location is in a different town or otherwise unfamiliar to you, it would be well to inquire the best route and learn something about the building.
- Relax the night before the test – Allow your mind to rest. Do not study at all that night. Plan some mild recreation or diversion; then go to bed early and get a good night's sleep.
- Get up early enough to make a leisurely trip to the place for the test – This way unforeseen events, traffic snarls, unfamiliar buildings, etc. will not upset you.
- Dress comfortably – A written test is not a fashion show. You will be known by number and not by name, so wear something comfortable.

- Leave excess paraphernalia at home – Shopping bags and odd bundles will get in your way. You need bring only the items mentioned in the official notice you received; usually everything you need is provided. Do not bring reference books to the exam. They will only confuse those last minutes and be taken away from you when in the test room.
- Arrive somewhat ahead of time – If because of transportation schedules you must get there very early, bring a newspaper or magazine to take your mind off yourself while waiting.
- Locate the examination room – When you have found the proper room, you will be directed to the seat or part of the room where you will sit. Sometimes you are given a sheet of instructions to read while you are waiting. Do not fill out any forms until you are told to do so; just read them and be prepared.
- Relax and prepare to listen to the instructions
- If you have any physical problem that may keep you from doing your best, be sure to tell the test administrator. If you are sick or in poor health, you really cannot do your best on the exam. You can come back and take the test some other time.

VII. AT THE TEST

The day of the test is here and you have the test booklet in your hand. The temptation to get going is very strong. Caution! There is more to success than knowing the right answers. You must know how to identify your papers and understand variations in the type of short-answer question used in this particular examination. Follow these suggestions for maximum results from your efforts:

1) Cooperate with the monitor

The test administrator has a duty to create a situation in which you can be as much at ease as possible. He will give instructions, tell you when to begin, check to see that you are marking your answer sheet correctly, and so on. He is not there to guard you, although he will see that your competitors do not take unfair advantage. He wants to help you do your best.

2) Listen to all instructions

Don't jump the gun! Wait until you understand all directions. In most civil service tests you get more time than you need to answer the questions. So don't be in a hurry. Read each word of instructions until you clearly understand the meaning. Study the examples, listen to all announcements and follow directions. Ask questions if you do not understand what to do.

3) Identify your papers

Civil service exams are usually identified by number only. You will be assigned a number; you must not put your name on your test papers. Be sure to copy your number correctly. Since more than one exam may be given, copy your exact examination title.

4) Plan your time

Unless you are told that a test is a "speed" or "rate of work" test, speed itself is usually not important. Time enough to answer all the questions will be provided, but this does not mean that you have all day. An overall time limit has been set. Divide the total time (in minutes) by the number of questions to determine the approximate time you have for each question.

5) Do not linger over difficult questions

If you come across a difficult question, mark it with a paper clip (useful to have along) and come back to it when you have been through the booklet. One caution if you do this – be sure to skip a number on your answer sheet as well. Check often to be sure that you have not lost your place and that you are marking in the row numbered the same as the question you are answering.

6) Read the questions

Be sure you know what the question asks! Many capable people are unsuccessful because they failed to *read* the questions correctly.

7) Answer all questions

Unless you have been instructed that a penalty will be deducted for incorrect answers, it is better to guess than to omit a question.

8) Speed tests

It is often better NOT to guess on speed tests. It has been found that on timed tests people are tempted to spend the last few seconds before time is called in marking answers at random – without even reading them – in the hope of picking up a few extra points. To discourage this practice, the instructions may warn you that your score will be "corrected" for guessing. That is, a penalty will be applied. The incorrect answers will be deducted from the correct ones, or some other penalty formula will be used.

9) Review your answers

If you finish before time is called, go back to the questions you guessed or omitted to give them further thought. Review other answers if you have time.

10) Return your test materials

If you are ready to leave before others have finished or time is called, take ALL your materials to the monitor and leave quietly. Never take any test material with you. The monitor can discover whose papers are not complete, and taking a test booklet may be grounds for disqualification.

VIII. EXAMINATION TECHNIQUES

1) Read the general instructions carefully. These are usually printed on the first page of the exam booklet. As a rule, these instructions refer to the timing of the examination; the fact that you should not start work until the signal and must stop work at a signal, etc. If there are any *special* instructions, such as a choice of questions to be answered, make sure that you note this instruction carefully.

2) When you are ready to start work on the examination, that is as soon as the signal has been given, read the instructions to each question booklet, underline any key words or phrases, such as *least, best, outline, describe* and the like. In this way you will tend to answer as requested rather than discover on reviewing your paper that you *listed without describing*, that you selected the *worst* choice rather than the *best* choice, etc.

3) If the examination is of the objective or multiple-choice type – that is, each question will also give a series of possible answers: A, B, C or D, and you are called upon to select the best answer and write the letter next to that answer on your answer paper – it is advisable to start answering each question in turn. There may be anywhere from 50 to 100 such questions in the three or four hours allotted and you can see how much time would be taken if you read through all the questions before beginning to answer any. Furthermore, if you come across a question or group of questions which you know would be difficult to answer, it would undoubtedly affect your handling of all the other questions.

4) If the examination is of the essay type and contains but a few questions, it is a moot point as to whether you should read all the questions before starting to answer any one. Of course, if you are given a choice – say five out of seven and the like – then it is essential to read all the questions so you can eliminate the two that are most difficult. If, however, you are asked to answer all the questions, there may be danger in trying to answer the easiest one first because you may find that you will spend too much time on it. The best technique is to answer the first question, then proceed to the second, etc.

5) Time your answers. Before the exam begins, write down the time it started, then add the time allowed for the examination and write down the time it must be completed, then divide the time available somewhat as follows:
   - If 3-1/2 hours are allowed, that would be 210 minutes. If you have 80 objective-type questions, that would be an average of 2-1/2 minutes per question. Allow yourself no more than 2 minutes per question, or a total of 160 minutes, which will permit about 50 minutes to review.
   - If for the time allotment of 210 minutes there are 7 essay questions to answer, that would average about 30 minutes a question. Give yourself only 25 minutes per question so that you have about 35 minutes to review.

6) The most important instruction is to *read each question* and make sure you know what is wanted. The second most important instruction is to *time yourself properly* so that you answer every question. The third most important instruction is to *answer every question*. Guess if you have to but include something for each question. Remember that you will receive no credit for a blank and will probably receive some credit if you write something in answer to an essay question. If you guess a letter – say "B" for a multiple-choice question – you may have guessed right. If you leave a blank as an answer to a multiple-choice question, the examiners may respect your feelings but it will not add a point to your score. Some exams may penalize you for wrong answers, so in such cases *only*, you may not want to guess unless you have some basis for your answer.

7) Suggestions
   a. Objective-type questions
      1. Examine the question booklet for proper sequence of pages and questions
      2. Read all instructions carefully
      3. Skip any question which seems too difficult; return to it after all other questions have been answered
      4. Apportion your time properly; do not spend too much time on any single question or group of questions

5. Note and underline key words – *all, most, fewest, least, best, worst, same, opposite*, etc.
6. Pay particular attention to negatives
7. Note unusual option, e.g., unduly long, short, complex, different or similar in content to the body of the question
8. Observe the use of "hedging" words – *probably, may, most likely*, etc.
9. Make sure that your answer is put next to the same number as the question
10. Do not second-guess unless you have good reason to believe the second answer is definitely more correct
11. Cross out original answer if you decide another answer is more accurate; do not erase until you are ready to hand your paper in
12. Answer all questions; guess unless instructed otherwise
13. Leave time for review

b. Essay questions
1. Read each question carefully
2. Determine exactly what is wanted. Underline key words or phrases.
3. Decide on outline or paragraph answer
4. Include many different points and elements unless asked to develop any one or two points or elements
5. Show impartiality by giving pros and cons unless directed to select one side only
6. Make and write down any assumptions you find necessary to answer the questions
7. Watch your English, grammar, punctuation and choice of words
8. Time your answers; don't crowd material

8) Answering the essay question

Most essay questions can be answered by framing the specific response around several key words or ideas. Here are a few such key words or ideas:

M's: manpower, materials, methods, money, management
P's: purpose, program, policy, plan, procedure, practice, problems, pitfalls, personnel, public relations

a. Six basic steps in handling problems:
1. Preliminary plan and background development
2. Collect information, data and facts
3. Analyze and interpret information, data and facts
4. Analyze and develop solutions as well as make recommendations
5. Prepare report and sell recommendations
6. Install recommendations and follow up effectiveness

b. Pitfalls to avoid
1. *Taking things for granted* – A statement of the situation does not necessarily imply that each of the elements is necessarily true; for example, a complaint may be invalid and biased so that all that can be taken for granted is that a complaint has been registered

2. *Considering only one side of a situation* – Wherever possible, indicate several alternatives and then point out the reasons you selected the best one
3. *Failing to indicate follow up* – Whenever your answer indicates action on your part, make certain that you will take proper follow-up action to see how successful your recommendations, procedures or actions turn out to be
4. *Taking too long in answering any single question* – Remember to time your answers properly

IX. AFTER THE TEST

Scoring procedures differ in detail among civil service jurisdictions although the general principles are the same. Whether the papers are hand-scored or graded by machine we have described, they are nearly always graded by number. That is, the person who marks the paper knows only the number – never the name – of the applicant. Not until all the papers have been graded will they be matched with names. If other tests, such as training and experience or oral interview ratings have been given, scores will be combined. Different parts of the examination usually have different weights. For example, the written test might count 60 percent of the final grade, and a rating of training and experience 40 percent. In many jurisdictions, veterans will have a certain number of points added to their grades.

After the final grade has been determined, the names are placed in grade order and an eligible list is established. There are various methods for resolving ties between those who get the same final grade – probably the most common is to place first the name of the person whose application was received first. Job offers are made from the eligible list in the order the names appear on it. You will be notified of your grade and your rank as soon as all these computations have been made. This will be done as rapidly as possible.

People who are found to meet the requirements in the announcement are called "eligibles." Their names are put on a list of eligible candidates. An eligible's chances of getting a job depend on how high he stands on this list and how fast agencies are filling jobs from the list.

When a job is to be filled from a list of eligibles, the agency asks for the names of people on the list of eligibles for that job. When the civil service commission receives this request, it sends to the agency the names of the three people highest on this list. Or, if the job to be filled has specialized requirements, the office sends the agency the names of the top three persons who meet these requirements from the general list.

The appointing officer makes a choice from among the three people whose names were sent to him. If the selected person accepts the appointment, the names of the others are put back on the list to be considered for future openings.

That is the rule in hiring from all kinds of eligible lists, whether they are for typist, carpenter, chemist, or something else. For every vacancy, the appointing officer has his choice of any one of the top three eligibles on the list. This explains why the person whose name is on top of the list sometimes does not get an appointment when some of the persons lower on the list do. If the appointing officer chooses the second or third eligible, the No. 1 eligible does not get a job at once, but stays on the list until he is appointed or the list is terminated.

X. HOW TO PASS THE INTERVIEW TEST

The examination for which you applied requires an oral interview test. You have already taken the written test and you are now being called for the interview test – the final part of the formal examination.

You may think that it is not possible to prepare for an interview test and that there are no procedures to follow during an interview. Our purpose is to point out some things you can do in advance that will help you and some good rules to follow and pitfalls to avoid while you are being interviewed.

What is an interview supposed to test?

The written examination is designed to test the technical knowledge and competence of the candidate; the oral is designed to evaluate intangible qualities, not readily measured otherwise, and to establish a list showing the relative fitness of each candidate – as measured against his competitors – for the position sought. Scoring is not on the basis of "right" and "wrong," but on a sliding scale of values ranging from "not passable" to "outstanding." As a matter of fact, it is possible to achieve a relatively low score without a single "incorrect" answer because of evident weakness in the qualities being measured.

Occasionally, an examination may consist entirely of an oral test – either an individual or a group oral. In such cases, information is sought concerning the technical knowledges and abilities of the candidate, since there has been no written examination for this purpose. More commonly, however, an oral test is used to supplement a written examination.

Who conducts interviews?

The composition of oral boards varies among different jurisdictions. In nearly all, a representative of the personnel department serves as chairman. One of the members of the board may be a representative of the department in which the candidate would work. In some cases, "outside experts" are used, and, frequently, a businessman or some other representative of the general public is asked to serve. Labor and management or other special groups may be represented. The aim is to secure the services of experts in the appropriate field.

However the board is composed, it is a good idea (and not at all improper or unethical) to ascertain in advance of the interview who the members are and what groups they represent. When you are introduced to them, you will have some idea of their backgrounds and interests, and at least you will not stutter and stammer over their names.

What should be done before the interview?

While knowledge about the board members is useful and takes some of the surprise element out of the interview, there is other preparation which is more substantive. It *is* possible to prepare for an oral interview – in several ways:

1) Keep a copy of your application and review it carefully before the interview

This may be the only document before the oral board, and the starting point of the interview. Know what education and experience you have listed there, and the sequence and dates of all of it. Sometimes the board will ask you to review the highlights of your experience for them; you should not have to hem and haw doing it.

2) Study the class specification and the examination announcement

Usually, the oral board has one or both of these to guide them. The qualities, characteristics or knowledges required by the position sought are stated in these documents. They offer valuable clues as to the nature of the oral interview. For example, if the job involves supervisory responsibilities, the announcement will usually indicate that knowledge of modern supervisory methods and the qualifications of the candidate as a supervisor will be tested. If so, you can expect such questions, frequently in the form of a hypothetical situation which you are expected to solve. NEVER go into an oral without knowledge of the duties and responsibilities of the job you seek.

3) Think through each qualification required

Try to visualize the kind of questions you would ask if you were a board member. How well could you answer them? Try especially to appraise your own knowledge and background in each area, *measured against the job sought*, and identify any areas in which you are weak. Be critical and realistic – do not flatter yourself.

4) Do some general reading in areas in which you feel you may be weak

For example, if the job involves supervision and your past experience has NOT, some general reading in supervisory methods and practices, particularly in the field of human relations, might be useful. Do NOT study agency procedures or detailed manuals. The oral board will be testing your understanding and capacity, not your memory.

5) Get a good night's sleep and watch your general health and mental attitude

You will want a clear head at the interview. Take care of a cold or any other minor ailment, and of course, no hangovers.

What should be done on the day of the interview?

Now comes the day of the interview itself. Give yourself plenty of time to get there. Plan to arrive somewhat ahead of the scheduled time, particularly if your appointment is in the fore part of the day. If a previous candidate fails to appear, the board might be ready for you a bit early. By early afternoon an oral board is almost invariably behind schedule if there are many candidates, and you may have to wait. Take along a book or magazine to read, or your application to review, but leave any extraneous material in the waiting room when you go in for your interview. In any event, relax and compose yourself.

The matter of dress is important. The board is forming impressions about you – from your experience, your manners, your attitude, and your appearance. Give your personal appearance careful attention. Dress your best, but not your flashiest. Choose conservative, appropriate clothing, and be sure it is immaculate. This is a business interview, and your appearance should indicate that you regard it as such. Besides, being well groomed and properly dressed will help boost your confidence.

Sooner or later, someone will call your name and escort you into the interview room. *This is it.* From here on you are on your own. It is too late for any more preparation. But remember, you asked for this opportunity to prove your fitness, and you are here because your request was granted.

What happens when you go in?

The usual sequence of events will be as follows: The clerk (who is often the board stenographer) will introduce you to the chairman of the oral board, who will introduce you to the other members of the board. Acknowledge the introductions before you sit down. Do not be surprised if you find a microphone facing you or a stenotypist sitting by. Oral interviews are usually recorded in the event of an appeal or other review.

Usually the chairman of the board will open the interview by reviewing the highlights of your education and work experience from your application – primarily for the benefit of the other members of the board, as well as to get the material into the record. Do not interrupt or comment unless there is an error or significant misinterpretation; if that is the case, do not hesitate. But do not quibble about insignificant matters. Also, he will usually ask you some question about your education, experience or your present job – partly to get you to start talking and to establish the interviewing "rapport." He may start the actual questioning, or turn it over to one of the other members. Frequently, each member undertakes the questioning on a particular area, one in which he is perhaps most competent, so you can expect each member to participate in the examination. Because time is limited, you may also expect some rather abrupt switches in the direction the questioning takes, so do not be upset by it. Normally, a board member will not pursue a single line of questioning unless he discovers a particular strength or weakness.

After each member has participated, the chairman will usually ask whether any member has any further questions, then will ask you if you have anything you wish to add. Unless you are expecting this question, it may floor you. Worse, it may start you off on an extended, extemporaneous speech. The board is not usually seeking more information. The question is principally to offer you a last opportunity to present further qualifications or to indicate that you have nothing to add. So, if you feel that a significant qualification or characteristic has been overlooked, it is proper to point it out in a sentence or so. Do not compliment the board on the thoroughness of their examination – they have been sketchy, and you know it. If you wish, merely say, "No thank you, I have nothing further to add." This is a point where you can "talk yourself out" of a good impression or fail to present an important bit of information. Remember, *you close the interview yourself.*

The chairman will then say, "That is all, Mr. _____, thank you." Do not be startled; the interview is over, and quicker than you think. Thank him, gather your belongings and take your leave. Save your sigh of relief for the other side of the door.

How to put your best foot forward

Throughout this entire process, you may feel that the board individually and collectively is trying to pierce your defenses, seek out your hidden weaknesses and embarrass and confuse you. Actually, this is not true. They are obliged to make an appraisal of your qualifications for the job you are seeking, and they want to see you in your best light. Remember, they must interview all candidates and a non-cooperative candidate may become a failure in spite of their best efforts to bring out his qualifications. Here are 15 suggestions that will help you:

1) Be natural – Keep your attitude confident, not cocky

If you are not confident that you can do the job, do not expect the board to be. Do not apologize for your weaknesses, try to bring out your strong points. The board is interested in a positive, not negative, presentation. Cockiness will antagonize any board member and make him wonder if you are covering up a weakness by a false show of strength.

2) Get comfortable, but don't lounge or sprawl

Sit erectly but not stiffly. A careless posture may lead the board to conclude that you are careless in other things, or at least that you are not impressed by the importance of the occasion. Either conclusion is natural, even if incorrect. Do not fuss with your clothing, a pencil or an ashtray. Your hands may occasionally be useful to emphasize a point; do not let them become a point of distraction.

3) Do not wisecrack or make small talk

This is a serious situation, and your attitude should show that you consider it as such. Further, the time of the board is limited – they do not want to waste it, and neither should you.

4) Do not exaggerate your experience or abilities

In the first place, from information in the application or other interviews and sources, the board may know more about you than you think. Secondly, you probably will not get away with it. An experienced board is rather adept at spotting such a situation, so do not take the chance.

5) If you know a board member, do not make a point of it, yet do not hide it

Certainly you are not fooling him, and probably not the other members of the board. Do not try to take advantage of your acquaintanceship – it will probably do you little good.

6) Do not dominate the interview

Let the board do that. They will give you the clues – do not assume that you have to do all the talking. Realize that the board has a number of questions to ask you, and do not try to take up all the interview time by showing off your extensive knowledge of the answer to the first one.

7) Be attentive

You only have 20 minutes or so, and you should keep your attention at its sharpest throughout. When a member is addressing a problem or question to you, give him your undivided attention. Address your reply principally to him, but do not exclude the other board members.

8) Do not interrupt

A board member may be stating a problem for you to analyze. He will ask you a question when the time comes. Let him state the problem, and wait for the question.

9) Make sure you understand the question

Do not try to answer until you are sure what the question is. If it is not clear, restate it in your own words or ask the board member to clarify it for you. However, do not haggle about minor elements.

10) Reply promptly but not hastily

A common entry on oral board rating sheets is "candidate responded readily," or "candidate hesitated in replies." Respond as promptly and quickly as you can, but do not jump to a hasty, ill-considered answer.

11) Do not be peremptory in your answers

A brief answer is proper – but do not fire your answer back. That is a losing game from your point of view. The board member can probably ask questions much faster than you can answer them.

12) Do not try to create the answer you think the board member wants

He is interested in what kind of mind you have and how it works – not in playing games. Furthermore, he can usually spot this practice and will actually grade you down on it.

13) Do not switch sides in your reply merely to agree with a board member

Frequently, a member will take a contrary position merely to draw you out and to see if you are willing and able to defend your point of view. Do not start a debate, yet do not surrender a good position. If a position is worth taking, it is worth defending.

14) Do not be afraid to admit an error in judgment if you are shown to be wrong

The board knows that you are forced to reply without any opportunity for careful consideration. Your answer may be demonstrably wrong. If so, admit it and get on with the interview.

15) Do not dwell at length on your present job

The opening question may relate to your present assignment. Answer the question but do not go into an extended discussion. You are being examined for a *new* job, not your present one. As a matter of fact, try to phrase ALL your answers in terms of the job for which you are being examined.

Basis of Rating

Probably you will forget most of these "do's" and "don'ts" when you walk into the oral interview room. Even remembering them all will not ensure you a passing grade. Perhaps you did not have the qualifications in the first place. But remembering them will help you to put your best foot forward, without treading on the toes of the board members.

Rumor and popular opinion to the contrary notwithstanding, an oral board wants you to make the best appearance possible. They know you are under pressure – but they also want to see how you respond to it as a guide to what your reaction would be under the pressures of the job you seek. They will be influenced by the degree of poise you display, the personal traits you show and the manner in which you respond.

ABOUT THIS BOOK

This book contains tests divided into Examination Sections. Go through each test, answering every question in the margin. We have also attached a sample answer sheet at the back of the book that can be removed and used. At the end of each test look at the answer key and check your answers. On the ones you got wrong, look at the right answer choice and learn. Do not fill in the answers first. Do not memorize the questions and answers, but understand the answer and principles involved. On your test, the questions will likely be different from the samples. Questions are changed and new ones added. If you understand these past questions you should have success with any changes that arise. Tests may consist of several types of questions. We have additional books on each subject should more study be advisable or necessary for you. Finally, the more you study, the better prepared you will be. This book is intended to be the last thing you study before you walk into the examination room. Prior study of relevant texts is also recommended. NLC publishes some of these in our Fundamental Series. Knowledge and good sense are important factors in passing your exam. Good luck also helps. So now study this Passbook, absorb the material contained within and take that knowledge into the examination. Then do your best to pass that exam.

EXAMINATION SECTION

EXAMINATION SECTION

TEST 1

DIRECTIONS: Each question or incomplete statement is followed by several suggested answers or completions. Select the one that BEST answers the question or completes the statement. *PRINT THE LETTER OF THE CORRECT ANSWER IN THE SPACE AT THE RIGHT.*

Questions 1-4.

DIRECTIONS: Questions 1 through 4 measure your ability to recognize objects, people, events, parts of maps, or crime, accident, or other scenes to which you have been exposed.

Below and on the following pages are twenty illustrations. Study them carefully. In the test, you will be shown pairs of drawings. For each pair, you will be asked which is or are from the twenty illustrations in this part.

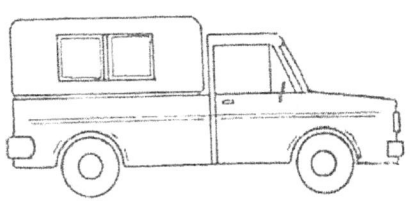

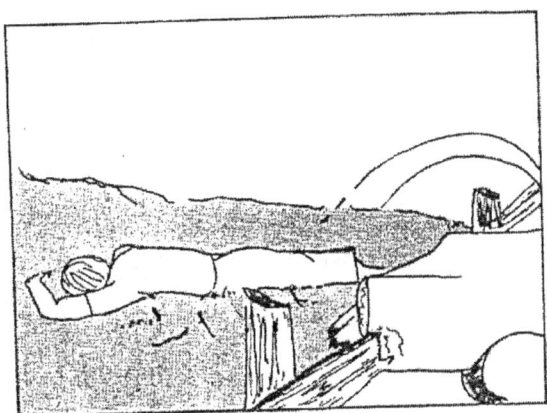

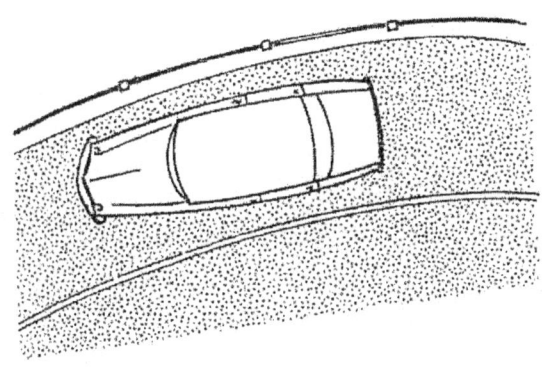

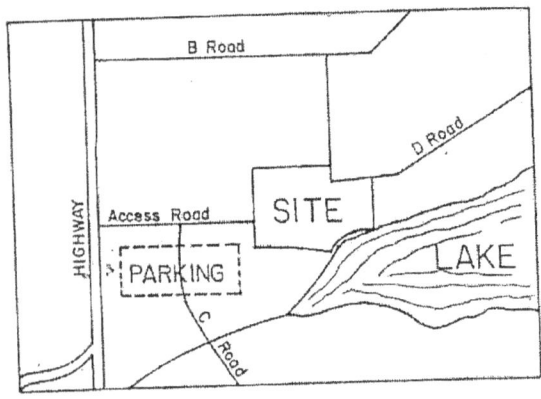

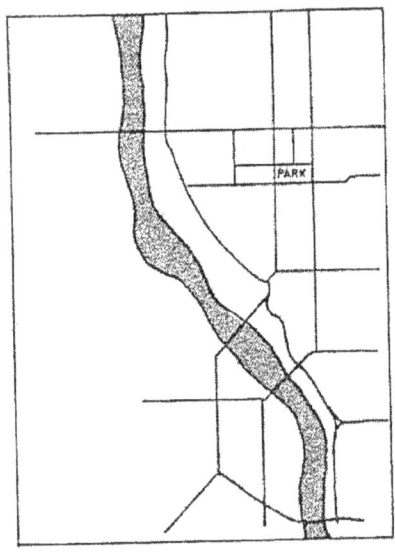

5 (#1)

Questions 1-4.

DIRECTIONS: In Questions 1 through 4, select the choice that corresponds to the scene(s) that is(are) from the illustrations for this section. *PRINT THE LETTER OF THE CORRECT ANSWER IN THE SPACE AT THE RIGHT.*

1.   I   II   2.____

   A. I only   B. II only
   C. Both I and II   D. Neither I nor II

2.   I   II   2.

   A. I only   B. II only
   C. Both I and II   D. Neither I nor II

5

3.

A. I only
C. Both I and II
B. II only
D. Neither I nor II

4.

A. I only
C. Both I and II
B. II only
D. Neither I nor II

Questions 5-6.

DIRECTIONS: Questions 5 and 6 measure your ability to notice and interpret details accurately. You will be shown a picture, below, and then asked a set of questions about the picture. You do NOT need to memorize this picture. You may look at the picture when answering the questions.

5.

Details in the picture lend some support to or do NOT tend to contradict which of the following statements about the person who occupies the room?
I. The person is very careless.
II. The person smokes.
The CORRECT answer is:
A. I only
B. II only
C. Both I and II
D. Neither I nor II

6. The number on the piece of paper on the desk is MOST likely a
A. ZIP code
B. street number
C. social security number
D. telephone area code

6._____

Questions 7-10.

DIRECTIONS: Questions 7 through 10 measure your ability to recognize objects or people in differing views, contexts, or situations. Each question consists of three pictures; one labeled I and one labeled II. In each question, you are to determine whether A – I only, B – II only, C – Both I and II, and D – Neither I nor II COULD be the subject.

The Subject is *always* ONE person or ONE object. The Subject picture shows the object or person as it, he, or she appeared at the time of initial contact. Pictures I and II show objects from a different viewpoint than that of the Subject picture. For example, if the Subject picture presents a front view, I and II may present back views, side views, or a back and a side view. Also, art objects may be displayed differently, may have a different base or frame or method of hanging.

When the subject is a person, I or II will be a picture of a different person or will be a picture of the same person after some change has taken place. The person may have made a deliberate attempt to alter his or her appearance, such as wearing (or taking off a wig, growing (or shaving off) a beard or mustache, or dressing as a member of the opposite sex. The change may also be a natural one, such as changing a hair style, changing from work clothes to play clothes, or from play clothes to work clothes, or growing older, thinner, or fatter. None has had cosmetic surgery.

7. Subject   7._____

A. I only B. II only
C. Both I and II D. Neither I nor II

8. Subject    8._____

A. I only B. II only
C. Both I and II D. Neither I nor II

9. Subject 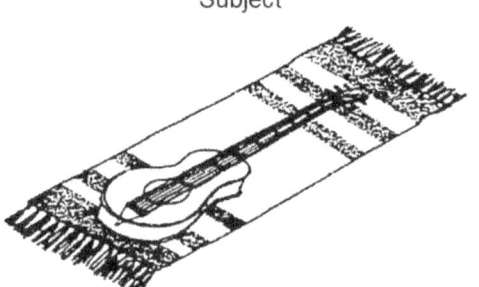 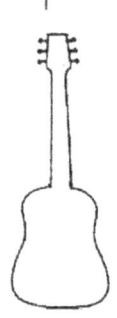  9._____

A. I only B. II only
C. Both I and II D. Neither I nor II

10. Subject I II 10._____

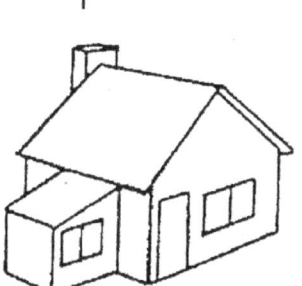

A. I only
B. II only
C. Both I and II
D. Neither I nor II

KEY (CORRECT ANSWERS)

1.	B	6.	B
2.	D	7.	D
3.	A	8.	A
4.	A	9.	D
5.	B	10.	D

EXAMINATION SECTION
TEST 1

DIRECTIONS: Each question or incomplete statement is followed by several suggested answers or completions. Select the one that BEST answers the question or completes the statement. *PRINT THE LETTER OF THE CORRECT ANSWER IN THE SPACE AT THE RIGHT.*

Questions 1-3.

DIRECTIONS: Questions 1 to 3 measure your ability to fill out forms correctly and to remember information and ideas. Below and on the following two pages are directions for completing two kinds of forms, a correctly completed sample of each form, and a section from a procedures manual. You should memorize the sets of directions and the section from the procedures manual.

In the test, you will be (1) asked questions about the information and ideas in the manual and (2) presented with completed forms and asked to identify entries that are INCORRECT (contain wrong information, incomplete information, information in wrong order, etc.).

DIRECTIONS FOR COMPLETING CASE REPORT FORM

A case report form (see completed sample) is to be filled out by each officer at the time of the preliminary investigation. The entry for each numbered box is as follows:

Box 1 - The time the assignment was received.

Box 2 - The day, date, and time of the occurrence, in that order. Names of months and days may be abbreviated.

Box 3 - The manner in which the report was received. Use P = person, TOC = Through Official Channels (911 or other emergency numbers), M = mail, or T = telephone.

Box 4 - Name of the person notifying the department.

Box 5 - The address of the occurrence. include number, street, and village, and name of establishment, if appropriate. Do NOT abbreviate the name of a street, village, or establishment. If no street address is available, supply directions.

Box 6 - Victim's name, last name first.

Box 7 - Victim's birthdate - month, day, and year. Use the style shown in the completed sample.

Box 8 - Victim's sex and race: F = female, M = male, B = black, W = white, Y = yellow, O = other.

Box 9 - Relationship of victim to the offender (be as specific as possible):
HU = husband, WI = wife, MO = mother, FA = father,

SO = son, DA = daughter, BR = brother, SI = sister,
AQ = acquaintance, ST = stranger, UN = unknown.

SAMPLE OF COMPLETED CASE REPORT FORM

1. Time Received 5:57 PM		2. Date and Time of Occurrence Wed., Oct. 17, 2017, 1:00 PM	
3. Original Complaint Received TOC		4. Reported by Jeffrey Greene	
5. Place of Occurrence Sam's Stationery Shop, 130 Main St., Brooketown			
6. Victim's Name Silver, Sam	7. Date of Birth 3/17/72		8. Sex and Race M - W
7. Relationship to the Offender ST			

DIRECTIONS FOR COMPLETING
AUTOMOBILE FIELD INTERVIEW FORM

An automobile field interview form (see completed sample on the following page) is to be filled out when a car is stopped under suspicious circumstances, but no arrests are made. The entry for each numbered box is as follows:

Box 1 - Driver's name, last name first.

Box 2 - Village of residence, if within the county

Box 3 - Type of vehicle: S = sedan, C = convertible, SW = station wagon, V = van, T = truck.

Box 4 - Vehicle registration number.

Box 5 - Time and place of interview: location (street address only), time (per 24-hour clock), date, in that order.

Box 6 - Type of area: C = commercial, H = highway, R = residential, I = industrial, S = school

Box 7 - Patrol post number: precinct number is first digit; sector number is last two digits.

Box 8 - Officer's name and shield number, in that order.

SAMPLE OF COMPLETED AUTOMOBILE FIELD INTERVIEW FORM

1. Operator Robbins, Susan		2. Village Shady Brook	
3. Type of Vehicle C		4. Registration C 7237	
5. Time and Place of Interview Merry Road at Elm Street, 1428, 2/7/17			
6. Type of Area R	7. Post No. 221		8. Officer Sally Dodd, 2212

CASE REPORT MANUAL
Section 1 - Solvability Factors

A solvability factor can be defined as any information about a crime that can provide a means to determine who committed it. In other words, a solvability factor is a useful clue to the identity of the perpetrator.

Based on national-level research, the following twelve universal factors have been identified:

1. Existence of witnesses to the crime
2. Knowledge of a perpetrator's name
3. Knowledge of a perpetrator's whereabouts
4. Description of a perpetrator
5. Identification of a perpetrator
6. Property that has traceable characteristics such as a registration number
7. Existence of a distinctive MO
8. Presence of significant physical evidence such as a set of burglar's tools
9. Description of a perpetrator's automobile
10. Positive results from a crime scene evidence search, such as fingerprints or footprints
11. Belief that a crime may be solved with publicity and/or reasonable investigative effort
12. Opportunity for only one person to have committed the crime

The presence of at least one of these solvability factors is necessary for there to be a reasonable chance for a solution to the crime. When there is no solvability factor, the chance of crime solution is limited. Therefore, the police officer who arrives at the scene of a crime first must make the greatest possible effort to identify solvability factors. This effort should include identification of witnesses and a thorough search of the crime scene.

DIRECTIONS: After you have memorized the directions and manual section, try to answer the following questions without referring to the study materials.

1. Which of the following crimes is *most likely* to have a solvability factor?

    A. A pickpocket takes several wallets on a crowded bus.
    B. Two muggers take money from a blind man in an alley.
    C. A hospital drug cabinet is broken into during a major emergency.
    D. A kidnapper escapes in a van decorated with pink, yellow, and avocado-green paint.

2. At 7:30 AM on Wednesday, February 6, 2017, Patrol Officer Alex White was assigned to investigate a suspected child-beating. The boy had been brought to the hospital, and Dr. Paul Cohen called the local station house at 7:20 AM. David Pepson, a White boy born on June 27, 2015, was brought from his home by his mother, who claims that her husband had punished David an hour earlier for making loud noises. David resides with his parents at 86 Whitewood Lane in Middletown.

4 (#1)

	CASE REPORT FORM			
1.	Time Received 7:30 AM	2.	Date and Time of Occurrence Wed., February 6, 2017, 5:00 AM	
3.	Original Complaint Received T	4.	Reported by Dr. Paul Cohen	
5.	Place of Occurrence 86 Whitewood Lane, Middletown			
6.	Victim's Name David Pepson	7.	Date of Birth 6/27/15	8. Sex and Race M - W
9.	Relationship to the Offender FA			

Of the following, the box in the form above which is filled out INCORRECTLY is Box
  A. 3   B. 4   C. 8   D. 9

3. Officer Steven Brown, 7234, stopped a station wagon in the business section of Westville. He talked to the driver, John Caseman, on Rocky Road near South Bend and the western boundary of section 16 of precinct 2 at 8:20 PM on 3/8/17. The vehicle, registration number 2729H belongs to Mr. Caseman, who resides in Silverton.

3.___

AUTOMOBILE FIELD INTERVIEW FORM

1. Operator Caseman, John		2. Village Westville	
3. Type of Vehicle V		4. Registration 2729H	
5. Time and Place of Interview Rocky Road near South Bend, 2020, 3/8/17			
6. Type of Area C	7. Post No. 216	8. Officer Steven Brown, 7234	

Of the following, the box in the form above which is filled out INCORRECTLY is Box
  A. 1   B. 3   C. 5   D. 7

Questions 4-6.

DIRECTIONS: Questions 4 to 6 measure your ability to recall information in a set of bulletins. To do well in the test, you must memorize both the pictorial and the written portions of each of the following eight bulletins.

Date of Issuance 5/13/17

INFORMATION WANTED

by

Police Department, County of Allamin
Hooblertown, Indiana 43102

The Allamin County Police Department homicide squad requests all auto repair shops, dealers and General Motors parts dealers in the precinct be contacted and questioned relative to the below described vehicle which is wanted for a felony - leaving the scene of a fatality. If vehicle is located, contact the homicide squad, (731) 624-1372. Refer to Homicide Case 130.

Place of Occurrence:	Midway State Road, South Strata, Indiana
Time of Occurrence:	0240 hours on March 3, 2017
Vehicle Wanted:	1980 Oldsmobile Cutlass Supreme, color green
Damage:	The Vehicle will have damage to the plastic grill located in the vicinity of the right front headlights. The chrome strip which is affixed to the center of the hood was recovered at the scene.
Parts:	The following parts will be needed to repair the vehicle: 1. Hood - GM Part No. 557547 or 557557 2. Plastic Grill - GM Part No. 22503156

WANTED
by

BULLETIN NO. 9-17

Police Department. County of Paradise
Cobbs Cove, Louisiana 41723
for
MURDER

No. FJ110M

Note
Seiko watch with Gold Face and three section band is not a standard import into this area.

Occurrence:	Blue Jay Way and Nickel Drive, Yellowbird, 0530 hours on April 12, 2017.
Modus Operandi:	The deceased returned to his home at 2 Blue Jay Way, Yellowbird, at about 0530 hours, April 12, 2017. Four male whites were waiting in the vicinity of his garage and robbed him of U.S. currency and the above watch. They ran to the intersection of Blue Jay Way and Nickel Drive and got into a late model, shiny dark color, four door sedan with large tail-lights. The deceased chased them to the corner. One shot was fired causing his death.
Subjects:	Four Male Whites, dark hair.
Property:	One Seiko Quartz - Sports 100 - wrist watch, yellow metal face and crystal retainer. The band is an expandable three-section, white, yellow, white metal.
Note:	Anyone with information is requested to contact the Paradise County Homicide Squad.

<u>W A N T E D</u>
<u>by</u>
<u>Police Department. County of Whitewall</u>
<u>Short Hills, Kentucky 27135</u>

<u>for</u>
<u>MURDER</u>

BULLETIN NO. 15-17

RC-550JW/C

Occurrence:	Public street, Brown Avenue, 60 ft. north of Camino Street, South Hill, KY, at 2340 hours, 6/25/17.
Modus Operandi:	The victim of the murder was walking south on Brown Avenue when he was accosted by the suspect and shot in the head by the suspect.
Subject:	Male, Black, 25-28 years, 5'9"-6' tall, thin build, short dark hair, medium dark skin, wearing a dark waist-length jacket, sneakers - armed with a gun.
Property:	The above property, a JVC AM-FM cassette radio, Model RC 550JW/C made of black plastic with chrome trim was stolen during the commission of a murder on Brown Avenue in South Hill. The battery compartment door is missing from the radio.
Note:	Anyone with information concerning the murder or the radio is asked to call the Whitewall Homicide Squad.

8 (#1)

WANTED
by
Police Department, County of Larinda
Blue Ridge, CA 97235

BULLETIN NO. 6-17

for
BURGLARY

#1

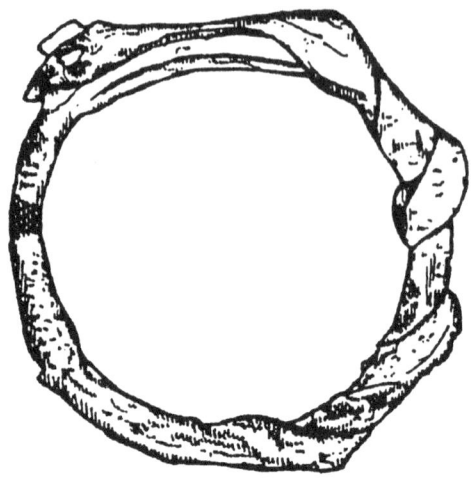
#2

Date of Occurrence: August 17, 2017 - 1930 to 2230 hours.
Place of Occurrence: Private home, 37 Cliffmount Dr., Palasino, CA
Property: Two distinctive, original designer rings taken.
1. Ladies, yellow gold, 18K ring, size 8, an alligator with green emerald eye.
2. Mans, yellow gold ring, a snake with 1/4 carat white diamond head and white diamond chips for eyes.
Value: 1. $5,000   2. $7,500
Note: Any information - contact Burglary Squad, Refer to DD 4-25.

9 (#1)

<u>W A N T E D</u>
<u>by</u>

BULLETIN NO.
12-17

<u>Police Department, County of Canton</u>
<u>Midship, Texas 84290</u>

<u>for</u>
<u>BURGLARY</u>

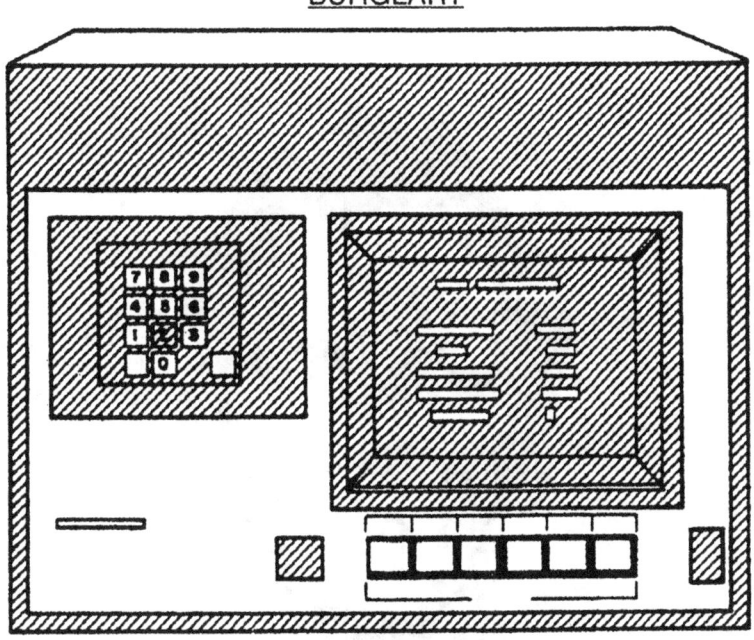

Date of Occurrence: July 31, 2017 - 1640 hours to August 1 - 0720 hours.
Place of Occurrence: 606 Hillmont Drive, Alston, TX Freemont Testing Systems
Property: Three engine analysers, color red, measuring 14" x 20" x 19"
Serial Numbers: 1. AN-0059 2. BP-0079 3. CR-0099
Value: $6,666.00 each.
Note: Request officers on patrol check service stations on post for the above items. Any information contact Detective Bryant, Third Squad, and refer to DD 3-52.

10 (#1)

WANTED by

Police Department, County of Marina
Waterford, CT 03612

for
ROBBERY

BULLETIN NO. 5-17

2014 PHOTO

Occurrences:	Robberies of gas stations and boutiques in North End precincts of Marina County.
Modus Operandi:	Subject enters store and uses telephone or shops. He then produces sawed-off shotgun or revolver from under his coat and announces robbery.
Subject:	Harry Hamilton, Male, White, DOB 6/22/73, 5'10", 180 lbs., medium complexion, severely pockmarked face.
Further Details:	Contact Robbery Squad at (203) 832-7663. Refer to Robbery Case 782. Robbery Squad has warrant for subject. IF THIS PERSON ENTERS YOUR STORE DIAL 911 OR THE ABOVE NUMBER

11 (#1)

WANTED
by

BULLETIN NO. 30-17

Police Department, County of Panfield
Lanser, South Carolina 30012

for
ROBBERY

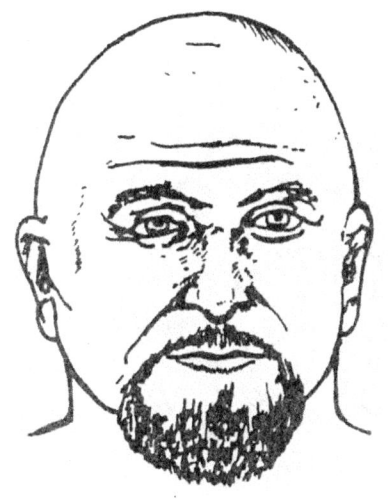

#1

2014 PHOTO
#2

Occurrence:	3 North Avenue, Anita, South Carolina, on 11/26/17 at 2310 hours.
Modus Operandi:	The above subjects forced their way into the private residence of a rug dealer, accosted the dealer, his wife, and brother, demanding jewelry, currency, escaped on foot after binding victims.
Subjects:	No. 1 - Male, White, 40-45 years, 200 lbs., heavy build, bald shaved head, fair complexion, mustache, goatee, large hooked nose, black leather jacket, armed with a knife. No. 2 - Male, White, 6'1" tall, medium build, brown hair, subject identified as Mark Nine, DOB 4/16/78, last known address 1275 East 61st Street, Brooklyn, NY in 2011, hard drug user, armed with a hand gun, subject has been indicted for residence robbery. See Wanted Bulletin 21-12.
Possible 3rd Suspect:	Male, Hispanic, 30-35 years, 5'6", thin build, collar-length black wavy hair, eyes close together, with a large Doberman. Subject observed in the area before robbery talking to bald, stocky male. Also seen entering a vehicle containing 3 or 4 males after the robbery.
Loss:	U.S. currency and jewelry valued at $3,000 to $4,000.

Further Details: Contact Robbery Squad.

12 (#1)

WANTED
by
Police Department, County of Fantail
Sweet Waters, Vermont 04610

BULLETIN NO.
1-17

for
HI-JACKING

Occurrence: Vicinity of Nikon Plaza, off Jewel Avenue & Brook Bubble Road, Sweet Waters, VT at 1820 hours, 2/6/17.

Modus Operandi: Subjects accosted the driver of a United Parcel tractor/trailer, forcing him into a pale yellow van-type vehicle, make and year unknown. Vehicle contained a black and yellow leopard rug. Driver released after two (2) hours, in the vicinity of West Lake, VT. Tractor/trailer recovered in White River, New Hampshire.

Subjects: Four (4) male Whites, one possibly named Joe, armed with hand guns. No further description.

Loss: Photo of above item: one (1) of four (4) broadcasting TV zoom lenses made by Nikon, valued at $7,000. Also included in the Nikon loss were current models of cameras, lenses, calculators, valued at $196,000. Medical supplies, mfg. by True Tell Inc., value $49,000. High quality medical examination scopes, industrial fiberscopes, cassette recorders and cameras, all mgf. by Canon Inc. valued at over $250,000. Sweaters, young mens, vee-neck design, mfg. Milford, Inc., labeled Dimension, Robt. Klein, J.C. Penney. Valued at over $20,450. Above items bearing serial numbers have been entered in NCIC.

Further Details: Contact Robbery Squad.

DIRECTIONS: After you have memorized both the pictorial and written portions of the bulletins, try to answer the following questions WITHOUT referring to the study materials.

4. Which of the following statements about the contents of the *Information Wanted* bulletin is or are true?
    I. The subject vehicle is involved in a felony.
    II. The subject vehicle is green-colored.
   The CORRECT answer is:

   A. I *only*
   C. Both I and II
   B. II *only*
   D. Neither I nor II

5.

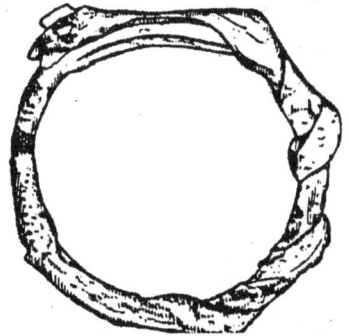

Which of the following statements about the object above is or are true?
   I. It was taken in the robbery of a residence.
   II. Its value is between $1,000 and $2,000.
The CORRECT answer is:

   A. I *only*
   C. Both I and II
   B. II *only*
   D. Neither I nor II

6. Which of the following, if any, fits the description of the individual who is wanted for the robbery of several gas stations?

   A.
   B.

C.  D. None of these

Questions 7-10.

DIRECTIONS: Questions 7 to 10 measure your ability to memorize and recall addresses, identification numbers and codes, and similar data.
In the test, you will be asked questions about the following body of information. You will NOT have the information in front of you when you take the test.

RADIO SIGNALS
01 - Back in Service
02 - Acknowledgement(OK)
06 - On Coffee
08 - Off Meal, Coffee, Personal
27 - Valid License
33 - Clear Channel (Any Emergency Request)
41 - One-Car Assistance Request
63 - Responding to Command
78 - Police Officer in Danger
99 - Possible Emergency Situation, Respond Quietly

TRUCK-TRACTOR IDENTIFICATION NUMBERS
VIN* Plate

Make	Location
Autocar	8
Brockway	2
Diamond Reo	9
Ford	10
GMC	4
Kenworth	1
Peterbuilt	7
White	5

*Vehicle Identification Number

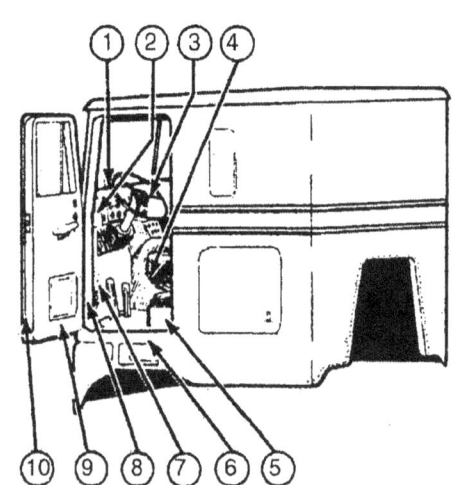

15 (#1)

Location of County Precinct Houses

First -   In H,* on S side of Merrick Rd., just E of Grand Avenue.
Second - In OB,* 1/8 mi. E of Seaford-Oyster Bay Expressway, 1/8 mi.S. of Jericho Trnpk.
Third -   In NH,* 1/8 mi. N of Hillside Ave., 1/8 mi. W of Willis Avenue
Fourth -   In H, on E side of Broadway, just N of Rockaway Avenue
Fifth -   In H, on S side of Dutch Broadway, 1/4 mi. N of Exit 14 of Southern State Parkway
Six -   In NH, just E of Community Drive, and just S of Whitney Pond Park. Seventh - In H,
           on side of Merrick Rd., just W of Seaford-Oyster Bay Expressway
Eighth -   In H, on E side of Wantagh Ave., just N of Hempstead Farmingdale Trnpk.

Location of Universities, Colleges, and Institutes
Adelphi U. -   In H,* 1/4 mi. E of Nassau Blvd., 1/4 mi. S of Stewart Ave.
Hofstra U. -   In H, at Oak and Fulton Streets.
Molloy College -   In H, on Hempstead Ave., just S of Southern State Pkway., and midway
                     between Exits 19 and 20.
C. W. Post College - In OB,* on Northern Blvd., 1 1/2 mi. W of Massapequa-Glen Cove Rd.
Nassau Community College - In H, on Stewart Ave., 1/2 mi. E of Clinton Rd.
Long Island Agri. & Tech. Institute - In OB, 1/2 mi. E of Round Swamp Rd., between Bethpage
     State Park and Old Bethpage Village Restoration.
N.Y. Inst. of Technology - In OB, on Northern Blvd., just E of line dividing OB and NH.
U.S. Merchant Marine Acad. - In NH,* at NW end of Elm Point Rd.

*H - Town of Hempstead; NH - Town of North Hempstead; OB - Town of Oyster Bay.

DIRECTIONS: After you have memorized the listed data, try to answer the following questions
              WITHOUT referring to the list.

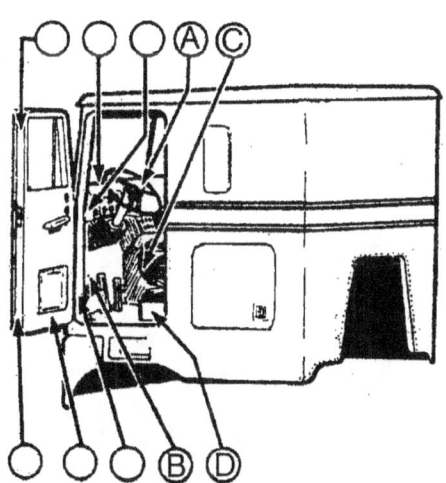

7. On a GMC truck-tractor, above, the VIN is located at

    A. A   B. B   C. C   D. D

8. The radio signal for *back in service* is

    A. 01   B. 04   C. 08   D. none of these

9. The Third Precinct House is located in 9.___

    A. NH, 1/8 mi. N of Hillside Ave., 1/8 mi. W of Willis Ave.
    B. NH, 1/4 mi. S of I.U. Willets Rd., 1/4 mi. E of Herricks Rd.
    C. Williston Park, on Willis Ave., 1/4 mi. S of Northern State Parkway
    D. Mineola, on Mineola Blvd., 1/2 mi. N of Jericho Trnpk.

10. The U.S. Merchant Marine Academy is at the NW end of _____ Rd. 10.___

    A. Sands Point   B. Mill Neck
    C. Kings Point   D. Elm Point

KEY (CORRECT ANSWERS)

1. D
2. D
3. B
4. C
5. A

6. D
7. C
8. A
9. A
10. D

EXAMINATION SECTION
TEST 1

DIRECTIONS: Each question or incomplete statement is followed by several suggested answers or completions. Select the one that BEST answers the question or completes the statement. *PRINT THE LETTER OF THE CORRECT ANSWER IN THE SPACE AT THE RIGHT.*

Questions 1-10.   MEMORY

DIRECTIONS: Questions 1 through 10 are to be answered SOLELY on the basis of the following passage, which contains a story about an incident involving police officers. You will have ten minutes to read and study the story. You may not write or make any notes while studying it. After ten minutes, close the memory booklet and do not look at it again. Then, answer the questions that follow.

You are one of a number of police officers who have been assigned to help control a demonstration inside Baldwin Square, a major square in the city. The demonstration is to protest the U.S. involvement in Iraq. As was expected, the demonstration has become nasty. You and nine other officers have been assigned to keep the demonstrators from going up Bell Street which enters the Square from the northwest. During the time you have been assigned to Bell Street, you have observed a number of things.

Before the demonstration began, three vans and a wagon entered the Square from the North on Howard Avenue. The first van was a 1989 blue Ford, plate number 897-JLK. The second van was a 1995 red Ford, plate number 899-LKK. The third van was a 1997 green Dodge step-van, plate number 997-KJL. The wagon was a blue 1998 Volvo with a luggage rack on the roof, plate number 989-LKK. The Dodge had a large dent in the left-hand rear door and was missing its radiator grill. The Ford that was painted red had markings under the paint which made you believe that it had once been a telephone company truck. Equipment for the speakers' platform was unloaded from the van, along with a number of demonstration signs. As soon as the vans and wagon were unloaded, a number of demonstrators picked up the signs and started marching around the square. A sign reading *U.S. Out Now* was carried by a woman wearing red jeans, a black tee shirt, and blue sneakers. A man with a beard, a blue shirt, and Army pants began carrying a poster reading *To Hell With Davis.* A tall, Black male and a Hispanic male had been carrying a large sign with *This Is How Vietnam Started* in big black letters with red dripping off the bottom of each letter.

A number of the demonstrators are wearing black armbands and green tee shirts with the peace symbol on the front. A woman with very short hair who was dressed in green and yellow fatigues is carrying a triangular-shaped blue sign with white letters. The sign says *Out Of Iraq*.

A group of 12 demonstrators have been carrying six fake coffins back and forth across the Square between Apple Street on the West and Webb Street on the East. They are shouting *Death to Hollis and his Henchmen.* Over where Victor Avenue enters the Square from the South, a small group of demonstrators (two men and three women) just started painting slogans on the walls surrounding the construction of the First National Union Bank and Trust.

1. Which street is on the opposite side of the Square from Victor Avenue?   1._____
   A. Bell   B. Howard   C. Apple   D. Webb

2. How many officers are assigned with you?   2._____
   A. 8   B. 6   C. 9   D. 5

3. Howard Avenue enters the Square from which direction?   3._____
   A. Northwest   B. North   C. East   D. Southwest

4. The van that had PROBABLY been a telephone truck had plate number   4._____
   A. 899-LKK   B. 989-LKK   C. 897-JKL   D. 997-KJL

5. What is the color of the sign carried by the woman with very short hair?   5._____
   A. Blue   B. White   C. Black   D. Red

6. The man wearing the army pants has a(n)   6._____
   A. Afro   B. beard
   C. triangular-shaped sign   D. black armband

7. Which vehicle had plate number 989-LKK? The   7._____
   A. red Ford   B. blue Ford   C. Volvo   D. Dodge

8. The bank under construction is located _____ of the Square.   8._____
   A. north   B. south   C. east   D. west

9. How many people are painting slogans on the walls surrounding the construction site?   9._____
   A. 4   B. 5   C. 6   D. 7

10. What is the name of the bank under construction?   10._____
    A. National Union Bank and Trust
    B. First National Bank and Trust
    C. First Union National Bank and Trust
    D. First National Union Bank and Trust

KEY (CORRECT ANSWERS)

1. B   6. B
2. C   7. C
3. B   8. B
4. A   9. B
5. A   10. D

TEST 2

DIRECTIONS: Each question or incomplete statement is followed by several suggested answers or completions. Select the one that BEST answers the question or completes the statement. *PRINT THE LETTER OF THE CORRECT ANSWER IN THE SPACE AT THE RIGHT.*

Questions 1-15.

DIRECTIONS: Questions 1 through 15 are to be answered SOLELY on the basis of the Memory Booklet given below.

MEMORY BOOKLET

The following passage contains a story about an incident involving police officers. You will have ten minutes to read and study the story. You may not write or make any notes while studying it. The first questions in the examination will be based on the passage. After ten minutes, close the memory booklet, and do not look at it again. Then, answer the questions that follow.

Police Officers Boggs and Thomas are patrolling in a radio squad car on a late Saturday afternoon in the spring. They are told by radio that a burglary is taking place on the top floor of a six-story building on the corner of 5th Street and Essex and that they should deal with the incident.

The police officers know the location and know that the Gold Jewelry Company occupies the entire sixth floor. They also know that, over the weekends, the owner has gold bricks in his office safe worth $500,000.

When the officers arrive at the location, they lock their radio car. They then find the superintendent of the building who opens the front door for them. He indicates he has neither seen nor heard anything suspicious in the building. However, he had just returned from a long lunch hour. The officers take the elevator to the sixth floor. As the door of the elevator with the officers opens on the sixth floor, the officers hear the door of the freight elevator in the rear of the building closing and the freight elevator beginning to move. They leave the elevator and proceed quickly through the open door of the office of the Gold Jewelry Company. They see that the office safe is open and empty. The officers quickly proceed to the rear staircase. They run down six flights of stairs, and they see four suspects leaving through the rear entrance of the building.

They run through the rear door and out of the building after the suspects. The four suspects are running quickly through the parking lot at the back of the building. The suspects then make a right-hand turn onto 5th Street and are clearly seen by the officers. The officers see one white male, one Hispanic male, one Black male, and one white female.

The white male has a beard and sunglasses. He is wearing blue jeans, a dark red and blue jacket, and white jogging shoes. He is carrying a large green duffel bag over his shoulder.

The Hispanic male limps slightly and has a dark moustache. He is wearing dark brown slacks, a dark green sweat shirt, and brown shoes. He is carrying a large blue duffel bag.

The Black male is clean-shaven, wearing black corduroy pants, a multi-colored shirt, a green beret, and black boots. He is carrying a tool box.

The white female has long dark hair and is wear-ing light-colored blue jeans, a white blouse, sneakers, and a red kerchief around her neck. She is carrying a shotgun.

The officers chase the suspects for three long blocks without getting any closer to them. At the intersection of 5th Street and Pennsylvania Avenue, the suspects separate. The white male and the Black male rapidly get into a 1992 brown Ford stationwagon. The stationwagon has a roof rack on top and a Connecticut license plate with the letters *JEAN* on it. The stationwagon departs even before the occupants close the door completely.

The Hispanic male and the white female get into an old blue Dodge van. The van has a CB antenna on top, a picture of a cougar on the back doors, a dented right rear fender, and a New Jersey license plate. The officers are not able to read the plate numbers on the van.

The officers then observe the stationwagon turn left and enter an expressway going to Connecticut. The van turns right onto Illinois Avenue and proceeds toward the tunnel to New Jersey.

The officers immediately run back to their radio car to radio in what happened.

1. Which one of the following suspects had sunglasses on?   1.____

    A. White male   B. Hispanic male
    C. Black male   D. White female

2. Which one of the following suspects was carrying a shotgun?   2.____

    A. White male   B. Hispanic male
    C. Black male   D. White female

3. Which one of the following suspects was wearing a green beret?   3.____

    A. White male   B. Hispanic male
    C. Black male   D. White femal

4. Which one of the following suspects limped slightly?   4.____

    A. White male   B. Hispanic male
    C. Black male   D. White female

5. Which one of the following BEST describes the stationwagon used?   5.____
A

    A. 1992 brown Ford   B. 1992 blue Dodge
    C. 1979 brown Ford   D. 1979 blue Dodge

6. Which one of the following BEST describes the suspect or suspects who used the stationwagon?
   A
   A. Black male and a Hispanic male
   B. white male and a Hispanic male
   C. Black male and a white male
   D. Black male and a white female

7. The van had a license plate from which of the following states?
   A. Connecticut
   B. New Jersey
   C. New York
   D. Pennsylvania

8. The license plate on the stationwagon read as follows:
   A. JANE
   B. JOAN
   C. JEAN
   D. JUNE

9. The van used had a dented _____ fender.
   A. left rear
   B. right rear
   C. right front
   D. left front

10. When last seen by the officers, the van was headed toward
    A. Connecticut
    B. New Jersey
    C. Pennsylvania
    D. Long Island

11. The female suspect's hair can BEST be described as
    A. long and dark-colored
    B. short and dark-colored
    C. long and light-colored
    D. short and light-colored

12. Which one of the following suspects was wearing a multicolored shirt?
    A. White male
    B. Hispanic male
    C. Black male
    D. White female

13. Blue jeans were worn by the _____ male suspect and the suspect.
    A. Hispanic; white female
    B. Black; Hispanic male
    C. white; white female
    D. Black; white male

14. The color of the duffel bag carried by the Hispanic male suspect was
    A. blue
    B. green
    C. brown
    D. red

15. The Hispanic male suspect was wearing
    A. brown shoes
    B. black shoes
    C. black boots
    D. jogging shoes

KEY (CORRECT ANSWERS)

1. A
2. D
3. C
4. B
5. A

6. C
7. B
8. C
9. B
10. B

11. A
12. C
13. C
14. A
15. A

PROBLEM SENSITIVITY

This section of the exam measures your ability to choose the course of action that should be taken first in critical situations.

Sample Questions

1. What should an officer do first when investigating an incident?

    A. Write a report of the incident.
    B. Inform other police officers of the incident.
    C. Proceed to the scene of the incident.
    D. Interview witnesses.

Getting the correct information to the emergency medical personnel is extremely important. It is suggested that you, the police officer, make the call if possible, or assign the task to a person who appears calm. If you are alone at the accident scene, do not leave the victim until breathing is restored, all bleeding has been stopped, the victim is no longer in danger of further injury, and all precautions have been taken against shock. When the emergency medical personnel arrive, brief them as to what happened to the victim, the type of first aid you have administered, and the physical status of the victim.

2. When the emergency medical personnel arrives at the accident scene, you first should tell them:

    A. how long the victim's breathing has been restored.
    B. how long the bleeding has been stopped.
    C. that the victim appeared to be going into shock.
    D. the type of first aid you administered.

KEY (CORRECT ANSWERS)

1. C
2. D

EXAMINATION SECTION
TEST 1

DIRECTIONS: Each question or incomplete statement is followed by several suggested answers or completions. Select the one that BEST answers the question or completes the statement. *PRINT THE LETTER OF THE CORRECT ANSWER IN THE SPACE AT THE RIGHT.*

Questions 1-9.

DIRECTIONS: Questions 1 through 9 measure your ability to (1) determine whether statements from witnesses say essentially the same thing, and (2) determine the evidence need to make it reasonably certain that a particular conclusion is true.

1. Which of the following pairs of statements say essentially the same thing in two different ways?
   I. The only time the machine's red light is on is when the door is locked.
      If the machine's door is locked, the red light is on.
   II. Some gray-jacketed cables are connected to the blower.
      If a cable is connected to the blower, it must be gray-jacketed.
   The CORRECT answer is:
   A. I only   B. I and II   C. II only   D. Neither I nor II

2. Which of the following pairs of statements say essentially the same thing in two different ways?
   I. If you live on Maple Street, your child is in the Valley District.
      If your child is in the Valley District, you must live on Maple Street.
   II. All the Smith children are brown-eyed.
      If a child is brown-eyed, it is not one of the Smith children.
   The CORRECT answer is:
   A. I only   B. I and II   C. II only   D. Neither I nor II

3. Which of the following pairs of statements say essentially the same thing in two different ways?
   I. If it's Monday, Mrs. James will be here.
      Mrs. James is here every Monday.
   II. Most people in the Drama Club do not have stage fright, but everyone in the Drama Club wants to be noticed.
      Some people in the Drama Club have stage fright and want to be noticed.
   The CORRECT answer is:
   A. I only   B. I and II   C. II only   D. Neither I nor II

4. Which of the following pairs of statements say essentially the same thing in two different ways?
   I. If you are older than 65, you will get a senior's discount.
      Either you will get a senior's discount, or you are not older than 65.
   II. Every cadet in Officer Johnson's class has passed the firearms safety course.
       No cadet that has failed the firearms safety course is in Officer Johnson's class.
   The CORRECT answer is:
   A. I only   B. I and II   C. II only   D. Neither I nor II

5. Summary of Evidence Collected to Date:
   Most people in the Greenlawn housing project do not have criminal records.
   Prematurely Drawn Conclusion:
   Some people in Greenlawn who have been crime victims have criminal records themselves.
   Which of the following pieces of evidence, if any, would make it *reasonably certain* that the conclusion drawn is TRUE?
   A. Some of those who live in the Greenlawn project have been arrested or convicted of "victimless" crimes.
   B. Most people in Greenlawn have been the victims of crime.
   C. Everyone in Greenlawn has been the victim of crime.
   D. None of the above

6. Summary of Evidence Collected to Date:
   Every drug dealer in the Oak Lawn neighborhood wears blue and carries a Glock.
   Prematurely Drawn Conclusion:
   A person in the Oak Lawn neighborhood who carries a Glock is a drug dealer.
   Which of the following pieces of evidence, if any, would make it *reasonably certain* that the conclusion drawn is TRUE?
   A. In the Oak Lawn neighborhood, only drug dealers wear blue.
   B. Drug dealers in Oak Lawn only carry Glocks when they're dealing drugs.
   C. In the Oak Lawn neighborhood, only drug dealers carry Glocks.
   D. None of the above

7. Summary of Evidence Collected to Date:
   I. Dr. Jones is older than Dr. Gupta.
   II. Dr. Gupta and Dr. Unruh were born on the same day.
   Prematurely Drawn Conclusion:
   Dr. Gupta does not work in the emergency room.
   Which of the following pieces of evidence, if any, would make it *reasonably certain* that the conclusion drawn is TRUE?
   A. Dr. Jones is older than Dr. Unruh.
   B. Dr. Jones works in the emergency room.
   C. Every doctor in the emergency room is older than Dr. Unruh.
   D. None of the above

8. Summary of Evidence Collected to Date:
   I. On the street, a "dose" of a certain drug contains four "drams."
   II. A person can trade three "rolls" of a drug for a "plunk."
   Prematurely Drawn Conclusion:
   A plunk is the most valuable amount of the drug on the street.
   Which of the following pieces of evidence, if any, would make it *reasonably certain* that the conclusion drawn is TRUE?
   A. A person can trade five doses for two rolls.
   B. A dram contains two rolls.
   C. A roll is larger than a dram.
   D. None of the above

   8.____

9. Summary of Evidence Collected to Date:
   Sam is a good writer and editor.
   Prematurely Drawn Conclusion:
   Sam is qualified for the job.
   Which of the following pieces of evidence, if any, would make it *reasonably certain* that the conclusion drawn is TRUE?
   A. The job calls for good writing and editing skills.
   B. A person who is not a good editor could still apply for the job on the strength of his/her writing skills.
   C. If Sam applies for the job, he must be both a good writer and editor.
   D. None of the above

   9.____

Questions 10-14.

DIRECTIONS: Questions 10 through 14 refer to Map #7 and measure your ability to orient yourself within a given section of town, neighborhood or particular area. Each of the questions describes a starting point and a destination. Assume that you are driving a car in the area shown on the map accompanying the questions. Use the map as a basis for the shortest way to get from one point to another without breaking the law.
On the map, a street marked by arrows, or by arrows and the words "One Way," indicates one-way travel, and should be assumed to be one-way for the entire length, even when there are breaks or jogs in the street. EXCEPTION: A street that does not have the same name over the full length.

Map #7.

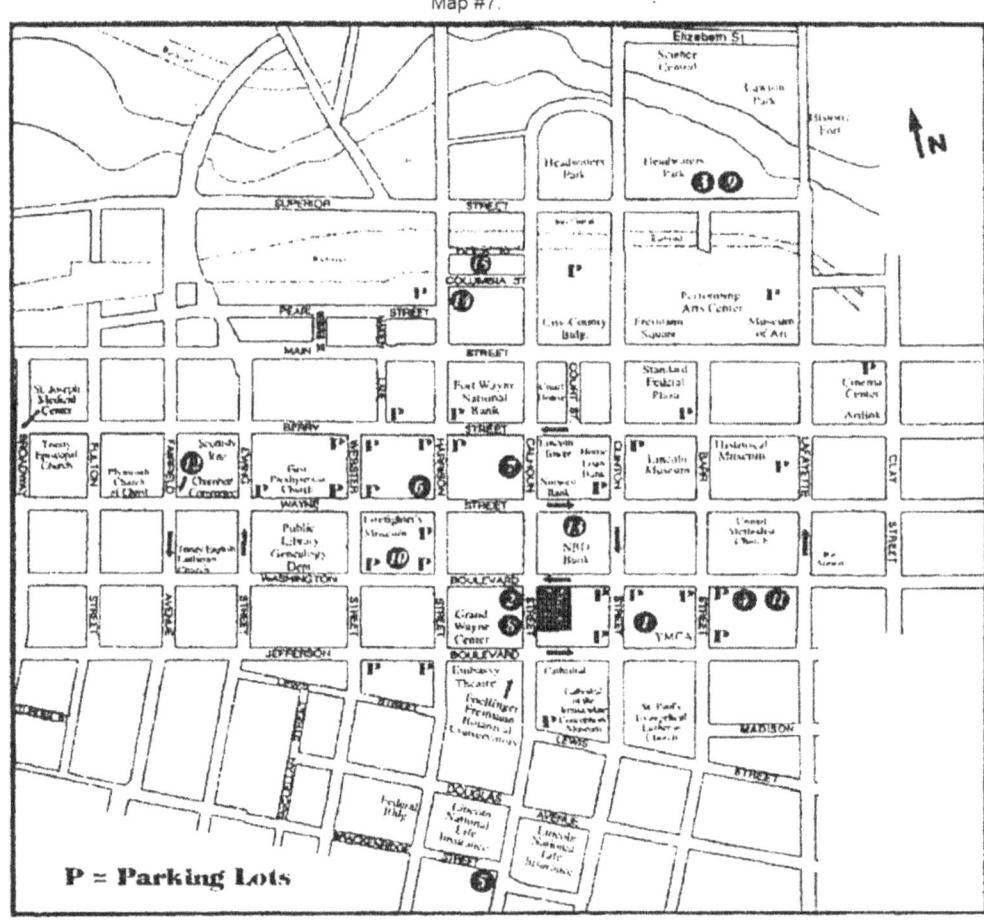

10. The SHORTEST legal way from Trinity Episcopal Church to Science Central is
    A. east on Berry, north on Clinton, east on Elizabeth
    B. east on Berry, north on Lafayette, west on Elizabeth
    C. north on Fulton, east on Main, north on Lafayette, west on Elizabeth
    D. north on Fulton, east on Main, north on Calhoun

11. The SHORTEST legal way from the Grand Wayne Center to the Museum of Art is
    A. north on Harrison, east on Superior, south on Lafayette
    B. east on Washington Blvd., north on Lafayette
    C. east on Jefferson Blvd., north on Clinton, east on Main
    D. east on Jefferson Blvd., north on Lafayette

12. The SHORTEST legal way from the Embassy Theatre too the City/County Building is
    A. west on Jefferson Blvd., north on Ewing, east on Main
    B. east on Jefferson Blvd., north on Lafayette, west on Main
    C. east on Jefferson Blvd., north on Clinton
    D. north on Harrison, east on Main

5 (#1)

13. The SHORTEST legal way from the YMCA to the Firefighter's Museum is   13._____
    A. west on Jefferson Blvd., north on Webster
    B. north on Barr, west on Washington Blvd., north on Webster
    C. north on Barr, west on Wayne
    D. north on Barr, west on Berry, south on Webster

14. The SHORTEST legal way from the Historic Fort to Freimann Square is   14._____
    A. north on Lafayette, west on Elizabeth, south on Clinton
    B. north on Lafayette, west on Elizabeth, west/south on Calhoun, east on Main
    C. south on Lafayette, west on Main
    D. south on Lafayette, west on Superior, south on Clinton

Questions 15-19.

DIRECTIONS: Questions 15 through 19 refer to Figure #7, on the following page, and measure your ability to understand written descriptions of events. Each question presents a description of an accident or event and asks you which of the five drawings in Figure #7 BEST represents it.

In the drawings, the following symbols are used:

Moving Vehicle: ⌂   Non-moving Vehicle: ▮

Pedestrian or Bicyclist: ●

The path and direction of travel of a vehicle or pedestrian is indicated by a solid line.

The path and direction of travel of each vehicle or pedestrian directly involved in a collision from the point of impact is indicated by a dotted line.

In the space at the right, print the letter of the drawing that BEST fits the descriptions written below:

15. A driver headed northeast on Cary strikes a car in the intersection and is   15._____
    diverted north, where he collides with the rear of a car that is traveling north on Park. The northbound car is knocked into the rear of another car that is traveling north ahead of it.

16. A driver headed northeast on Cary strikes a car in the intersection and is   16._____
    diverted north, where he collides head-on with a car stopped at a traffic light in the southbound lane on Park.

17. A driver headed northeast on Cary strikes a car in the intersection and is   17._____
    diverted east, where he collides head-on with a car stopped at a traffic light in the westbound lane on Roble.

18. A driver headed east on Roble collides with the left front of a car that is turning right from Knox onto Roble. The driver swerves right after the collision and collides head-on with another car headed north on Park.

18.____

19. A driver headed northeast on Cary strikes a car in the intersection and is diverted north, where he collides with the rear of a car parked on the northbound lane on Park.

19.____

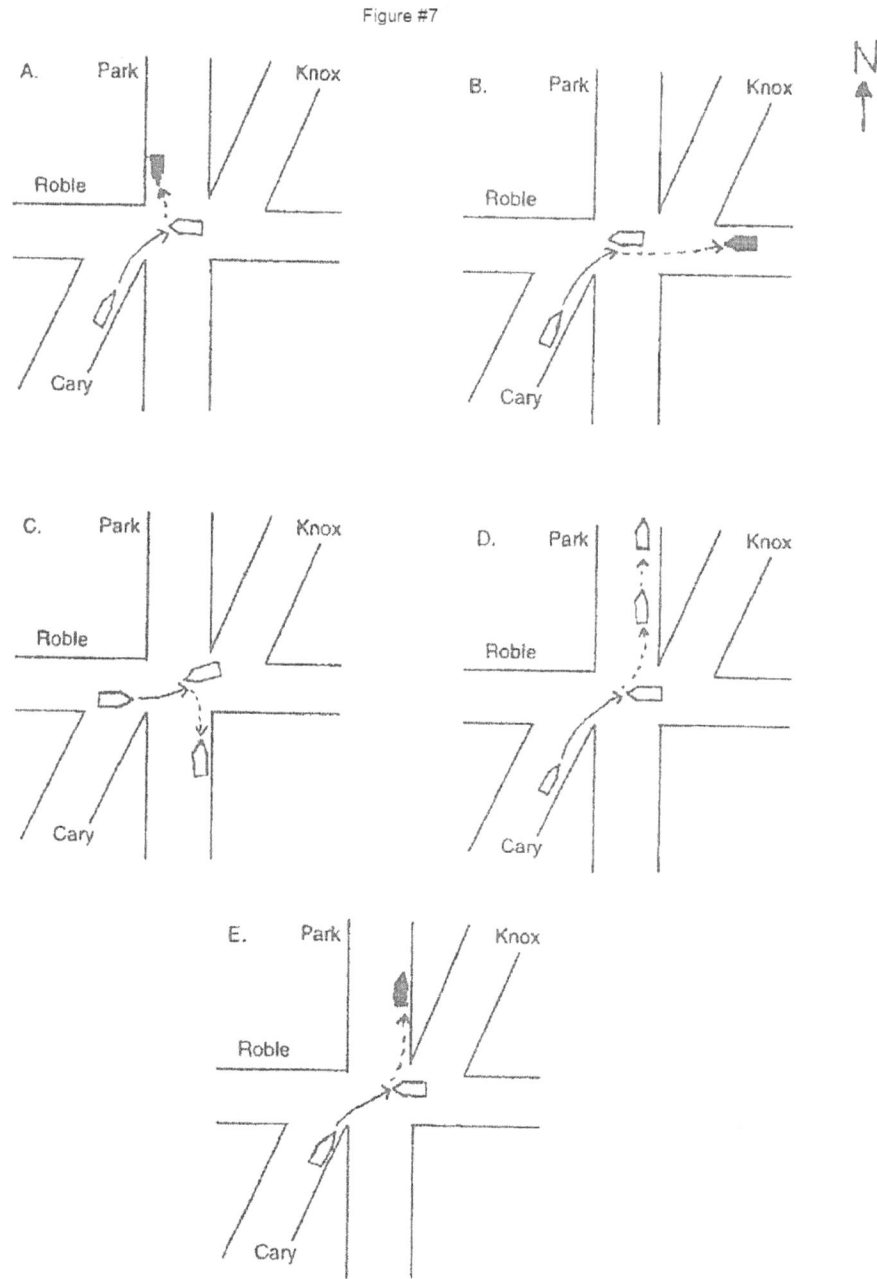

Figure #7

Questions 20-22.

DIRECTIONS: In Questions 20 through 22, choose the word or phrase CLOSEST in meaning to the word or phrase printed in capital letters.

20. JURISDICTION
    A. authority   B. decision   C. judgment   D. argument

21. PROXY
    A. neighbor   B. agent   C. enforcer   D. impostor

22. LARCENY
    A. theft   B. assault   C. deceit   D. gentleness

Questions 23-25.

DIRECTIONS: Questions 22 through 25 measure your ability to do fieldwork-related arithmetic. Each question presents a separate arithmetic problem for you to solve.

23. Mr. Long has 14 employees. He has four more male employees than female employees.
    How many female employees does he have?
    A. 4   B. 5   C. 9   D. 10

24. A box of latex gloves costs $18. A crate has 12 boxes, each of which contains 48 gloves.
    How much does a crate of latex gloves cost?
    A. $216   B. $328   C. $576   D. $864

25. In a single week, the Department of Parking collected 540 quarter, 623 dimes, and 146 nickels from its parking meters.
    What was the TOTAL revenue collected from the meters during the week?
    A. $135.00   B. $154.00   C. $204.60   D. $270.30

KEY (CORRECT ANSWERS)

1.	A	11.	D
2.	D	12.	D
3.	B	13.	B
4.	B	14.	A
5.	C	15.	D
6.	C	16.	A
7.	C	17.	B
8.	A	18.	C
9.	A	19.	E
10.	C	20.	A

21. B
22. A
23. B
24. A
25. C

SOLUTIONS (QUESTIONS 1-9)

P implies Q = original statement

Not Q implies not P = contrapositive of the original statement. A statement and its contrapositive are logically equivalent.

Q implies P = converse of the original statement.

Not P implies not Q = inverse of the original statement. The converse and inverse of an original statement are logically equivalent.

P implies Q = Not P or Q

1. CORRECT ANSWER: A
   For Item I, the equivalent of the first statement would be "If the red light is on, the door is locked." This is the converse of the second statement, so it is not equivalent to the first statement. For Item II, the first statement does not guarantee that all cables that are connected to the blower must be gray-jacketed. There may very well be other cables that are connected to the blower that are not gray-jacketed. Equally possible, some gray-jacketed cables are not necessarily connected to the blower.

2. CORRECT ANSWER: D
   For Item I, the second statement is the converse of the first statement, so it is not logically equivalent. For Item II, the equivalent of the first statement is "If a child is not brown-eyed, then it is not one of the Smith children." Thus, statement II as it stands is not equivalent to statement I.

3. CORRECT ANSWER: B
   For Item I, Mrs. James is here every Monday, so we conclude that if it is Monday, she is here. (She may be here on other days as well.) For Item II, we can conclude that there are some people in the Drama Club who do have stage fright. Since everyone in the Drama Club wants to be noticed, this would include those who have stage fright.

4. CORRECT ANSWER: B
   For Item I, these two statements represent "P implies Q" and "Not P or Q," where P = Older than 65 and Q = Get a senior discount. These are equivalent statements. For Item II, these statements are contrapositive of each other and so must be equivalent. (P = Cadet in Johnson's class and Q = Passes the safety course.)

5. CORRECT ANSWER: C
   If everyone in the housing project has been a victim of crime and most of these people do not have a criminal record, we can conclude that some of them do have a criminal record. Thus, we have the situation that some of the people who live in this housing project are both a victim of crime as well as a perpetrator of crime.

6. **CORRECT ANSWER: C**
This choice can be written as "In this neighborhood, if a person carries a Glock, he is a drug dealer." This would lead directly to the drawn conclusion.

7. **CORRECT ANSWER: C**
We know that every doctor in the emergency room is older than Dr. Unruh; it is not possible for Dr. Gupta to be working in the emergency room since he is the same age as Dr. Unruh.

8. **CORRECT ANSWER: A**
From statement I, a dose is worth more than a dram. If 5 doses is equal to 2 rolls, then a roll is worth more than a dose. So of these three, a roll is worth the most. Finally, statement II tells us that a plunk is worth more than a roll. This means that a plunk is worth the most among all four of these categories.

9. **CORRECT ANSWER: A**
Sam has the qualifications of being a good writer and editor, which is exactly what is needed for the job. Therefore, Sam is qualified for this job.

TEST 2

DIRECTIONS: Each question or incomplete statement is followed by several suggested answers or completions. Select the one that BEST answers the question or completes the statement. *PRINT THE LETTER OF THE CORRECT ANSWER IN THE SPACE AT THE RIGHT.*

Questions 1-9.

DIRECTIONS: Questions 1 through 9 measure your ability to (1) determine whether statements from witnesses say essentially the same thing, and (2) determine the evidence need to make it reasonably certain that a particular conclusion is true.

To do well on this part of the test, you do NOT have to have a working knowledge of police procedures and techniques. Nor do you have to have any more familiarity with criminals and criminal behavior than that acquired from reading newspapers, listening to radio or watching TV. To do well in this part, you must read and reason carefully.

1. Which of the following pairs of statements say essentially the same thing in two different ways?
   I. If the garbage is collected today, it is definitely Wednesday.
      The garbage is collected every Wednesday.
   II. Nobody has no answer to the question.
       Everybody has at least one answer to the question.
   The CORRECT answer is:
   A. I only   B. I and II   C. II only   D. Neither I nor II

2. Which of the following pairs of statements say essentially the same thing in two different ways?
   I. If it trains, the streets will be wet.
      If the streets are wet, it has rained.
   II. All of the Duluth Five are immune from prosecution.
       No member of the Duluth Five can be prosecuted.
   The CORRECT answer is:
   A. I only   B. I and II   C. II only   D. Neither I nor II

3. Which of the following pairs of statements say essentially the same thing in two different ways?
   I. Ms. Friar will accept her promotion if and only if she is offered a 10% raise.
      For Ms. Friar to accept her promotion, it is necessary that she be offered a 10% raise.
   II. If the hydraulic lines are flushed, it is definitely inspection day.
       The hydraulic lines are flushed only on inspection days.
   The CORRECT answer is:
   A. I only   B. I and II   C. II only   D. Neither I nor II

4. Which of the following pairs of statements say essentially the same thing in two different ways?
   I. If you are tall you will get onto the basketball team.
      Unless you are tall, you will not get onto the basketball team.
   II. That raven is black.
       If that bird is black, it's a raven.
   The CORRECT answer is:
   A. I only   B. I and II   C. II only   D. Neither I nor II

5. Summary of Evidence Collected to Date:
   Every member of the Rotary Club is retired.
   Prematurely Drawn Conclusion:
   At least some people in the planning commission are retired.
   Which of the following pieces of evidence, if any, would make it *reasonably certain* that the conclusion drawn is TRUE?
   A. Retirement is a condition for membership in the Rotary Club.
   B. Every member of the planning commission has been in the Rotary Club at one time.
   C. Every member of the Rotary Club is also on the planning commission.
   D. None of the above

6. Summary of Evidence Collected to Date:
   Some of the SWAT team snipers have poor aim.
   Prematurely Drawn Conclusion:
   The snipers on the SWAT team with the worst aim also have 20/20 vision.
   Which of the following pieces of evidence, if any, would make it *reasonably certain* that the conclusion drawn is TRUE?
   A. Some of the SWAT team snipers have 20/20 vision.
   B. Every sniper on the SWAT team has 20/20 vision.
   C. Some snipers on the SWAT team wear corrective lenses.
   D. None of the above

7. Summary of Evidence Collected to Date:
   The only time Garson hears voices is on a day when he doesn't take his medication.
   Prematurely Drawn Conclusion:
   On Fridays, Garson never hears voices.
   Which of the following pieces of evidence, if any, would make it *reasonably certain* that the conclusion drawn is TRUE?
   A. Garson is supposed to take his medication every day.
   B. Garson usually undergoes shock therapy on Fridays.
   C. Garson usually takes his medication and undergoes shock therapy on Fridays.
   D. None of the above

8. Summary of Evidence Collected to Date:
Among the three maintenance workers, Frank, Lily and Jean, Frank is not the tallest.
Premhaturely Drawn Conclusion:
Lily is the tallest.
Which of the following pieces of evidence, if any, would make it *reasonably certain* that the conclusion drawn is TRUE?
  A. Jean is not the tallest.
  B. Frank is the shortest.
  C. Jean is the shortest.
  D. None of the above

8.____

9. Summary of Evidence Collected to Date:
Doctor Lyons went to the cafeteria for lunch today and did not eat dessert.
Prematurely Drawn Conclusion:
The cafeteria did not serve dessert.
Which of the following pieces of evidence, if any, would make it *reasonably certain* that the conclusion drawn is TRUE?
  A. Dr. Lyons never eats dessert.
  B. When the cafeteria serves dessert, Dr. Lyons always eats it.
  C. The cafeteria rarely serves dessert when Dr. Lyons eats there.

9.____

Questions 10-14.

DIRECTIONS: Questions 10 through 14 refer to Map #8 and measure your ability to orient yourself within a given section of town, neighborhood or particular area. Each of the questions describes a starting point and a destination. Assume that you are driving a car in the area shown on the map accompanying the questions. Use the map as a basis for the shortest way to get from one point to another without breaking the law.
On the map, a street marked by arrows, or by arrows and the words "One Way," indicates one-way travel, and should be assumed to be one-way for the entire length, even when there are breaks or jogs in the street. EXCEPTION: A street that does not have the same name over the full length.

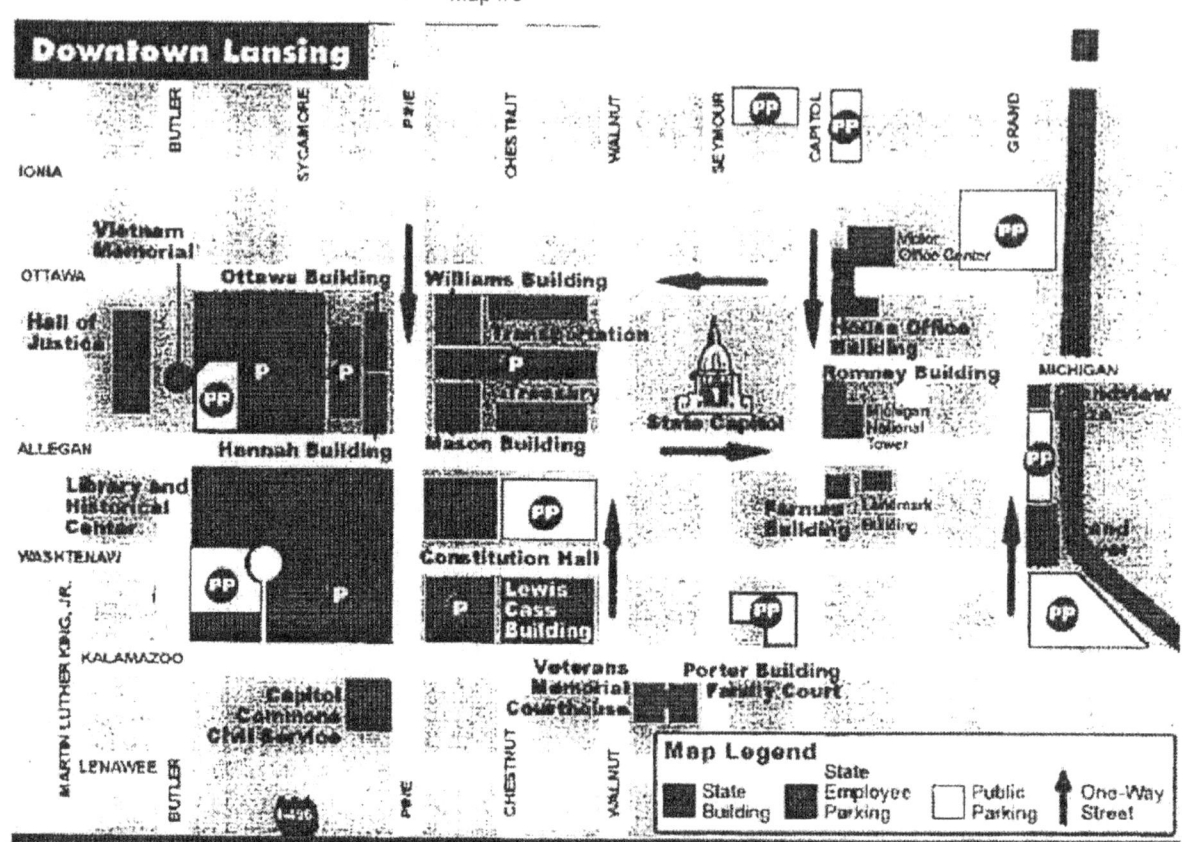

Map #8

10. The SHORTEST legal way from the Library and Historical Center to Grandview Plaza is
    A. south on Butler, east on Kalamazoo, north on Grand
    B. east on Allegan, north on Grand
    C. north on Butler, east on Ionia, south on Grand
    D. north on Martin Luther King, Jr., east on Ottawa, south on Pine, east on Allegan, north on Grand

11. The SHORTEST legal way from the Victor Office Center to the Mason Building is
    A. west on Ottawa, south on Pine
    B. south on Capitol, west on Allegan, north on Pine
    C. south on Capitol, west on Washtenaw, north on Walnut, west on Allegan
    D. west on Ottawa, north on Seymour, west on Ionia, south on Pine

12. The SHORTESST legal way from the Treasury to the Hall of Justice is
    A. north on Walnut, west on Ottawa, south on Martin Luther King, Jr.
    B. west on Allegan
    C. east on Allegan, north on Grand, west on Ottawa, south on Martin Luther King. Jr.
    D. south on Walnut, west on Kalamazoo, north on Martin Luther King, Jr.

13. The SHORTEST legal way from the Veterans Memorial Courthouse to the   13._____
    House Office Building is
    A. north on Walnut, east on Ottawa
    B. east on Kalamazoo, north on Capitol
    C. east on Kalamazoo, north on Grand, west on Ottawa
    D. north on Walnut, east on Allegan, north on Capitol

14. The SHORTEST legal way from Grand Tower to Constitution Hall is   14._____
    A. west on Washtenaw
    B. north on Grand, west on Allegan, south on Pine
    C. north on Grand, west on Ottaway, south on Pine
    D. south on Grand, west on Kalamazoo, north on Pine

Questions 15-19.

DIRECTIONS: Questions 15 through 19 refer to Figure #8, on the following page, and measure your ability to understand written descriptions of events. Each question presents a description of an accident or event and asks you which of the five drawings in Figure #8 BEST represents it.

In the drawings, the following symbols are used:

Moving Vehicle: ◯   Non-moving Vehicle: ▮

Pedestrian or Bicyclist: ●

The path and direction of travel of a vehicle or pedestrian is indicated by a solid line.

The path and direction of travel of each vehicle or pedestrian directly involved in a collision from the point of impact is indicated by a dotted line.

In the space at the right, print the letter of the drawing that BEST fits the descriptions written below:

15. A driver headed west on Holly runs a red light and turns left. He sideswipes   15._____
    a car headed south in the intersection, and then flees south on Bay. The southbound car is diverted into the rear end of a car parked in the southbound lane on Bay.

16. A driver headed east on Holly runs a red light. Another driver headed south   16._____
    through the intersection slams on her brakes just in time to avoid a serious collision. The eastbound driver glances off the front of the southbound car and continues east, where he collides with a car parked in the eastbound lane on Holly.

17. A driver headed east on Holly runs a red light. She strikes the left front of a   17._____
    westbound car that is turning left from Holly onto Bay, and then veers left and strikes the rear end of a car parked in the northbound lane on Bay.

18. A driver headed north on Bay strikes the right front of a car heading south in the intersection of Bay and Holly. After the collision, the driver veers left and collides with the rear end of a car parked in the westbound lane of Holly. The southbound car veers left and collides with the rear end of a car in the eastbound lane on Holly.

18._____

19. A driver headed north on Bay strikes the left front of a car heading south in the intersection of Bay and Holly. After the collision, the driver continues north and collides with the rear end of a car parked in the northbound lane. The southbound car continues south and collides with the rear end of a car in the southbound lane.

19._____

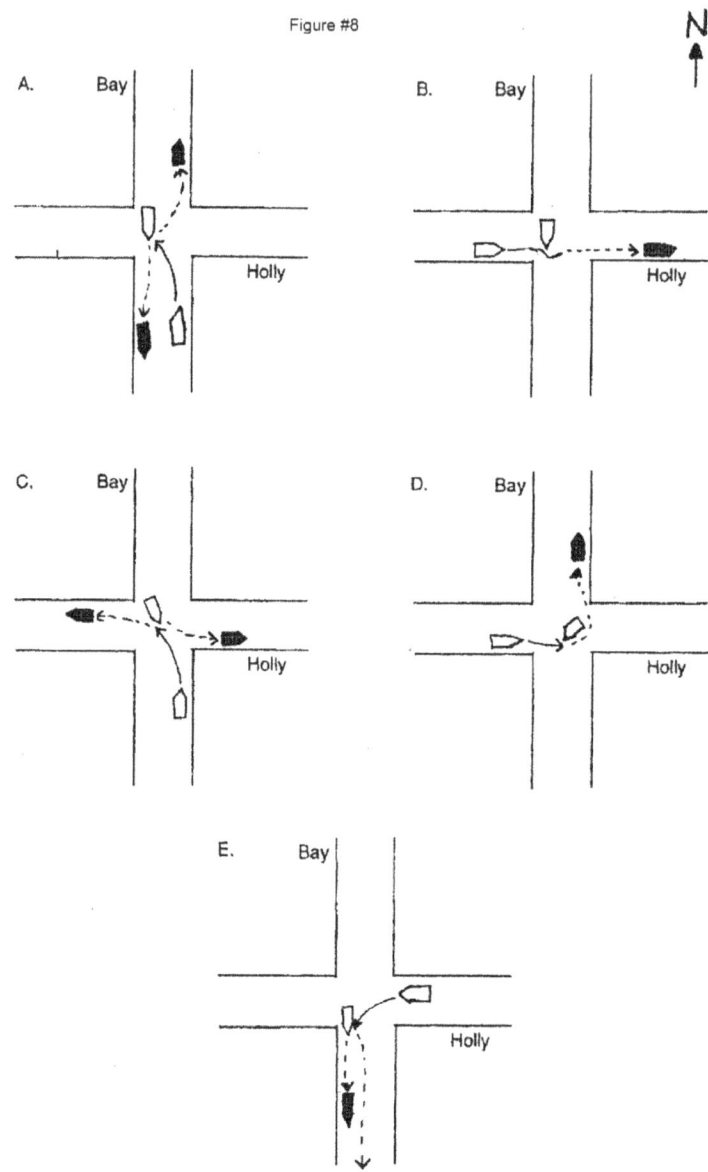

Figure #8

Questions 20-22.

DIRECTIONS: In Questions 20 through 22, choose the word or phrase CLOSEST in meaning to the word or phrase printed in capital letters.

20. LIABLE
    A. sensitive   B. dishonest   C. responsible   D. valid

21. CLAIM
    A. debt   B. period   C. denial   D. banishment

22. ADMISSIBLE
    A. false   B. conclusive   C. acceptable   D. indsputable

Questions 23-25.

DIRECTIONS: Questions 22 through 25 measure your ability to do fieldwork-related arithmetic. Each question presents a separate arithmetic problem for you to solve.

23. Three departments divide an $800 payment. Department 1 takes $270, and Department 2 takes $150 more than Department 3.
    How much does Department 2 take?
    A. $150   B. $190   C. $340   D. $490

24. Detective Smalley cleared 100 murder cases in five years. Each year he cleared six more than he cleared in the previous year.
    How many cases did he clear during the first year?
    A. 6   B. 8   C. 12   D. 18

25. The purchasing agent bought three binders for $2 each, four reams of copier paper for $3 each and five packs of black pens for $7 each.
    How much did the agent spend?
    A. $12.00   B. $25.20   C. $53.00   D. $72.00

KEY (CORRECT ANSWERS)

1.	B	11.	A
2.	C	12.	A
3.	B	13.	C
4.	D	14.	A
5.	C	15.	E
6.	B	16.	B
7.	D	17.	D
8.	A	18.	C
9.	B	19.	A
10.	B	20.	C

21.	A
22.	C
23.	C
24.	B
25.	C

9 (#2)

SOLUTIONS (QUESTIONS 1-9)

P implies Q = original statement

Not Q implies not P = contrapositive of the original statement. A statement and its contrapositive are logically equivalent.

Q implies P = converse of the original statement.

Not P implies not Q = inverse of the original statement. The converse and inverse of an original statement are logically equivalent.

P implies Q = Not P or Q

1. CORRECT ANSWER: B
    For Item I, we can conclude that it is Wednesday if and only if the garbage is collected. For Item II, the phrase "nobody has no" is equivalent to everybody has at least one."

2. CORRECT ANSWER: C
    For Item I, each statement is the converse of the other. Thus, they are not equivalent. For Item II, each statement says that each member of the Duluth Five is immune from prosecution.

3. CORRECT ANSWER: B
    For Item I, accepting a promotion is a necessary and sufficient condition for receiving a 10% raise. For Item II, we have the P implies Q condition, where P = hydraulic lines are flushed and Q = it is an inspection day.

4. CORRECT ANSWER: D
    For Item I, each statement is the converse of the other (so they are not equivalent). For Item II, the first statement simply states that a particular raven is black. The second statement says that all black birds are ravens. They are not equivalent.

5. CORRECT ANSWER: C
    The two scenarios are (a) a Rotary Club member is a subset of the set of all retirees, which is a subset of all planning commission member or (b) a Rotary Club member is a subset of all planning commission members, which is a subset of all retirees.

6. CORRECT ANSWER: B
    We know that some SWAT sniper members have poor aim. If we also know that all snipers on the SWAT team also have 20/20 vision, then we conclude that any sniper (including those with the worst aim) must have 20/20 vision.

7. CORRECT ANSWER: D
    The only way that Garson will not hear voices is if he takes his medication. The premature conclusion can only be correct if he takes his medication every Friday. None of choices A, B, or C mentions this specifically.

8. CORRECT ANSWER: A
   If Frank is not the tallest and Jean is not the tallest, then the conclusion that Lily is the tallest is correct. This is a reasonable conclusion, unless all three are the same height (very unlikely).

9. CORRECT ANSWER: B
   We are given that Dr. Lyons went to the cafeteria for lunch and that he did not have dessert. If Dr. Lyons always eats dessert when it is served in the cafeteria, we can conclude that the cafeteria did not serve dessert.

EVALUATING CONCLUSIONS IN LIGHT OF KNOWN FACTS
EXAMINATION SECTION
TEST 1

DIRECTIONS: Each question or incomplete statement is followed by several suggested answers or completions. Select the one that BEST answers the question or completes the statement. *PRINT THE LETTER OF THE CORRECT ANSWER IN THE SPACE AT THE RIGHT.*

Questions 1-9.

DIRECTIONS: In Questions 1 through 9, you will read a set of facts and a conclusion drawn from them. The conclusion may be valid or invalid, based on the facts—it's your task to determine the validity of the conclusion.

For each question, select the letter before the statement that BEST expresses the relationship between the given facts and the conclusion that has been drawn from them. Your choices are:
   A. The facts prove the conclusion;
   B. The facts disprove the conclusion; or
   C. The facts neither prove nor disprove the conclusion.

1. FACTS: If the supervisor retires, James, the assistant supervisor, will not be transferred to another department. James will be promoted to supervisor if he is not transferred. The supervisor retired.

   CONCLUSION: James will be promoted to supervisor.
   A. The facts prove the conclusion.
   B. The facts disprove the conclusion.
   C. The facts neither prove nor disprove the conclusion.

2. FACTS: In the town of Luray, every player on the softball team works at Luray National Bank. In addition, every player on the Luray softball team wear glasses.

   CONCLUSIONS: At least some of the people who work at Luray National Bank wear glasses.
   A. The facts prove the conclusion.
   B. The facts disprove the conclusion.
   C. The facts neither prove nor disprove the conclusion.

3. FACTS: The only time Henry and June go out to dinner is on an evening when they have childbirth classes. Their childbirth classes meet on Tuesdays and Thursdays.

CONCLUSION: Henry and June never go out to dinner on Friday or Saturday.
A. The facts prove the conclusion.
B. The facts disprove the conclusion.
C. The facts neither prove nor disprove the conclusion.

4. FACTS: Every player on the field hockey team has at least one bruise. Everyone on the field hockey team also has scarred knees.

   CONCLUSION: Most people with both bruises and scarred knees are field hockey players.
   A. The facts prove the conclusion.
   B. The facts disprove the conclusion.
   C. The facts neither prove nor disprove the conclusion.

4.____

5. FACTS: In the chess tournament, Lance will win his match against Jane if Jane wins her match against Mathias. If Lance wins his match against Jane, Christine will not win her match against Jane.

   CONCLUSION: Christine will not win her match against Jane if Jane wins her match against Mathias.
   A. The facts prove the conclusion.
   B. The facts disprove the conclusion.
   C. The facts neither prove nor disprove the conclusion.

5.____

6. FACTS: No green lights on the machine are indicators for the belt drive status. Not all of the lights on the machine's upper panel are green. Some lights on the machine's lower panel are green.

   CONCLUSION: The green lights on the machine's lower panel may be indicators for the belt drive status.
   A. The facts prove the conclusion.
   B. The facts disprove the conclusion.
   C. The facts neither prove nor disprove the conclusion.

6.____

7. FACTS: At a small, one-room country school, there are eight students: Amy, Ben, Carla, Dan, Elliot, Francine, Greg, and Hannah. Each student is in either the 6th, 7th, or 8th grade. Either two or three students are in each grade. Amy, Dan, and Francine are all in different grades. Ben and Elliot are both in the 7th grade. Hannah and Carl are in the same grade.

   CONCLUSION: Exactly three students are in the 7th grade.
   A. The facts prove the conclusion.
   B. The facts disprove the conclusion.
   C. The facts neither prove nor disprove the conclusion.

7.____

8. FACTS: Two married couples are having lunch together. Two of the four people are German and two are Russian, but in each couple the nationality of the spouse is not necessarily the same as the other's. One person in the group is a teacher, the other a lawyer, one an engineer, and the other a writer. The teacher is a Russian man. The writer is Russian, and her husband is an engineer. One of the people, Mr. Stern, is German.

   CONCLUSION: Mr. Stern's wife is a writer.
   A. The facts prove the conclusion.
   B. The facts disprove the conclusion.
   C. The facts neither prove nor disprove the conclusion.

   8.____

9. FACTS: The flume ride at the county fair is open only to children who are at least 36 inches tall. Lisa is 30 inches tall. John is shorter than Henry, but more than 10 inches taller than Lisa.

   CONCLUSION: Lisa is the only one who can't ride the flume ride.
   A. The facts prove the conclusion.
   B. The facts disprove the conclusion.
   C. The facts neither prove nor disprove the conclusion.

   9.____

Questions 10-17.

DIRECTIONS: Questions 10 through 17 are based on the following reading passage. It is not your knowledge of the particular topic that is being tested, but your ability to reason based on what you have read. The passage is likely to detail several proposed courses of action and factors affecting these proposals. The reading passage is followed by a conclusion or outcome based on the facts in the passage, or a description of a decision taken regarding the situation. The conclusion is followed by a number of statements that have a possible connection to the conclusion. For each statement, you are to determine whether:
   A. The statement proves the conclusion.
   B. The statement supports the conclusion but does not prove it.
   C. The statement disproves the conclusion.
   D. The statement weakens the conclusion but does not disprove it.
   E. The statement has no relevance to the conclusion.

Remember that the conclusion after the passage is to be accepted as the outcome of what actually happened, and that you are being asked to evaluate the impact each statement would have had on the conclusion.

PASSAGE:

The Grand Army of Foreign Wars, a national veteran's organization, is struggling to maintain its National Home, where the widowed spouses and orphans of deceased members are housed together in a small village-like community. The Home is open to spouses and children who are bereaved for any reason, regardless of whether the member's death was related to military service, but a new global conflict has led to a dramatic surge in the number of members' deaths: many veterans who re-enlisted for the conflict have been killed in action.

The Grand Army of Foreign Wars is considering several options for handling the increased number of applications for housing at the National Home, which has been traditionally supported by membership due. At its national convention, it will choose only one of the following:

The first idea is a one-time $50 tax on all members, above and beyond the dues they pay already. Since the organization has more than a million member, this tax should be sufficient for the construction and maintenance of new housing for applicants on the existing grounds of the National Home. The idea is opposed, however, by some older members who live on fixed incomes. These members object in principle to the taxation of Grand Army members. The Grand Army has never imposed a tax on its members.

The second idea is to launch a national fundraising drive the public relations campaign that will attract donations for the National Home. Several national celebrities are members of the organization, and other celebrities could be attracted to the cause. Many Grand Army members are wary of this approach, however: in the past, the net receipts of some fundraising efforts have been relatively insignificant, given the costs of staging them.

A third approach, suggested by many of the younger members, is to have new applicants share some of the costs of construction and maintenance. The spouses and children would pay an up-front "enrollment" fee, based on a sliding scale proportionate to their income and assets, and then a monthly fee adjusted similarly to contribute to maintenance costs. Many older members are strongly opposed to this idea, as it is in direct contradiction to the principles on which the organization was founded more than a century ago.

The fourth option is simply to maintain the status quo, focus the organization's efforts on supporting the families who already live at the National Home, and wait to accept new applicants based on attrition.

CONCLUSION: At its annual national convention, the Grand Army of Foreign Wars votes to impose a one-time tax of $10 on each member for the purpose of expanding and supporting the National Home to welcome a larger number of applicants. The tax is considered to be the solution most likely to produce the funds needed to accommodate the growing number of applicants.

10. Actuarial studies have shown that because the Grand Army's membership consists mostly of older veterans from earlier wars, the organization's membership will suffer a precipitous decline in numbers in about five years.
    A. The statement proves the conclusion.
    B. The statement supports the conclusion but does not prove it.
    C. The statement disproves the conclusion.
    D. The statement weakens the conclusion but does not disprove it.
    E. The statement has no relevance to the conclusion.

11. After passage of the funding measure, a splinter group of older members appeals for the "sliding scale" provision to be applied to the tax, so that some members may be allowed to contribute less based on their income.
    A. The statement proves the conclusion.
    B. The statement supports the conclusion but does not prove it.
    C. The statement disproves the conclusion.
    D. The statement weakens the conclusion but does not disprove it.
    E. The statement has no relevance to the conclusion.

5 (#1)

12. The original charter of the Grand Army of Foreign Wars specifically states that the organization will not levy taxes or duties on its members beyond its modest annual dues. It takes a super-majority of attending delegates at the national convention to make alterations to the charter.
    A. The statement proves the conclusion.
    B. The statement supports the conclusion but does not prove it.
    C. The statement disproves the conclusion.
    D. The statement weakens the conclusion but does not disprove it.
    E. The statement has no relevance to the conclusion.

12.____

13. Six months before Grand Army of Foreign Wars' national convention, the Internal Revenue Service rules that because it is an organization that engages in political lobbying, the Grand Army must no longer enjoy its own federal tax-exempt status.
    A. The statement proves the conclusion.
    B. The statement supports the conclusion but does not prove it.
    C. The statement disproves the conclusion.
    D. The statement weakens the conclusion but does not disprove it.
    E. The statement has no relevance to the conclusion.

13.____

14. Two months before the national convention, Dirk Rockwell, arguably the country's most famous film actor, announces in a nationally televised interview that he has been saddened to learn of the plight of the National Home, and that he is going to make it his own personal crusade to see that it is able to house and support a greater number of widowed spouses and orphans in the future.
    A. The statement proves the conclusion.
    B. The statement supports the conclusion but does not prove it.
    C. The statement disproves the conclusion.
    D. The statement weakens the conclusion but does not disprove it.
    E. The statement has no relevance to the conclusion.

14.____

15. The Grand Army's final estimate is that the cost of expanding the National Home to accommodate the increased number of applicants will be about $61 million.
    A. The statement proves the conclusion.
    B. The statement supports the conclusion but does not prove it.
    C. The statement disproves the conclusion.
    D. The statement weakens the conclusion but does not disprove it.
    E. The statement has no relevance to the conclusion.

15.____

16. Just before the national convention, the Federal Department of Veterans Affairs announces steep cuts in the benefits package that is currently offered to the widowed spouses and orphans of veterans.
    A. The statement proves the conclusion.
    B. The statement supports the conclusion but does not prove it.
    C. The statement disproves the conclusion.
    D. The statement weakens the conclusion but does not disprove it.
    E. The statement has no relevance to the conclusion.

16.____

17. After the national convention, the Grand Army of Foreign Wars begins charging a modest "start-up" fee to all families who apply for residence at the national home.
    A. The statement proves the conclusion.
    B. The statement supports the conclusion but does not prove it.
    C. The statement disproves the conclusion.
    D. The statement weakens the conclusion but does not disprove it.
    E. The statement has no relevance to the conclusion.

17._____

Questions 18-25.

DIRECTIONS: Questions 18 through 25 each provide four factual statements and a conclusion based on these statements. After reading the entire question, you will decide whether:
   A. The conclusion is proved by statements I-IV;
   B. The conclusion is disproved by statements I-IV.
   C. The facts are not sufficient to prove or disprove the conclusion.

18. FACTUAL STATEMENTS:
    I. In the Field Day high jump competition, Martha jumped higher than Frank.
    II. Carl jumped higher than Ignacio.
    III. Ignacio jumped higher than Frank.
    IV. Dan jumped higher than Carl.

    CONCLUSION: Frank finished last in the high jump competition.
    A. The conclusion is proved by statements I-IV;
    B. The conclusion is disproved by statements I-IV.
    C. The facts are not sufficient to prove or disprove the conclusion.

18._____

19. FACTUAL STATEMENTS:
    I. The door to the hammer mill chamber is locked if light 6 is red.
    II. The door to the hammer mill chamber is locked only when the mill is operating.
    III. If the mill is not operating, light 6 is blue.
    IV. Light 6 is blue.

    CONCLUSION: The door to the hammer mill chamber is locked.
    A. The conclusion is proved by statements I-IV;
    B. The conclusion is disproved by statements I-IV.
    C. The facts are not sufficient to prove or disprove the conclusion.

19._____

20. FACTUAL STATEMENTS:
    I. Ziegfried, the lion tamer at the circus, has demanded ten additional minutes of performance time during each show.
    II. If Ziegfried is allowed his ten additional minutes per show, he will attempt to teach Kimba the tiger to shoot a basketball.
    III. If Kimba learns how to shoot a basketball, then Ziegfried was not given his ten additional minutes.
    IV. Ziegfried was given his ten additional minutes.

20._____

7 (#1)

CONCLUSION: Despite Ziegfried's efforts, Kimba did not learn how to shoot a basketball.
   A. The conclusion is proved by statements I-IV;
   B. The conclusion is disproved by statements I-IV.
   C. The facts are not sufficient to prove or disprove the conclusion.

21. FACTUAL STATEMENTS:
    I. If Stan goes to counseling, Sara won't divorce him.
    II. If Sara divorces Stan, she'll move back to Texas.
    III. If Sara doesn't divorce Stan, Irene will be disappointed.
    IV. Stan goes to counseling.

    CONCLUSION: Irene will be disappointed.
       A. The conclusion is proved by statements I-IV;
       B. The conclusion is disproved by statements I-IV.
       C. The facts are not sufficient to prove or disprove the conclusion.

22. FACTUAL STATEMENTS:
    I. If Delia is promoted to district manager, Claudia will have to be promoted to team leader.
    II. Delia will be promoted to district manager unless she misses her fourth-quarter sales quota.
    III. If Claudia is promoted to team leader, Thomas will be promoted to assistant team leader.
    IV. Delia meets her fourth-quarter sales quota.

    CONCLUSION: Thomas is promoted to assistant team leader.
       A. The conclusion is proved by statements I-IV;
       B. The conclusion is disproved by statements I-IV.
       C. The facts are not sufficient to prove or disprove the conclusion.

23. FACTUAL STATEMENTS:
    I. Clone D is identical to Clone B.
    II. Clone B is not identical to Clone A.
    III. Clone D is not identical to Clone C.
    IV. Clone E is not identical to the clones that are identical to Clone B.

    CONCLUSION: Clone E is identical to Clone D.
       A. The conclusion is proved by statements I-IV;
       B. The conclusion is disproved by statements I-IV.
       C. The facts are not sufficient to prove or disprove the conclusion.

24. FACTUAL STATEMENTS:
    I. In the Stafford Tower, each floor is occupied by a single business.
    II. Big G Staffing is on a floor between CyberGraphics and MainEvent.
    III. Gasco is on the floor directly below CyberGraphics and three floors above Treehorn Audio.
    IV. MainEvent is five floors below EZ Tax and four floors below Treehorn Audio.

8 (#1)

CONCLUSION: EZ Tax is on a floor between Gasco and MainEvent.
  A. The conclusion is proved by statements I-IV;
  B. The conclusion is disproved by statements I-IV.
  C. The facts are not sufficient to prove or disprove the conclusion.

25. FACTUAL STATEMENTS:
  I. Only county roads lead to Nicodemus.
  II. All the roads from Hill City to Graham County are federal highways.
  III. Some of the roads from Plainville lead to Nicodemus.
  IV. Some of the roads running from Hill City lead to Strong City.

CONCLUSION: Some of the roads from Plainville are county roads.
  A. The conclusion is proved by statements I-IV;
  B. The conclusion is disproved by statements I-IV.
  C. The facts are not sufficient to prove or disprove the conclusion.

25.____

KEY (CORRECT ANSWERS)

1.	A	11.	A
2.	A	12.	D
3.	A	13.	E
4.	C	14.	D
5.	A	15.	B
6.	B	16.	B
7.	A	17.	C
8.	A	18.	A
9.	A	19.	B
10.	E	20.	A

21. A
22. A
23. B
24. A
25. A

SOLUTIONS TO PROBLEMS

1. CORRECT ANSWER: A
   Given Statement 3, we deduce that James will not be transferred to another department. By Statement 2, we can conclude that James will be promoted.

2. CORRECT ANSWER: A
   Since every player on the softball team wears glasses, these individuals compose some of the people who work at the bank. Although not every person who works at the bank plays softball, those bank employees who do play softball wear glasses.

3. CORRECT ANSWER: A
   If Henry and June go out to dinner, we conclude that it must be on Tuesday or Thursday, which are the only two days when they have childbirth classes. This implies that if it is not Tuesday or Thursday, then this couple does not go out to dinner.

4. CORRECT ANSWER: C
   We can only conclude that if a person plays on the field hockey team, then he or she has both bruises and scarred knees. But there are probably a great number of people who have both bruises and scarred knees but do not play on the field hockey team. The given conclusion can neither be proven or disproven.

5. CORRECT ANSWER: A
   From statement 1, if Jane beats Mathias, then Lance will beat Jane. Using statement 2, we can then conclude that Christine will not win her match against Jane.

6. CORRECT ANSWER: B
   Statement 1 tells us that no green light can be an indicator of the belt drive status. Thus, the given conclusion must be false.

7. CORRECT ANSWER: A
   We already know that Ben and Elliot are in the 7th grade. Even though Hannah and Carl are in the same grade, it cannot be the 7th grade because we would then have at least four students in this 7th grade. This would contradict the third statement, which states that either two or three students are in each grade. Since Amy, Dan, and Francine are in different grade, exactly one of them must be in the 7th grade. Thus, Ben, Elliot, and exactly one of Amy, Dan, and Francine are the three students in the 7th grade.

8. CORRECT ANSWER: A
   One man is a teacher, who is Russian. We know that the writer is female and is Russian. Since her husband is an engineer, he cannot be the Russian teacher. Thus, her husband is of German descent, namely Mr. Stern. This means that Mr. Stern's wife is the writer. Note that one couple consists of a male Russian teacher and a female German lawyer. The other couple consists of a male German engineer and a female Russian writer.

10 (#1)

9. **CORRECT ANSWER: A**
Since John is more than 10 inches taller than Lisa, his height is at least 46 inches. Also, John is shorter than Henry, so Henry's height must be greater than 46 inches. Thus, Lisa is the only one whose height is less than 36 inches. Therefore, she is the only one who is not allowed on the flume ride.

18. **CORRECT ANSWER: A**
Dan jumped higher than Carl, who jumped higher than Ignacio, who jumped higher than Frank. Since Martha jumped higher than Frank, every person jumped higher than Frank. Thus, Frank finished last.

19. **CORRECT ANSWER: B**
If the light is red, then the door is locked. If the door is locked, then the mill is operating. Reversing the logical sequence of these statements, if the mill is not operating, then the door is not locked, which means that the light is blue. Thus, the given conclusion is disproved.

20. **CORRECT ANSWER: A**
Using the contrapositive of statement III, Ziegfried was given his ten additional minutes, then Kimba did not learn how to shoot a basketball. Since statement IV is factual, the conclusion is proved.

21. **CORRECT ANSWER: A**
From Statements IV and I, we conclude that Sara doesn't divorce Stan. Then statement III reveals that Irene will be disappointed. Thus, the conclusion is proved.

22. **CORRECT ANSWER: A**
Statement II can be rewritten as "Delia is promoted to district manager or she misses her sales quota." Furthermore, this statement is equivalent to "If Delia makes her sales quota, then she is promoted to district manager." From statement I, we conclude that Claudia is promoted to team leader. Finally, by statement III, Thomas is promoted to assistant team leader.

23. **CORRECT ANSWER: B**
By statement IV, Clone E is not identical to any clones identical to Clone B. Statement I tells us that Clones B and D are identical. Therefore, Clone E cannot be identical to Clone D. The conclusion is disproved.

24. **CORRECT ANSWER: A**
Based on all four statements, CyberGraphics is somewhere below MainEvent. Gasco is one floor below CyberGraphics. EZ Tax is two floors below Gasco. Treehorn Audio is one floor below EZ Tax. MainEvent is four floors below Treehorn Audio. Thus, EZ Tax is two floors below Gasco and five floors above MainEvent. The conclusion is proved.

25. **CORRECT ANSWER: A**
From statement III, we know that some of the roads from Plainville lead to Nicodemus. But statement I tells us that only county roads lead to Nicodemus. Therefore, some of the roads from Plainville must be county roads. The conclusion is proved.

TEST 2

DIRECTIONS: Each question or incomplete statement is followed by several suggested answers or completions. Select the one that BEST answers the question or completes the statement. *PRINT THE LETTER OF THE CORRECT ANSWER IN THE SPACE AT THE RIGHT.*

Questions 1-9.

DIRECTIONS: In Questions 1 through 9, you will read a set of facts and a conclusion drawn from them. The conclusion may be valid or invalid, based on the facts—it's your task to determine the validity of the conclusion.

For each question, select the letter before the statement that BEST expresses the relationship between the given facts and the conclusion that has been drawn from them. Your choices are:
    A. The facts prove the conclusion;
    B. The facts disprove the conclusion; or
    C. The facts neither prove nor disprove the conclusion.

1. FACTS: Some employees in the testing department are statisticians. Most of the statisticians who work in the testing department are projection specialists. Tom Wilks works in the testing department.

    CONCLUSION: Tom Wilks is a statistician.
        A. The facts prove the conclusion.
        B. The facts disprove the conclusion.
        C. The facts neither prove nor disprove the conclusion.

2. FACTS: Ten coins are split among Hank, Lawrence, and Gail. If Lawrence gives his coins to Hank, then Hank will have more coins than Gail. If Gail gives her coins to Lawrence, then Lawrence will have more coins than Hank.

    CONCLUSION: Hank has six coins.
        A. The facts prove the conclusion.
        B. The facts disprove the conclusion.
        C. The facts neither prove nor disprove the conclusion.

3. FACTS: Nobody loves everybody. Janet loves Ken. Ken loves everybody who loves Janet.

    CONCLUSION: Everybody loves Janet.
        A. The facts prove the conclusion.
        B. The facts disprove the conclusion.
        C. The facts neither prove nor disprove the conclusion.

4. FACTS: Most of the Torres family lives in East Los Angeles. Many people in East Los Angeles celebrate Cinco de Mayo. Joe is a member of the Torres family.

   CONCLUSION: Joe lives in East Los Angeles.
   A. The facts prove the conclusion.
   B. The facts disprove the conclusion.
   C. The facts neither prove nor disprove the conclusion.

   4.____

5. FACTS: Five professionals each occupy one story of a five-story office building. Dr. Kane's office is above Dr. Assad's. Dr. Johnson's office is between Dr. Kane's and Dr. Conlon's. Dr. Steen's office is between Dr. Conlon's and Dr. Assad's. Dr. Johnson is on the fourth story.

   CONCLUSION: Dr. Kane occupies the top story.
   A. The facts prove the conclusion.
   B. The facts disprove the conclusion.
   C. The facts neither prove nor disprove the conclusion.

   5.____

6. FACTS: To be eligible for membership in the Yukon Society, a person must be able to either tunnel through a snowbank while wearing only a T-shirt and short, or hold his breath for two minutes under water that is 50°F. Ray can only hold his breath for a minute and a half.

   CONCLUSION: Ray can still become a member of the Yukon Society by tunneling through a snowbank while wearing a T-shirt and shorts.
   A. The facts prove the conclusion.
   B. The facts disprove the conclusion.
   C. The facts neither prove nor disprove the conclusion.

   6.____

7. FACTS: A mark is worth five plunks. You can exchange four sharps for a tinplot. It takes eight marks to buy a sharp.

   CONCLUSION: A sharp is the most valuable.
   A. The facts prove the conclusion.
   B. The facts disprove the conclusion.
   C. The facts neither prove nor disprove the conclusion.

   7.____

8. FACTS: There are gibbons, as well as lemurs, who like to play in the trees at the monkey house. All those who like to play in the trees at the monkey house are fed lettuce and bananas.

   CONCLUSION: Lemurs and gibbons are types of monkeys.
   A. The facts prove the conclusion.
   B. The facts disprove the conclusion.
   C. The facts neither prove nor disprove the conclusion.

   8.____

9. FACTS: None of the Blackfoot tribes is a Salishan Indian tribe. Salishan Indians came from the northern Pacific Coast. All Salishan Indians live each of the Continental Divide.

9.____

CONCLUSION: No Blackfoot tribes live east of the Continental Divide.
A. The facts prove the conclusion.
B. The facts disprove the conclusion.
C. The facts neither prove nor disprove the conclusion.

Questions 10-17.

DIRECTIONS: Questions 10 through 17 are based on the following reading passage. It is not your knowledge of the particular topic that is being tested, but your ability to reason based on what you have read. The passage is likely to detail several proposed courses of action and factors affecting these proposals. The reading passage is followed by a conclusion or outcome based on the facts in the passage, or a description of a decision taken regarding the situation. The conclusion is followed by a number of statements that have a possible connection to the conclusion. For each statement, you are to determine whether:
A. The statement proves the conclusion.
B. The statement supports the conclusion but does not prove it.
C. The statement disproves the conclusion.
D. The statement weakens the conclusion but does not disprove it.
E. The statement has no relevance to the conclusion.

Remember that the conclusion after the passage is to be accepted as the outcome of what actually happened, and that you are being asked to evaluate the impact each statement would have had on the conclusion.

PASSAGE:

On August 12, Beverly Willey reported that she was in the elevator late on the previous evening after leaving her office on the 16th floor of a large office building. In her report, she states that a man got on the elevator at the 11th floor, pulled her off the elevator, assaulted her, and stole her purse. Ms. Willey reported that she had seen the man in the elevators and hallways of the building before. She believes that the man works in the building. Her description of him is as follows: he is tall, unshaven, with wavy brown hair and a scar on his left cheek. He walks with a pronounced limp, often dragging his left foot behind his right.

CONCLUSION: After Beverly Willey makes her report, the police arrest a 43-year-old man, Barton Black, and charge him with her assault.

10. Barton Black is a former Marine who served in Vietnam, where he sustained shrapnel wounds to the left side of his face and suffered nerve damage in his left leg.
    A. The statement proves the conclusion.
    B. The statement supports the conclusion but does not prove it.
    C. The statement disproves the conclusion.
    D. The statement weakens the conclusion but does not disprove it.
    E. The statement has no relevance to the conclusion.

    10.____

11. When they arrived at his residence to question him, detectives were greeted at the door by Barton Black, who was tall and clean-shaven.
    A. The statement proves the conclusion.
    B. The statement supports the conclusion but does not prove it.
    C. The statement disproves the conclusion.
    D. The statement weakens the conclusion but does not disprove it.
    E. The statement has no relevance to the conclusion.

    11.____

12. Barton Black was booked into the county jail several days after Beverly Willey's assault.
    A. The statement proves the conclusion.
    B. The statement supports the conclusion but does not prove it.
    C. The statement disproves the conclusion.
    D. The statement weakens the conclusion but does not disprove it.
    E. The statement has no relevance to the conclusion.

    12.____

13. Upon further investigation, detectives discover that Beverly Willey does not work at the office building.
    A. The statement proves the conclusion.
    B. The statement supports the conclusion but does not prove it.
    C. The statement disproves the conclusion.
    D. The statement weakens the conclusion but does not disprove it.
    E. The statement has no relevance to the conclusion.

    13.____

14. Upon further investigation, detectives discover that Barton Black does not work at the office building.
    A. The statement proves the conclusion.
    B. The statement supports the conclusion but does not prove it.
    C. The statement disproves the conclusion.
    D. The statement weakens the conclusion but does not disprove it.
    E. The statement has no relevance to the conclusion.

    14.____

15. In the spring of the following year, Barton Black is convicted of assaulting Beverly Willey on August 11.
    A. The statement proves the conclusion.
    B. The statement supports the conclusion but does not prove it.
    C. The statement disproves the conclusion.
    D. The statement weakens the conclusion but does not disprove it.
    E. The statement has no relevance to the conclusion.

    15.____

16. During their investigation of the assault, detectives determine that Beverly Willey was assaulted on the 12th floor of the office building.   16.____
    A. The statement proves the conclusion.
    B. The statement supports the conclusion but does not prove it.
    C. The statement disproves the conclusion.
    D. The statement weakens the conclusion but does not disprove it.
    E. The statement has no relevance to the conclusion.

17. The day after Beverly Willey's assault, Barton Black fled the area and was never seen again.   17.____
    A. The statement proves the conclusion.
    B. The statement supports the conclusion but does not prove it.
    C. The statement disproves the conclusion.
    D. The statement weakens the conclusion but does not disprove it.
    E. The statement has no relevance to the conclusion.

Questions 18-25.

DIRECTIONS: Questions 18 through 25 each provide four factual statements and a conclusion based on these statements. After reading the entire question, you will decide whether:
    A. The conclusion is proved by statements I-IV;
    B. The conclusion is disproved by statements I-IV.
    C. The facts are not sufficient to prove or disprove the conclusion.

18. FACTUAL STATEMENTS: 18.____
    I. Among five spice jars on the shelf, the sage is to the right of the parsley.
    II. The pepper is to the left of the basil.
    III. The nutmeg is between the sage and the pepper.
    IV. The pepper is the second spice from the left.

    CONCLUSION: The safe is the farthest to the right.
    A. The conclusion is proved by statements I-IV;
    B. The conclusion is disproved by statements I-IV.
    C. The facts are not sufficient to prove or disprove the conclusion.

19. FACTUAL STATEMENTS: 19.____
    I. Gear X rotates in a clockwise direction if Switch C is in the OFF position.
    II. Gear X will rotate in a counter-clockwise direction is Switch C is ON.
    III. If Gear X is rotating in a clockwise direction, then Gear Y will not be rotating at all.
    IV. Switch C is ON.

    CONCLUSION: Gear X is rotating in a counter-clockwise direction.
    A. The conclusion is proved by statements I-IV;
    B. The conclusion is disproved by statements I-IV.
    C. The facts are not sufficient to prove or disprove the conclusion.

20. FACTUAL STATEMENTS:
    I. Lane will leave for the Toronto meeting today only if Terence, Rourke, and Jackson all file their marketing reports by the end of the work day.
    II. Rourke will file her report on time only if Ganz submits last quarter's data.
    III. If Terence attends the security meeting, he will attend it with Jackson, and they will not file their marketing reports by the end of the work day.

    CONCLUSION: Lane will leave for the Toronto meeting today.
    A. The conclusion is proved by statements I-IV;
    B. The conclusion is disproved by statements I-IV.
    C. The facts are not sufficient to prove or disprove the conclusion.

21. FACTUAL STATEMENTS:
    I. Bob is in second place in the Boston Marathon.
    II. Gregory is winning the Boston Marathon.
    III. There are four miles to go in the race, and Bob is gaining on Gregory at the rate of 100 yards every minute.
    IV. There are 1760 yards in a mile and Gregory's usual pace during the Boston Marathon is one mile every six minutes.

    CONCLUSION: Bob wins the Boston Marathon.
    A. The conclusion is proved by statements I-IV;
    B. The conclusion is disproved by statements I-IV.
    C. The facts are not sufficient to prove or disprove the conclusion.

22. FACTUAL STATEMENTS:
    I. Four brothers are named Earl, John, Gary, and Pete.
    II. Earl and Pete are unmarried.
    III. John is shorter than the youngest of the four.
    IV. The oldest brother is married, and is also the tallest.

    CONCLUSION: Gary is the oldest brother.
    A. The conclusion is proved by statements I-IV;
    B. The conclusion is disproved by statements I-IV.
    C. The facts are not sufficient to prove or disprove the conclusion.

23. FACTUAL STATEMENTS:
    I. Brigade X is ten miles from the demilitarized zone.
    II. If General Woundwort gives the order, Brigade X will advance to the demilitarized zone, but not quickly enough to reach the zone before the conflict begins.
    III. Brigade Y, five miles behind Brigade X, will not advance unless General Woundwort gives the order.
    IV. Brigade Y advances.

7 (#2)

CONCLUSION: Brigade X reaches the demilitarized zone before the conflict begins.
  A. The conclusion is proved by statements I-IV;
  B. The conclusion is disproved by statements I-IV.
  C. The facts are not sufficient to prove or disprove the conclusion.

24. FACTUAL STATEMENTS: 24.____
  I. Jerry has decided to take a cab from Fullerton to Elverton.
  II. Chubby Cab charges $5 plus $3 a mile.
  III. Orange Cab charges $7.50 but gives free mileage for the first 5 miles.
  IV. After the first 5 miles, Orange Cab charges $2.50 a mile.

  CONCLUSION: Orange Cab is the cheaper fare from Fullerton to Elverton.
  A. The conclusion is proved by statements I-IV;
  B. The conclusion is disproved by statements I-IV.
  C. The facts are not sufficient to prove or disprove the conclusion.

25. FACTUAL STATEMENTS: 25.____
  I. Dan is never in class when his friend Lucy is absent.
  II. Lucy is never absent unless her mother is sick.
  III. If Lucy is in class, Sergio is in class also.
  IV. Sergio is never in class when Dalton is absent.

  CONCLUSION: If Lucy is absent, Dalton may be in class.
  A. The conclusion is proved by statements I-IV;
  B. The conclusion is disproved by statements I-IV.
  C. The facts are not sufficient to prove or disprove the conclusion.

KEY (CORRECT ANSWERS)

1. C
2. B
3. B
4. C
5. A

6. A
7. B
8. C
9. C
10. B

11. E
12. B
13. D
14. E
15. A

16. E
17. C
18. B
19. A
20. C

21. C
22. A
23. B
24. A
25. B

SOLUTIONS TO PROBLEMS

1. CORRECT ANSWER: C
   Statement 1 only tells us that some employees who work in the Testing Department are statisticians. This means that we need to allow the possibility that at least one person in this department is not a statistician. Thus, if a person works in the Testing Department, we cannot conclude whether or not this individual is a statistician.

2. CORRECT ANSWER: B
   If Hank had six coins, then the total of Gail's collection and Lawrence's collection would be four. Thus, if Gail gave all her coins to Lawrence, Lawrence would only have four coins. Thus, it would be impossible for Lawrence to have more coins than Hank.

3. CORRECT ANSWER: B
   Statement 1 tells us that nobody loves everybody. If everybody loved Janet, then Statement 3 would imply that Ken loves everybody. This would contradict statement 1. The conclusion is disproved.

4. CORRECT ANSWER: C
   Although most of the Torres family lives in East Los Angeles, we can assume that some members of this family do not live in East Los Angeles. Thus, we cannot prove or disprove that Joe, who is a member of the Torres family, lives in East Los Angeles.

5. CORRECT ANSWER: A
   Since Dr. Johnson is on the 4th floor, either (a) Dr. Kane is on the 5th floor and Dr. Conlon is on the 3rd floor, or (b) Dr. Kane is on the 3rd floor and Dr. Conlon is on the 5th floor. If option (b) were correct, then since Dr. Assad would be on the 1st floor, it would be impossible for Dr. Steen's office to be between Dr. Conlon and Dr. Assad's office. Therefore, Dr. Kane's office must be on the 5th floor. The order of the doctors' offices, from 5th floor down to the 1st floor is: Dr. Kane, Dr. Johnson, Dr. Conlon, Dr. Steen, Dr. Assad.

6. CORRECT ANSWER: A
   Ray does not satisfy the requirement of holding his breath for two minutes under water, since he can only hold is breath for one minute in that setting. But if he tunnels through a snowbank with just a T-shirt and shorts, he will satisfy the eligibility requirement. Note that the eligibility requirement contains the key word "or." So only one of the two clauses separated by "or" need to be fulfilled.

7. CORRECT ANSWER: B
   Statement 2 says that four sharps is equivalent to one tinplot. This means that a tinplot is worth more than a sharp. The conclusion is disproved. We note that the order of these items, from most valuable to least valuable are: tinplot, sharp, mark, plunk.

8. CORRECT ANSWER: C
   We can only conclude that gibbons and lemurs are fed lettuce and bananas. We can neither prove nor disprove that these animals are types of monkeys.

9. CORRECT ANSWER: C
We know that all Salishan Indians live east of the Continental Divide. But some non-members of this tribe of Indians may also live east of the Continental Divide. Since none of the members of the Blackfoot tribe belong to the Salishan Indian tribe, we cannot draw any conclusion about the location of the Blackfoot tribe with respect to the Continental Divide.

18. CORRECT ANSWER: B
Since the pepper is second from the left and the nutmeg is between the sage and the pepper, the positions 2, 3, and 4 (from the left) are pepper, nutmeg, sage. By statement II, the basil must be in position 5, which implies that the parsley is in position 1. Therefore, the basil, not the sage, is farthest to the right. The conclusion disproved.

19. CORRECT ANSWER: A
Statement II assures us that if switch C is ON, then Gear X is rotating in a counterclockwise direction. The conclusion is proved.

20. CORRECT ANSWER: C
Based on Statement IV, followed by Statement II, we conclude that Ganz and Rourke will file their reports on time. Statement III reveals that if Terence and Jackson attend the security meeting, they will fail to file their reports on time. We have no further information if Terence and Jackson attended the security meeting, so we are not able to either confirm or deny that their reports were filed on time. This implies that we cannot know for certain that Lane will leave for his meeting in Toronto.

21. CORRECT ANSWER: C
Although Bob is in second place behind Gregory, we cannot deduce how far behind Gregory he is running. At Gregory's current pace, he will cover four miles in 24 minutes. If Bob were only 100 yards behind Gregory, he would catch up to Gregory in one minute. But if Bob were very far behind Gregory, for example 5 miles, this is the equivalent of (5)(1760) = 8800 yards. Then Bob would need 8800/100 = 88 minutes to catch up to Gregory. Thus, the given facts are not sufficient to draw a conclusion.

22. CORRECT ANSWER: A
Statement II tells us that neither Earl nor Pete could be the oldest; also, either John or Gary is married. Statement IV reveals that the oldest brother is both married and the tallest. By Statement III, John cannot be the tallest. Since John is not the tallest, he is not the oldest. Thus, the oldest brother must be Gary. The conclusion is proved.

23. CORRECT ANSWER: B
By Statements III and IV, General Woundwort must have given the order to advance. Statement II then tells us that Brigade X will advance to the demilitarized zone, but not soon enough before the conflict begins. Thus, the conclusion is disproved.

24. CORRECT ANSWER: A
If the distance is 5 miles or less, then the cost for the Orange Cab is only $7.50, whereas the cost for the Chubby Cab is $5 + 3x, where x represents the number of miles traveled. For 1 to 5 miles, the cost of the Chubby Cab is between $8 and $20. This means that for a distance of 5 miles, the Orange Cab costs $7.50, whereas the Chubby Cab costs $20. After 5 miles, the cost per mile of the Chubby Cab exceeds the cost per mile of the Orange Cab. Thus, regardless of the actual distance between Fullerton and Elverton, the cost for the Orange Cab will be cheaper than that of the Chubby Cab.

25. CORRECT ANSWER: B
It looks like "Dalton" should be replaced by "Dan" in the conclusion. Then by statement I, if Lucy is absent, Dan is never in class. Thus, the conclusion is disproved.

REPORT WRITING

EXAMINATION SECTION
TEST 1

DIRECTIONS: Each question or incomplete statement is followed by several suggested answers or completions. Select the one that BEST answers the question or completes the statement. *PRINT THE LETTER OF THE CORRECT ANSWER IN THE SPACE AT THE RIGHT.*

1. Police Officer Johnson responds to the scene of an assault and obtains the following information:
    Time of Occurrence: 8:30 P.M.
    Place of Occurrence: 120-18 119th Avenue, Apt. 2A
    Suspects: John Andrews, victim's ex-husband and unknown white male
    Victim: Susan Andrews
    Injury: Broken right arm
    Officer Johnson is preparing a complaint report on the incident.
    Which one of the following expresses the above information MOST clearly and accurately?

    A. Susan Andrews was assaulted at 120-18 119th Avenue, Apt. 2A. At 8:30 P.M., her ex-husband, John Andrews, and an unknown white male broke her arm.
    B. At 8:30 P.M., Susan Andrews was assaulted at 120-18 119th Avenue, Apt. 2A, by her ex-husband, John Andrews, and an unknown white male. Her right arm was broken.
    C. John Andrews, an unknown white male, and Susan Andrews' ex-husband, assaulted and broke her right arm at 8:30 P.M., at 120-18 119th Avenue, Apt. 2A.
    D. John Andrews, ex-husband of Susan Andrews, broke her right arm with an unknown white male at 120-18 119th Avenue, at 8:30 P.M. in Apt. 2A.

2. While on patrol, Officers Banks and Thompson see a man lying on the ground bleeding. Officer Banks records the following details about the incident:
    Time of Incident: 3:15 P.M.
    Place of Incident: Sidewalk in front of 517 Rock Avenue
    Incident: Tripped and fell
    Name of Injured: John Blake
    Injury: Head wound
    Action Taken: Transported to Merry Hospital
    Officer Banks is completing a report on the incident.
    Which one of the following expresses the above information MOST clearly and accurately?

    A. At 3:15 P.M., Mr. John Blake was transported to Merry Hospital. He tripped and fell, injuring his head on sidewalk in front of 517 Rock Avenue.
    B. Mr. John Blake tripped and fell on the sidewalk at 3:15 P.M. in front of 517 Rock Avenue. He was transported to Merry Hospital while he sustained a head wound.
    C. Mr. John Blake injured his head when he tripped and fell on the sidewalk in front of 517 Rock Avenue at 3:15 P.M. He was transported to Merry Hospital.
    D. A head was wounded on the sidewalk in front of 517 Rock Avenue at 3:15 P.M. Mr. John Blake tripped and fell and was transported to Merry Hospital.

3. When assigned to investigate a complaint, a police officer should
   I. Interview witnesses and obtain facts
   II. Conduct a thorough investigation of circumstances concerning the complaint
   III. Prepare a complaint report
   IV. Determine if the complaint report should be closed or referred for further investigation
   V. Enter complaint report on the Complaint Report Index and obtain a complaint report number at the station house

   While on patrol, Police Officer John is instructed by his supervisor to investigate a complaint by Mr. Stanley Burns, who was assaulted by his brother-in-law, Henry Traub. After interviewing Mr. Burns, Officer John learns that Mr. Traub has been living with Mr. Burns for the past two years. Officer John accompanies Mr. Burns to his apartment but Mr. Traub is not there. Officer John fills out the complaint report and takes the report back to the station house where it is entered on the Complaint Report Index and assigned a complaint report number. Officer John's actions were

   A. *improper,* primarily because he should have stayed at Mr. Burns' apartment and waited for Mr. Traub to return in order to arrest him
   B. *proper,* primarily because after obtaining all the facts, he took the report back to the station house and was assigned a complaint report number
   C. *improper,* primarily because he should have decided whether to close the report or refer it for further investigation
   D. *proper,* primarily because he was instructed by his supervisor to take the report from Mr. Burns even though it involved his brother-in-law

4. Police Officer Waters was the first person at the scene of a fire which may have been the result of arson. He obtained the following information:

   Place of Occurrence: 35 John Street, Apt. 27
   Time of Occurrence: 4:00 P.M.
   Witness: Daisy Logan
   Incident: Fire (possible arson)
   Suspect: Male, white, approximately 18 years old, wearing blue jeans and a plaid shirt, running away from the incident Officer Waters is completing a report on the incident.

   Which one of the following expresses the above information MOST clearly and accurately?

   A. At 4:00 P.M., Daisy Logan saw a white male, approximately 18 years old who was wearing blue jeans and a plaid shirt, running from the scene of a fire at 35 John Street, Apt. 27.
   B. Seeing a fire at 35 John Street, a white male approximately 18 years old, wearing blue jeans and a plaid shirt, was seen running from Apt. 27 at 4:00 P.M. reported Daisy Logan.
   C. Approximately 18 years old and wearing blue jeans and a plaid shirt, Daisy Logan saw a fire and a white male running from 35 John Street, Apt. 27 at 4:00 P.M.
   D. Running from 35 John Street, Apt. 27, the scene of the fire, reported Daisy Logan at 4:00 P.M., was a white male approximately 18 years old and wearing blue jeans and a plaid shirt.

5. Police Officer Sullivan obtained the following information at the scene of a two-car accident:

Place of Occurrence:	2971 William Street
Drivers and Vehicles Involved:	Mrs. Wilson, driver of blue 2004 Toyota Camry; Mr. Bailey, driver of white 2001 Dodge
Injuries Sustained:	Mr. Bailey had a swollen right eye; Mrs. Wilson had a broken left hand

Which one of the following expresses the above information MOST clearly and accurately?

- A. Mr. Bailey, owner of a white 2001 Dodge, at 2971 William Street, had a swollen right eye. Mrs. Wilson, with a broken left hand, is the owner of the blue 2004 Toyota Camry. They were in a car accident.
- B. Mrs. Wilson got a broken left hand and Mr. Bailey a swollen right eye at 2971 William Street. The vehicles involved in the car accident were a 2001 Dodge, white, owned by Mr. Bailey, and Mrs. Wilson's blue 2004 Toyota Camry.
- C. Mrs. Wilson, the driver of the blue 2004 Toyota Camry, and Mr. Bailey, the driver of the white 2001 Dodge, were involved in a car accident at 2971 William Street. Mr. Bailey sustained a swollen right eye, and Mrs. Wilson broke her left hand.
- D. Mr. Bailey sustained a swollen right eye and Mrs. Wilson broke her left hand in a car accident at 2971 William Street. They owned a 2001 white Dodge and a 2004 blue Toyota Camry.

6. Officer Johnson has issued a summons to a driver and has obtained the following information:

Place of Occurrence: Corner of Foster Road and Woodrow Avenue
Time of Occurrence: 7:10 P.M.
Driver: William Grant
Offense: Driving through a red light
Age of Driver: 42
Address of Driver: 23 Richmond Avenue

Officer Johnson is making an entry in his Memo Book regarding the incident.
Which one of the following expresses the above information MOST clearly and accurately?

- A. William Grant, lives at 23 Richmond Avenue at 7:10 P.M., went through a red light. He was issued a summons at the corner of Foster Road and Woodrow Avenue. The driver is 42 years old.
- B. William Grant, age 42, who lives at 23 Richmond Avenue, was issued a summons for going through a red light at 7:10 P.M. at the corner of Foster Road and Woodrow Avenue.
- C. William Grant, age 42, was issued a summons on the corner of Foster Road and Woodrow Avenue for going through a red light. He lives at 23 Richmond Avenue at 7:10 P.M.
- D. A 42-year-old man who lives at 23 Richmond Avenue was issued a summons at 7:10 P.M. William Grant went through a red light at the corner of Foster Road and Woodrow Avenue.

7. Police Officer Frome has completed investigating a report of a stolen auto and obtained 7.____
the following information:
Date of Occurrence: October 26, 2004
Place of Occurrence: 51st Street and 8th Avenue
Time of Occurrence: 3:30 P.M.
Crime: Auto theft
Suspect: Michael Wadsworth
Action Taken: Suspect arrested
Which one of the following expresses the above information
MOST clearly and accurately?

   A. Arrested on October 26, 2004 was a stolen auto at 51st Street and 8th Avenue at 3:30 P.M. driven by Michael Wadsworth.
   B. For driving a stolen auto at 3:30 P.M., Michael Wadsworth was arrested at 51st Street and 8th Avenue on October 26, 2004.
   C. On October 26, 2004 at 3:30 P.M., Michael Wadsworth was arrested at 51st Street and 8th Avenue for driving a stolen auto.
   D. Michael Wadsworth was arrested on October 26, 2004 at 3:30 P.M. for driving at 51st Street and 8th Avenue. The auto was stolen.

8. Police Officer Wright has finished investigating a report of Grand Larceny and has 8.____
obtained the following information:
Time of Occurrence: Between 1:00 P.M. and 2:00 P.M.
Place of Occurrence: In front of victim's home, 85 Montgomery Avenue
Victim: Mr. Williams, owner of the vehicle
Crime: Automobile broken into
Property Taken: Stereo valued at $1,200
Officer Wright is preparing a report on the incident. Which one of the following
expresses the above information MOST clearly and accurately?

   A. While parked in front of his home Mr. Williams states that between 1:00 P.M. and 2:00 P.M. an unknown person broke into his vehicle. Mr. Williams, who lives at 85 Montgomery Avenue, lost his $1,200 stereo.
   B. Mr. Williams, who lives at 85 Montgomery Avenue, states that between 1:00 P.M. and 2:00 P.M. his vehicle was parked in front of his home when an unknown person broke into his car and took his stereo worth $1,200.
   C. Mr. Williams was parked in front of 85 Montgomery Avenue, which is his home, when it was robbed of a $1,200 stereo. When he came out, he observed between 1:00 P.M. and 2:00 P.M. that his car had been broken into by an unknown person.
   D. Mr. Williams states between 1:00 P.M. and 2:00 P.M. that an unknown person broke into his car in front of his home. Mr. Williams further states that he was robbed of a $1,200 stereo at 85 Montgomery Avenue.

9. Police Officer Fontaine obtained the following details relating to a suspicious package:

   Place of Occurrence: Case Bank, 2 Wall Street
   Time of Occurrence: 10:30 A.M.
   Date of Occurrence: October 10, 2004
   Complaint: Suspicious package in doorway
   Found By: Emergency Service Unit

   Officer Fontaine is preparing a report for department records.
   Which one of the following expresses the above information MOST clearly and accurately?

   A. At 10:30 A.M., the Emergency Service Unit reported they found a package on October 10, 2004 which appeared suspicious. This occurred in a doorway at 2 Wall Street, Case Bank.
   B. A package which appeared suspicious was in the doorway of Case Bank. The Emergency Service Unit reported this at 2 Wall Street at 10:30 A.M. on October 10, 2004 when found.
   C. On October 10, 2004 at 10:30 A.M., a suspicious package was found by the Emergency Service Unit in the doorway of Case Bank at 2 Wall Street.
   D. The Emergency Service Unit found a package at the Case Bank. It appeared suspicious at 10:30 A.M. in the doorway of 2 Wall Street on October 10, 2004.

10. Police Officer Reardon receives the following information regarding a case of child abuse:

    Victim: Joseph Mays
    Victim's Age: 10 years old
    Victim's Address: Resides with his family at 42 Columbia Street, Apt. 1B
    Complainant: Victim's uncle, Kevin Mays
    Suspects: Victim's parents

    Police Officer Reardon is preparing a report to send to the Department of Social Services.
    Which one of the following expresses the above information MOST clearly and accurately?

    A. Kevin Mays reported a case of child abuse to his ten-year-old nephew, Joseph Mays, by his parents. He resides with his family at 42 Columbia Street, Apt. 1B.
    B. Kevin Mays reported that his ten-year-old nephew, Joseph Mays, has been abused by the child's parents. Joseph Mays resides with his family at 42 Columbia Street, Apt. 1B.
    C. Joseph Mays has been abused by his parents. Kevin Mays reported that his nephew resides with his family at 42 Columbia Street, Apt. 1B. He is ten years old.
    D. Kevin Mays reported that his nephew is ten years old. Joseph Mays has been abused by his parents. He resides with his family at 42 Columbia Street, Apt. 1B.

11. While on patrol, Police Officer Hawkins was approached by Harry Roland, a store owner, who found a leather bag valued at $200.00 outside his store. Officer Hawkins took the property into custody and removed the following items:

2 Solex watches, each valued at	$500.00
4 14-kt. gold necklaces, each valued at	$315.00
Cash	$519.00
1 diamond ring, valued at	$400.00

    Officer Hawkins is preparing a report on the found property.
    Which one of the following is the TOTAL value of the property and cash found?

    A. $1,734 B. $3,171 C. $3,179 D. $3,379

12. While on patrol, Police Officer Blake observes a man running from a burning abandoned building. Officer Blake radios the following information:

Place of Occurrence:	310 Hall Avenue
Time of Occurrence:	8:30 P.M.
Type of Building:	Abandoned
Suspect:	Male, white, about 35 years old
Crime:	Arson

    Officer Blake is completing a report on the incident.
    Which one of the following expresses the above information MOST clearly and accurately?

    A. An abandoned building located at 310 Hall Avenue was on fire at 8:30 P.M. A white male, approximately 35 years old, was observed fleeing the scene.
    B. A white male, approximately 35 years old, at 8:30 P.M. was observed fleeing 310 Hall Avenue. The fire was set at an abandoned building.
    C. An abandoned building was set on fire. A white male, approximately 35 years old, was observed fleeing the scene at 8:30 P.M. at 310 Hall Avenue.
    D. Observed fleeing a building at 8:30 P.M. was a white male, approximately 35 years old. An abandoned building, located at 310 Hall Avenue, was set on fire.

13. Police Officer Winters responds to a call regarding a report of a missing person. The following information was obtained by the Officer:

Time of Occurrence:	3:30 P.M.
Place of Occurrence:	Harrison Park
Reported By:	Louise Dee - daughter
Description of Missing Person:	Sharon Dee, 70 years old, 5'5", brown eyes, black hair - mother

    Officer Winters is completing a report on the incident. Which one of the following expresses the above information MOST clearly and accurately?

    A. Mrs. Sharon Dee, reported missing by her daughter, Louise, was seen in Harrison Park. The last time she saw her was at 3:30 P.M. She is 70 years old with black hair, brown eyes, and 5'5".
    B. Louise Dee reported that her mother, Sharon Dee, is missing. Sharon Dee is 70 years old, has black hair, brown eyes, and is 5'5". She was last seen at 3:30 P.M. in Harrison Park.
    C. Louise Dee reported Sharon, her 70-year-old mother at 3:30 P.M., to be missing after being seen last at Harrison Park. Described as being 5'5", she has black hair and brown eyes.

D. At 3:30 P.M. Louise Dee's mother was last seen by her daughter in Harrison Park. She has black hair and brown eyes. Louise reported Sharon is 5'5" and 70 years old.

14. While on patrol, Police Officers Mertz and Gallo receive a call from the dispatcher regarding a crime in progress.
    When the Officers arrive, they obtain the following information:
    Time of Occurrence: 2:00 P.M.
    Place of Occurrence: In front of 2124 Bristol Avenue
    Crime: Purse snatch
    Victim: Maria Nieves
    Suspect: Carlos Ortiz
    Witness: Jose Perez, who apprehended the subject
    The Officers are completing a report on the incident.
    Which one of the following expresses the above information MOST clearly and accurately?

    14.____

    A. At 2:00 P.M., Jose Perez witnessed Maria Nieves. Her purse was snatched. The suspect, Carlos Ortiz, was apprehended in front of 2124 Bristol Avenue.
    B. In front of 2124 Bristol Avenue, Carlos Ortiz snatched the purse belonging to Maria Nieves. Carlos Ortiz was apprehended by a witness to the crime after Jose Perez saw the purse snatch at 2:00 P.M.
    C. At 2:00 P.M., Carlos Ortiz snatched a purse from Maria Nieves in front of 2124 Bristol Avenue. Carlos Ortiz was apprehended by Jose Perez, a witness to the crime.
    D. At 2:00 P.M., Carlos Ortiz was seen snatching the purse of Maria Nieves as seen and apprehended by Jose Perez in front of 2124 Bristol Avenue.

15. Police Officers Willis and James respond to a crime in progress and obtain the following information:
    Time of Occurrence: 8:30 A.M.
    Place of Occurrence: Corner of Hopkin Avenue and Amboy Place
    Crime: Chain snatch
    Victim: Mrs. Paula Evans
    Witness: Mr. Robert Peters
    Suspect: White male
    Officers Willis and James are completing a report on the incident.
    Which one of the following expresses the above information MOST clearly and accurately?

    15.____

    A. Mrs. Paula Evans was standing on the corner of Hopkin Avenue and Amboy Place at 8:30 A.M. when a white male snatched her chain. Mr. Robert Peters witnessed the crime.
    B. At 8:30 A.M., Mr. Robert Peters witnessed Mrs. Paula Evans and a white male standing on the corner of Hopkin Avenue and Amboy Place. Her chain was snatched.
    C. At 8:30 A.M., a white male was standing on the corner of Hopkin Avenue and Amboy Place. Mrs. Paula Evans' chain was snatched, and Mr. Robert Peters witnessed the crime.

D. At 8:30 A.M., Mr. Robert Peters reported he witnessed a white male snatching Mrs. Paula Evans' chain while standing on the corner of Hopkin Avenue and Amboy Place.

16. Police Officers Cleveland and Logan responded to an assault that had recently occurred. The following information was obtained at the scene:

    Place of Occurrence: Broadway and Roosevelt Avenue
    Time of Occurrence: 1:00 A.M.
    Crime: Attempted robbery, assault
    Victim: Chuck Brown, suffered a broken tooth
    Suspect: Lewis Brown, victim's brother

    Officer Logan is completing a report on the incident.
    Which one of the following expresses the above information MOST clearly and accurately?

    A. Lewis Brown assaulted his brother Chuck on the corner of Broadway and Roosevelt Avenue. Chuck Brown reported his broken tooth during the attempted robbery at 1:00 A.M.
    B. Chuck Brown had his tooth broken when he was assaulted at 1:00 A.M. on the corner of Broadway and Roosevelt Avenue by his brother, Lewis Brown, while Lewis was attempting to rob him.
    C. An attempt at 1:00 A.M. to rob Chuck Brown turned into an assault at the corner of Broadway and Roosevelt Avenue when his brother Lewis broke his tooth.
    D. At 1:00 A.M., Chuck Brown reported that he was assaulted during his brother's attempt to rob him. Lewis Brown broke his tooth. The incident occurred on the corner of Broadway and Roosevelt Avenue.

17. Police Officer Mannix has just completed an investigation regarding a hit-and-run accident which resulted in a pedestrian being injured. Officer Mannix has obtained the following information:

    Make and Model of Car: Pontiac, Trans Am
    Year and Color of Car: 2006, white
    Driver of Car: Male, black
    Place of Occurrence: Corner of E. 15th Street and 8th Avenue
    Time of Occurrence: 1:00 P.M.

    Officer Mannix is completing a report on the accident.
    Which one of the following expresses the above information MOST clearly and accurately?

    A. At 1:00 P.M., at the corner of E. 15th Street and 8th Avenue, a black male driving a white 2006 Pontiac Trans Am was observed leaving the scene of an accident after injuring a pedestrian with the vehicle.
    B. On the corner of E. 15th Street and 8th Avenue, a white Pontiac, driven by a black male, a 2006 Trans Am injured a pedestrian and left the scene of the accident at 1:00 P.M.
    C. A black male driving a white 2006 Pontiac Trans Am injured a pedestrian and left with the car while driving on the corner of E. 15th Street and 8th Avenue at 1:00 P.M.
    D. At the corner of E. 15th Street and 8th Avenue, a pedestrian was injured by a black male. He fled in his white 2006 Pontiac Trans Am at 1:00 P.M.

18. The following details were obtained by Police Officer Dwight at the scene of a family dispute:

    Place of Occurrence: 77 Baruch Drive
    Victim: Andrea Valdez, wife of Walker
    Violator: Edward Walker
    Witness: George Valdez, victim's brother
    Crime: Violation of Order of Protection
    Action Taken: Violator arrested

    Police Officer Dwight is preparing a report on the incident.
    Which one of the following expresses the above information MOST clearly and accurately?

    A. George Valdez saw Edward Walker violate his sister's Order of Protection at 77 Baruch Drive. Andrea Valdez's husband was arrested for this violation.
    B. Andrea Valdez's Order of Protection was violated at 77 Baruch Drive. George Valdez saw his brother-in-law violate his sister's Order. Edward Walker was arrested.
    C. Edward Walker was arrested for violating an Order of Protection held by his wife, Andrea Valdez. Andrea's brother, George Valdez, witnessed the violation at 77 Baruch Drive.
    D. An arrest was made at 77 Baruch Drive when an Order of Protection held by Andrea Valdez was violated by her husband. George Valdez, her brother, witnessed Edward Walker.

19. The following details were obtained by Police Officer Jackson at the scene of a robbery:

    Place of Occurrence: Chambers Street, northbound A platform
    Victim: Mr. John Wells
    Suspect: Joseph Miller
    Crime: Robbery, armed with knife, wallet taken
    Action Taken: Suspect arrested

    Officer Jackson is completing a report on the incident.
    Which one of the following expresses the above information MOST clearly and accurately?

    A. At Chambers Street northbound A platform, Joseph Miller used a knife to remove the wallet of John Wells while waiting for the train. Police arrested him.
    B. Mr. John Wells, while waiting for the northbound A train at Chambers Street, had his wallet forcibly removed at knifepoint by Joseph Miller. Joseph Miller was later arrested.
    C. Joseph Miller was arrested for robbery. At Chambers Street, John Wells stated that his wallet was taken. The incident occurred at knifepoint while waiting on a northbound A platform.
    D. At the northbound Chambers Street platform, John Wells was waiting for the A train. Joseph Miller produced a knife and removed his wallet. He was arrested.

20. Police Officer Bellows responds to a report of drugs being sold in the lobby of an apartment building. He obtains the following information at the scene:

Time of Occurrence: 11:30 P.M.
Place of Occurrence: 1010 Bath Avenue
Witnesses: Mary Markham, John Silver
Suspect: Harry Stoner
Crime: Drug sales
Action Taken: Suspect was gone when police arrived

Officer Bellows is completing a report of the incident. Which one of the following expresses the above information MOST clearly and accurately?

- A. Mary Markham and John Silver witnessed drugs being sold and the suspect flee at 1010 Bath Avenue. Harry Stoner was conducting his business at 11:30 P.M. before police arrival in the lobby.
- B. In the lobby, Mary Markham reported at 11:30 P.M. she saw Harry Stoner, along with John Silver, selling drugs. He ran from the lobby at 1010 Bath Avenue before police arrived.
- C. John Silver and Mary Markham reported that they observed Harry Stoner selling drugs in the lobby of 1010 Bath Avenue at 11:30 P.M. The witnesses stated that Stoner fled before police arrived.
- D. Before police arrived, witnesses stated that Harry Stoner was selling drugs. At 1010 Bath Avenue, in the lobby, John Silver and Mary Markham said they observed his actions at 11:30 P.M.

21. While on patrol, Police Officer Fox receives a call to respond to a robbery. Upon arriving at the scene, he obtains the following information:

Time of Occurrence: 6:00 P.M.
Place of Occurrence: Sal's Liquor Store at 30 Fordham Road
Victim: Sal Jones
Suspect: White male wearing a beige parka
Description of Crime: Victim was robbed in his store at gunpoint

Officer Fox is completing a report on the incident. Which one of the following expresses the above information MOST clearly and accurately?

- A. I was informed at 6:00 P.M. by Sal Jones that an unidentified white male robbed him at gunpoint at 30 Fordham Road while wearing a beige parka at Sal's Liquor Store.
- B. At 6:00 P.M., Sal Jones was robbed at gunpoint in his store. An unidentified white male wearing a beige parka came into Sal's Liquor Store at 30 Fordham Road, he told me.
- C. I was informed at 6:00 P.M. while wearing a beige parka an unidentified white male robbed Sal Jones at gunpoint at Sal's Liquor Store at 30 Fordham Road.
- D. Sal Jones informed me that at 6:00 P.M. he was robbed at gunpoint in his store, Sal's Liquor Store, located at 30 Fordham Road, by an unidentified white male wearing a beige parka.

22. The following details were obtained by Police Officer Connors at the scene of a bank robbery: 22.____

    Time of Occurrence: 10:21 A.M.
    Place of Occurrence: Westbury Savings and Loan
    Crime: Bank Robbery
    Suspect: Male, dressed in black, wearing a black woolen face mask
    Witness: Mary Henderson of 217 Westbury Ave.
    Amount Stolen: $6141 U.S. currency

    Officer Connors is completing a report on the incident. Which one of the following expresses the above information MOST clearly and accurately?

    A. At 10:21 A.M., the Westbury Savings and Loan was witnessed being robbed by Mary Henderson of 217 Westbury Avenue. The suspect fled dressed in black with a black woolen face mask. He left the bank with $6141 in U.S. currency.
    B. Dressed in black wearing a black woolen face mask, Mary Henderson of 217 Westbury Avenue saw a suspect flee with $6141 in U.S. currency after robbing the Westbury Savings and Loan. The robber was seen at 10:21 A.M.
    C. At 10:21 A.M., Mary Henderson of 217 Westbury Avenue, witness to the robbery of the Westbury Savings and Loan, reports that a male, dressed in black, wearing a black face mask, did rob said bank and fled with $6141 in U.S. currency.
    D. Mary Henderson, of 217 Westbury Avenue, witnessed the robbery of the Westbury Savings and Loan at 10:21 A.M. The suspect, a male, was dressed in black and was wearing a black woolen face mask. He fled with $6141 in U.S. currency.

23. At the scene of a dispute, Police Officer Johnson made an arrest after obtaining the following information: 23.____

    Place of Occurrence: 940 Baxter Avenue
    Time of Occurrence: 3:40 P.M.
    Victim: John Mitchell
    Suspect: Robert Holden, arrested at scene
    Crime: Menacing
    Weapon: Knife
    Time of Arrest: 4:00 P.M.

    Officer Johnson is completing a report of the incident.
    Which one of the following expresses the above information
    MOST clearly and accurately?

    A. John Mitchell was menaced by a knife at 940 Baxter Avenue. Robert Holden, owner of the weapon, was arrested at 4:00 P.M., twenty minutes later, at the scene.
    B. John Mitchell reports at 3:40 P.M. he was menaced at 940 Baxter Avenue by Robert Holden. He threatened him with his knife and was arrested at 4:00 P.M. at the scene.
    C. John Mitchell stated that at 3:40 P.M. at 940 Baxter Avenue he was menaced by Robert Holden, who was carrying a knife. Mr. Holden was arrested at the scene at 4:00 P.M.
    D. With a knife, Robert Holden menaced John Mitchell at 3:40 P.M. The knife belonged to him, and he was arrested at the scene of 940 Baxter Avenue at 4:00 P.M.

24. Officer Nieves obtained the following information after he was called to the scene of a large gathering:

Time of Occurrence: 2:45 A.M.
Place of Occurrence: Mulberry Park
Complaint: Loud music
Complainant: Mrs. Simpkins, 42 Mulberry Street, Apt. 25
Action Taken: Police officer dispersed the crowd

Officer Nieves is completing a report on the incident. Which one of the following expresses the above information MOST clearly and accurately?

A. Mrs. Simpkins, who lives at 42 Mulberry Street, Apt. 25, called the police to make a complaint. A large crowd of people were playing loud music in Mulberry Park at 2:45 A.M. Officer Nieves responded and dispersed the crowd.
B. Officer Nieves responded to Mulberry Park because Mrs. Simpkins, the complainant, lives at 42 Mulberry Street, Apt. 25. Due to a large crowd of people who were playing loud music at 2:45 A.M., he immediately dispersed the crowd.
C. Due to a large crowd of people who were playing loud music in Mulberry Park at 2:45 A.M., Officer Nieves responded and dispersed the crowd. Mrs. Simpkins called the police and complained. She lives at 42 Mulberry Street, Apt. 25.
D. Responding to a complaint by Mrs. Simpkins, who resides at 42 Mulberry Street, Apt. 25, Officer Nieves dispersed a large crowd in Mulberry Park. They were playing loud music. It was 2:45 A.M.

25. While patroling the subway, Police Officer Clark responds to the scene of a past robbery where he obtains the following information:

Place of Occurrence: Northbound E train
Time of Occurrence: 6:30 P.M.
Victim: Robert Brey
Crime: Wallet and jewelry taken
Suspects: 2 male whites armed with knives

Officer Clark is completing a report on the incident.
Which one of the following expresses the above information MOST clearly and accurately?

A. At 6:30 P.M., Robert Brey reported he was robbed of his wallet and jewelry. On the northbound E train, two white males approached Mr. Brey. They threatened him before taking his property with knives.
B. While riding the E train northbound, two white men approached Robert Brey at 6:30 P.M. They threatened him with knives and took his wallet and jewelry.
C. Robert Brey was riding the E train at 6:30 P.M. when he was threatened by two whites. The men took his wallet and jewelry as he was traveling northbound.
D. Robert Brey reports at 6:30 P.M. he lost his wallet to two white men as well as his jewelry. They were carrying knives and threatened him aboard the northbound E train.

KEY (CORRECT ANSWERS)

1.	B	11.	D
2.	C	12.	A
3.	C	13.	B
4.	A	14.	C
5.	C	15.	A
6.	B	16.	B
7.	C	17.	A
8.	B	18.	C
9.	C	19.	B
10.	B	20.	C

21. D
22. D
23. C
24. A
25. B

TEST 2

DIRECTIONS: Each question or incomplete statement is followed by several suggested answers or completions. Select the one that BEST answers the question or completes the statement. *PRINT THE LETTER OF THE CORRECT ANSWER IN THE SPACE AT THE RIGHT.*

1. Police Officer Johnson has just finished investigating a report of a burglary and has obtained the following information: 1.____

   Place of Occurrence: Victim's residence
   Time of Occurrence: Between 8:13 P.M. and 4:15 A.M.
   Victim: Paul Mason of 1264 Twentieth Street, Apt. 3D
   Crime: Burglary
   Damage: Filed front door lock

   Officer Johnson is preparing a report of the incident. Which one of the following expresses the above information MOST clearly and accurately?

   A. Paul Mason's residence was burglarized at 1264 Twentieth Street, Apt. 3D, between 8:13 P.M. and 4:15 A.M. by filing the front door lock.
   B. Paul Mason was burglarized by filing the front door lock and he lives at 1264 Twentieth Street, Apt. 3D, between 8:13 P.M. and 4:15 A.M.
   C. Between 8:13 P.M. and 4:15 A.M., the residence of Paul Mason, located at 1264 Twentieth Street, Apt. 3D, was burglarized after the front door lock was filed.
   D. Between 8:13 P.M. and 4:15 A.M., at 1264 Twentieth Street, Apt. 3D, after the front door lock was filed, the residence of Paul Mason was burglarized.

2. Police Officer Lowell has just finished investigating a burglary and has received the following information: 2.____

   Place of Occurrence: 117-12 Sutphin Boulevard
   Time of Occurrence: Between 9:00 A.M. and 5:00 P.M.
   Victim: Mandee Cotton
   Suspects: Unknown

   Officer Lowell is completing a report on this incident.
   Which one of the following expresses the above information MOST clearly and accurately?

   A. Mandee Cotton reported that her home was burglarized between 9:00 A.M. and 5:00 P.M. Ms. Cotton resides at 117-12 Sutphin Boulevard. Suspects are unknown.
   B. A burglary was committed at 117-12 Sutphin Boulevard reported Mandee Cotton between 9:00 A.M. and 5:00 P.M. Ms. Cotton said unknown suspects burglarized her home.
   C. Unknown suspects burglarized a home at 117-12 Sutphin Boulevard between 9:00 A.M. and 5:00 P.M. Mandee Cotton, homeowner, reported.
   D. Between the hours of 9:00 A.M. and 5:00 P.M., it was reported that 117-12 Sutphin Boulevard was burglarized. Mandee Cotton reported that unknown suspects are responsible.

3. Police Officer Dale has just finished investigating a report of attempted theft and has obtained the following information:

Place of Occurrence: In front of 103 W. 105th Street
Time of Occurrence: 11:30 A.M.
Victim: Mary Davis
Crime: Attempted theft
Suspect: Male, black, scar on right side of face
Action Taken: Drove victim around area to locate suspect

Officer Dale is preparing a report on the incident. Which one of the following expresses the above information MOST clearly and accurately?

- A. Mary Davis was standing in front of 103 W. 105th Street when Officer Dale arrived after an attempt to steal her pocketbook failed at 11:30 A.M. Officer Dale canvassed the area looking for a black male with a scar on the right side of his face with Ms. Davis in the patrol car.
- B. Mary Davis stated that, at 11:30 A.M., she was standing in front of 103 W. 105th Street when a black male with a scar on the right side of his face attempted to steal her pocketbook. Officer Dale canvassed the area with Ms. Davis in the patrol car.
- C. Officer Dale canvassed the area by putting Mary Davis in a patrol car looking for a black male with a scar on the right side of his face. At 11:30 A.M. in front of 103 W. 105th Street, she said he attempted to steal her pocketbook.
- D. At 11:30 A.M., in front of 103 W. 105th Street, Officer Dale canvassed the area with Mary Davis in a patrol car who said that a black male with a scar on the right side of his face attempted to steal her pocketbook.

4. While on patrol, Police Officer Santoro received a call to respond to the scene of a shooting. The following details were obtained at the scene:

Time of Occurrence: 4:00 A.M.
Place of Occurrence: 232 Senator Street
Victim: Mike Nisman
Suspect: Howard Conran
Crime: Shooting
Witness: Sheila Norris

Officer Santoro is completing a report on the incident.
Which one of the following expresses the above information MOST clearly and accurately?

- A. Sheila Norris stated at 4:00 A.M. she witnessed a shooting of her neighbor in front of her building. Howard Conran shot Mike Nisman and ran from 232 Senator Street.
- B. Mike Nisman was the victim of a shooting incident seen by his neighbor. At 4:00 A.M., Sheila Norris saw Howard Conran shoot him and run in front of their building. Norris and Nisman reside at 232 Senator Street.
- C. Sheila Norris states that at 4:00 A.M. she witnessed Howard Conran shoot Mike Nisman, her neighbor, in front of their building at 232 Senator Street. She further states she saw the suspect running from the scene.
- D. Mike Nisman was shot by Howard Conran at 4:00 A.M. His neighbor, Sheila Norris, witnessed him run from the scene in front of their building at 232 Senator Street.

5. Police Officer Taylor responds to the scene of a serious traffic accident in which a car struck a telephone pole, and obtains the following information:
Place of Occurrence: Intersection of Rock Street and Amboy Place
Time of Occurrence: 3:27 A.M.
Name of Injured: Carlos Black
Driver of Car: Carlos Black
Action Taken: Injured taken to Beth-El Hospital
Officer Taylor is preparing a report on the accident. Which one of the following expresses the above information MOST clearly and accurately?

   A. At approximately 3:27 A.M., Carlos Black drove his car into a telephone pole located at the intersection of Rock Street and Amboy Place. Mr. Black, who was the only person injured, was taken to Beth-El Hospital.
   B. Carlos Black, injured at the intersection of Rock Street and Amboy Place, hit a telephone pole. He was taken to Beth-El Hospital after the car accident which occurred at 3:27 A.M.
   C. At the intersection of Rock Street and Amboy Place, Carlos Black injured himself and was taken to Beth-El Hospital. His car hit a telephone pole at 3:27 A.M.
   D. At the intersection of Rock Street and Amboy Place at 3:27 A.M., Carlos Black was taken to Beth-El Hospital after injuring himself by driving into a telephone pole.

6. While on patrol in the Jefferson Housing Projects, Police Officer Johnson responds to the scene of a Grand Larceny.
The following information was obtained by Officer Johnson:
Time of Occurrence: 6:00 P.M.
Place of Occurrence: Rear of Building 12A
Victim: Maria Lopez
Crime: Purse snatched
Suspect: Unknown
Officer Johnson is preparing a report on the incident.
Which one of the following expresses the above information MOST clearly and accurately?

   A. At the rear of Building 12A, at 6:00 P.M., by an unknown suspect, Maria Lopez reported her purse snatched in the Jefferson Housing Projects.
   B. Maria Lopez reported that at 6:00 P.M. her purse was snatched by an unknown suspect at the rear of Building 12A in the Jefferson Housing Projects.
   C. At the rear of Building 12A, Maria Lopez reported at 6:00 P.M. that her purse had been snatched by an unknown suspect in the Jefferson Housing Projects.
   D. In the Jefferson Housing Projects, Maria Lopez reported at the rear of Building 12A that her purse had been snatched by an unknown suspect at 6:00 P.M.

7. Criminal Possession of Stolen Property 2nd Degree occurs when a person knowingly possesses stolen property with intent to benefit himself or a person other than the owner, or to prevent its recovery by the owner, and when the
   I. value of the property exceeds two hundred fifty dollars; or
   II. property consists of a credit card; or
   III. person is a pawnbroker or is in the business of buying, selling, or otherwise dealing in property; or
   IV. property consists of one or more firearms, rifles, or shotguns.

   Which one of the following is the BEST example of Criminal Possession of Stolen Property in the Second Degree?

   A. Mary knowingly buys a stolen camera valued at $225 for her mother's birthday.
   B. John finds a wallet containing $100 and various credit cards. John keeps the money and turns the credit cards in at his local precinct.
   C. Mr. Varrone, a pawnbroker, refuses to buy Mr. Cutter's stolen VCR valued at $230.
   D. Mr. Aquista, the owner of a toy store, knowingly buys a crate of stolen water pistols valued at $260.

8. Police Officer Dale has just finished investigating a report of menacing and obtained the following information:
   Time of Occurrence: 10:30 P.M.
   Place of Occurrence: (Hallway) 77 Hill Street
   Victim: Grace Jackson
   Suspect: Susan, white female, 30 years of age
   Crime: Menacing with a knife

   Officer Dale is preparing a report on the incident.
   Which one of the following expresses the above information MOST clearly and accurately?

   A. At 10:30 P.M., Grace Jackson was stopped in the hallway of 77 Hill Street by a 30-year-old white female known to Grace as Susan. Susan put a knife to Grace's throat and demanded that Grace stay out of the building or Susan would hurt her.
   B. Grace Jackson was stopped in the hallway at knifepoint and threatened to stay away from the building located at 77 Hill Street. The female who is 30 years of age known as Susan by Jackson stopped her at 10:30 P.M.
   C. At 10:30 P.M. in the hallway of 77 Hill Street, Grace Jackson reported a white female 30 years of age put a knife to her throat. She knew her as Susan and demanded she stay away from the building or she would get hurt.
   D. A white female 30 years of age known to Grace Jackson as Susan stopped her in the hallway of 77 Hill Street. She put a knife to her throat and at 10:30 P.M. demanded she stay away from the building or she would get hurt.

9. Police Officer Bennett responds to the scene of a car accident and obtains the following information from the witness:
   Time of Occurrence: 3:00 A.M.
   Victim: Joe Morris, removed to Methodist Hospital
   Crime: Struck pedestrian and left the scene of accident
   Description of Auto: Blue 2008 Pontiac, license plate BOT-3745

   Officer Bennett is preparing an accident report. Which one of the following expresses the above information MOST clearly and accurately?

5 (#2)

- A. Joe Morris, a pedestrian, was hit at 3:00 A.M. and removed to Methodist Hospital. Also a blue Pontiac, 2008 model left the scene, license plate BOT-3745.
- B. A pedestrian was taken to Methodist Hospital after being struck at 3:00 A.M. A blue automobile was seen leaving the scene with license plate BOT-3745. Joe Morris was knocked down by a 2008 Pontiac.
- C. At 3:00 A.M., Joe Morris, a pedestrian, was struck by a blue 2008 Pontiac. The automobile, license plate BOT-3745, left the scene. Mr. Morris was taken to Methodist Hospital.
- D. Joe Morris, a pedestrian at 3:00 A.M. was struck by a Pontiac. A 2008 model, license plate BOT-3745, blue in color, left the scene and the victim was taken to Methodist Hospital.

10. At 11:30 A.M., Police Officers Newman and Johnson receive a radio call to respond to a reported robbery. The Officers obtained the following information: 10.____

    Time of Occurrence: 11:20 A.M.
    Place of Occurrence: Twenty-four hour newsstand at 2024 86th Street
    Victim: Sam Norris, owner
    Amount Stolen: $450.00
    Suspects: Two male whites

    Officer Newman is completing a complaint report on the incident.
    Which one of the following expresses the above information MOST clearly and accurately?

    - A. At 11:20 A.M., it was reported by the newsstand owner that two male whites robbed $450.00 from Sam Norris. The Twenty-four hour newsstand is located at 2024 86th Street.
    - B. At 11:20 A.M., Sam Norris, the newsstand owner, reported that the Twenty-four hour newsstand located at 2024 86th Street was robbed by two male whites who took $450.00.
    - C. Sam Norris, the owner of the Twenty-four hour newsstand located at 2024 86th Street, reported that at 11:20 A.M. two white males robbed his newsstand of $450.00.
    - D. Sam Norris reported at 11:20 A.M. that $450.00 had been taken from the owner of the Twenty-four hour newsstand located at 2024 86th Street by two male whites.

11. While on patrol, Police Officers Carter and Popps receive a call to respond to an assault in progress. Upon arrival, they receive the following information: 11.____

    Place of Occurrence: 27 Park Avenue
    Victim: John Dee
    Suspect: Michael Jones
    Crime: Stabbing during a fight
    Action Taken: Suspect arrested

    The Officers are completing a report on the incident.
    Which one of the following expresses the above information MOST clearly and accurately?

    - A. In front of 27 Park Avenue, Michael Jones was arrested for stabbing John Dee during a fight.
    - B. Michael Jones was arrested for stabbing John Dee during a fight in front of 27 Park Avenue.

C. During a fight, Michael Jones was arrested for stabbing John Dee in front of 27 Park Avenue.

D. John Dee was stabbed by Michael Jones, who was arrested for fighting in front of 27 Park Avenue.

12. Police Officer Gattuso responded to a report of a robbery and obtained the following information regarding the incident:

Place of Occurrence: Princess Grocery, 6 Button Place
Time of Occurrence: 6:00 P.M.
Crime: Robbery of $200
Victim: Sara Davidson, owner of Princess Grocery
Description of Suspect: White, female, red hair, blue jeans, and white T-shirt
Weapon: Knife

Officer Gattuso is preparing a report on the incident.
Which one of the following expresses the above information MOST clearly and accurately?

A. Sara Davidson reported at 6:00 P.M. her store Princess Grocery was robbed at knifepoint at 6 Button Place. A white woman with red hair took $200 from her wearing blue jeans and a white T-shirt.

B. At 6:00 P.M., a red-haired woman took $200 from 6 Button Place at Princess Grocery owned by Sara Davidson, who was robbed by the white woman. She was wearing blue jeans and a white T-shirt and used a knife.

C. In a robbery that occurred at knifepoint, a red-haired white woman robbed the owner of Princess Grocery. Sara Davidson, the owner of the 6 Button Place store which was robbed of $200, said she was wearing blue jeans and a white T-shirt at 6:00 P.M.

D. At 6:00 P.M., Sara Davidson, owner of Princess Grocery, located at 6 Button Place, was robbed of $200 at knifepoint. The suspect is a white female with red hair wearing blue jeans and a white T-shirt.

13. Police Officer Martinez responds to a report of an assault and obtains the following information regarding the incident:

Place of Occurrence: Corner of Frank and Lincoln Avenues
Time of Occurrence: 9:40 A.M.
Crime: Assault
Victim: Mr. John Adams of 31 20th Street
Suspect: Male, white, 5'11", 170 lbs., dressed in gray
Injury: Victim suffered a split lip
Action Taken: Victim transported to St. Mary's Hospital

Officer Martinez is completing a report on the incident. Which one of the following expresses the above information MOST clearly and accurately?

A. At 9:40 A.M., John Adams was assaulted on the corner of Frank and Lincoln Avenues by a white male, 5'11", 170 lbs., dressed in gray, suffering a split lip. Mr. Adams lives at 31 20th Street and was transported to St. Mary's Hospital.

B. At 9:40 A.M., John Adams was assaulted on the corner of Frank and Lincoln Avenues by a white male, 5'11", 170 lbs., dressed in gray, and lives at 31 20th Street. Mr. Adams suffered a split lip and was transported to St. Mary's Hospital.

C. John Adams, who lives at 31 20th Street, was assaulted at 9:40 A.M. on the corner of Frank and Lincoln Avenues by a white male, 5'11", 170 lbs., dressed in gray. Mr. Adams suffered a split lip and was transported to St. Mary's Hospital.

D. Living at 31 20th Street, Mr. Adams suffered a split lip and was transported to St. Mary's Hospital. At 9:40 A.M., Mr. Adams was assaulted by a white male, 5'11", 170 lbs., dressed in gray.

14. The following information was obtained by Police Officer Adams at the scene of an auto accident:

    Date of Occurrence: August 7, 2004
    Place of Occurrence: 541 W. Broadway
    Time of Occurrence: 12:45 P.M.
    Drivers: Mrs. Liz Smith and Mr. John Sharp
    Action Taken: Summons served to Mrs. Liz Smith

    Officer Adams is completing a report on the accident. Which one of the following expresses the above information MOST clearly and accurately?

    A. At 541 W. Broadway, Mr. John Sharp and Mrs. Liz Smith had an auto accident at 12:45 P.M. Mrs. Smith received a summons on August 7, 2004.
    B. Mrs. Liz Smith received a summons at 12:45 P.M. on August 7, 2004 for an auto accident with Mr. John Sharp at 541 W. Broadway.
    C. Mr. John Sharp and Mrs. Liz Smith were in an auto accident. At 541 W. Broadway on August 7, 2004 at 12:45 P.M., Mrs. Smith received a summons.
    D. On August 7, 2004 at 12:45 P.M. at 541 W. Broadway, Mrs. Liz Smith and Mr. John Sharp were involved in an auto accident. Mrs. Smith received a summons.

14.____

15. Police Officer Gold and his partner were directed by the radio dispatcher to investigate a report of a past burglary. They obtained the following information at the scene:

    Date of Occurrence: April 2, 2004
    Time of Occurrence: Between 7:30 A.M. and 6:15 P.M.
    Place of Occurrence: 124 Haring Street, residence of victim
    Victim: Mr. Gerald Palmer
    Suspect: Unknown
    Crime: Burglary
    Items Stolen: Assorted jewelry, $150 cash, TV, VCR

    Officer Gold must complete a report on the incident. Which one of the following expresses the above information MOST clearly and accurately?

    A. Mr. Gerald Palmer stated that on April 2, 2004, between 7:30 A.M. and 6:15 P.M., while he was at work, someone broke into his house at 124 Haring Street and removed assorted jewelry, a VCR, $150 cash, and a TV.
    B. Mr. Gerald Palmer stated while he was at work that somebody broke into his house on April 2, 2004 and between 7:30 A.M. and 6:15 P.M. took his VCR, TV, assorted jewelry, and $150 cash. His address is 124 Haring Street.
    C. Between 7:30 A.M. and 6:15 P.M. on April 2, 2004, Mr. Gerald Palmer reported an unknown person at 124 Haring Street took his TV, VCR, $150 cash, and assorted jewelry from his house. Mr. Palmer said he was at work at the time.
    D. An unknown person broke into the house at 124 Haring Street and stole a TV, VCR, assorted jewelry, and $150 cash from Mr. Gerald Palmer. The suspect broke in on April 2, 2004 while he was at work, reported Mr. Palmer between 7:30 A.M. and 6:15 P.M.

15.____

16. While on patrol, Police Officers Morris and Devine receive a call to respond to a reported burglary. The following information relating to the crime was obtained by the Officers:

Time of Occurrence: 2:00 A.M.
Place of Occurrence: 2100 First Avenue
Witness: David Santiago
Victim: John Rivera
Suspect: Joe Ryan
Crime: Burglary, DVD player stolen

The Officers are completing a report on the incident.
Which one of the following expresses the above information MOST clearly and accurately?

    A. David Santiago, the witness reported at 2:00 A.M. he saw Joe Ryan leave 2100 First Avenue, home of John Rivera, with a DVD player.
    B. At 2:00 A.M. David Santiago reported that he had seen Joe Ryan go into 2100 First Avenue and steal a DVD player. John Rivera lives at 2100 First Avenue.
    C. David Santiago stated that Joe Ryan burglarized John Rivera's house at 2100 First Avenue. He saw Joe Ryan leaving his house at 2:00 A.M. with a DVD player.
    D. David Santiago reported that at 2:00 A.M. he saw Joe Ryan leave John Rivera's house, located at 2100 First Avenue, with Mr. Rivera's DVD player.

17. When a police officer responds to an incident involving the victim of an animal bite, the officer should do the following in the order given:
    I. Determine the owner of the animal
    II. Obtain a description of the animal and attempt to locate it for an examination if the owner is unknown
    III. If the animal is located and the owner is unknown, comply with the Care and Disposition of Animal procedure
    IV. Prepare a Department of Health Form 480BAA and deliver it to the Desk Officer with a written report
    V. Notify the Department of Health by telephone if the person has been bitten by an animal other than a dog or cat.

Police Officer Rosario responds to 1225 South Boulevard where someone has been bitten by a dog. He is met by John Miller who informs Officer Rosario that he was bitten by a large German Shepard. Mr. Miller also states that he believes the dog belongs to someone in the neighborhood but does not know who owns it. Officer Rosario searches the area for the dog but is unable to find it.
What should Officer Rosario do NEXT?

    A. Locate the owner of the animal.
    B. Notify the Department of Health by telephone.
    C. Prepare a Department of Health Form 480BAA.
    D. Comply with the Care and Disposition of Animal procedure.

18. The following details were obtained by Police Officer Howard at the scene of a hit-and-run accident:

Place of Occurrence: Intersection of Brown Street and Front Street
Time of Occurrence: 11:15 A.M.
Victim: John Lawrence
Vehicle: Red Chevrolet, license plate 727PQA
Crime: Leaving the scene of an accident

Officer Howard is completing a report on the incident. Which one of the following expresses the above information MOST clearly and accurately?

 A. A red Chevrolet, license plate 727PQA, hit John Lawrence. It left the scene of the accident at 11:15 A.M. at the intersection of Brown and Front Streets.
 B. At 11:15 A.M., John Lawrence was walking at the intersection of Brown Street and Front Street when he was struck by a red Chevrolet, license plate 727PQA, which left the scene.
 C. It was reported at 11:15 A.M. that John Lawrence was struck at the intersection of Brown Street and Front Street. The red Chevrolet, license plate 727PQA, left the scene.
 D. At the intersection of Brown Street and Front Street, John Lawrence was the victim of a car at 11:15 A.M. which struck him and left the scene. It was a red Chevrolet, license plate 727PQA.

19. Police Officer Donnelly has transported an elderly male to Mt. Hope Hospital after finding him lying on the street. At the hospital, Nurse Baker provided Officer Donnelly with the following information:

Name: Robert Jones
Address: 1485 E. 97th St.
Date of Birth: May 13, 1935
Age: 73 years old
Type of Ailment: Heart condition

Officer Donnelly is completing an Aided Report.
Which one of the following expresses the above information MOST clearly and accurately?

 A. Mr. Robert Jones, who is 73 years old, born on May 13, 1935, collapsed on the street. Mr. Jones, who resides at 1485 E. 97th Street, suffers from a heart condition.
 B. Mr. Robert Jones had a heart condition and collapsed today on the street, and resides at 1485 E. 97th Street. He was 73 years old and born on May 13, 1935.
 C. Mr. Robert Jones, who resides at 1485 E. 97th Street, was born on May 13, 1935, and is 73 years old, was found lying on the street from a heart condition.
 D. Mr. Robert Jones, born on May 13, 1935, suffers from a heart condition at age 73 and was found lying on the street residing at 1485 E. 97th Street.

20. Police officers on patrol are often called to a scene where a response from the Fire Department might be necessary.
In which one of the following situations would a request to the Fire Department to respond be MOST critical?

A. A film crew has started a small fire in order to shoot a scene on an October evening.
B. Two manhole covers blow off on a September afternoon.
C. Homeless persons are gathered around a trash can fire on a February morning.
D. A fire hydrant has been opened by people in the neighborhood on a July afternoon.

21. Police Officer Johnson arrives at the National Savings Bank five minutes after it has been robbed at gunpoint.
The following are details provided by eyewitnesses: <u>Suspect</u>
Sex: Male
Ethnicity: White
Height: 5'10" to 6'2"
Weight: 180 lbs. to 190 lbs.
Hair Color: Blonde
Clothing: Black jacket, blue dungarees
Weapon: .45 caliber revolver
Officer Johnson is completing a report on the incident.
Which one of the following expresses the above information MOST clearly and accurately?
A white male

A. weighing 180-190 lbs. robbed the National Savings Bank. He was white with a black jacket with blonde hair, is 5'10" to 6'2", and blue dungarees. The robber was armed with a .45 caliber revolver.
B. weighing around 180 or 190 lbs. was wearing a black jacket and blue dungarees. He had blonde hair and had a .45 caliber revolver, and was 5'10" to 6'2". He robbed the National Savings Bank.
C. who was 5'10" to 6'2" and was weighing 180 to 190 lbs., and has blonde hair and wearing blue dungarees and a black jacket with a revolver, robbed the National Savings Bank.
D. armed with a .45 caliber revolver robbed the National Savings Bank. The robber was described as being between 180-190 lbs., 5'10" to 6'2", with blonde hair. He was wearing a black jacket and blue dungarees.

22. While on patrol, Police Officer Rogers is approached by Terry Conyers, a young woman whose pocketbook has been stolen. Ms. Conyers tells Officer Rogers that the following items were in her pocketbook at the time it was taken:
   4 Traveler's checks, each valued at $20.00
   3 Traveler's checks, each valued at $25.00
   Cash of $212.00
   1 wedding band valued at $450.00
Officer Rogers is preparing a Complaint Report on the robbery.
Which one of the following is the TOTAL value of the property and cash taken from Ms. Conyers?

A. $707   B. $807   C. $817   D. $837

23. While on patrol, Police Officer Scott is dispatched to respond to a reported burglary. Two burglars entered the home of Mr. and Mrs. Walker and stole the following items:
    3 watches valued at $65.00 each
    1 amplifier valued at $340.00
    1 television set valued at $420.00
    Officer Scott is preparing a Complaint Report on the burglary.
    Which one of the following is the TOTAL value of the property stolen?

    A. $707   B. $825   C. $920   D. $955

24. While on patrol, Police Officer Smith is dispatched to investigate a grand larceny. Deborah Paisley, a businesswoman, reports that her 2000 Porsche was broken into. The following items were taken:
    1 car stereo system valued at $2,950.00
    1 car phone valued at $1,060.00
    Ms. Paisley's attache case valued at $200.00 was also taken from the car in the incident. The attache case contained two new solid gold pens valued at $970.00 each. Officer Smith is completing a Complaint Report.
    Which one of the following is the TOTAL dollar value of the property stolen from Ms. Paisley's car?

    A. $5,180   B. $5,980   C. $6,040   D. $6,150

25. Police Officer Grundig is writing a Complaint Report regarding a burglary and assault case. Officer Grundig has obtained the following facts:
    Place of Occurrence: 2244 Clark Street
    Victim: Mrs. Willis
    Suspect: Mr. Willis, victim's ex-husband
    Complaint: Unlawful entry; head injury inflicted with a bat
    Officer Grundig is completing a report on the incident. Which one of the following expresses the above information MOST clearly and accurately?

    A. He had no permission or authority to do so and it caused her head injuries, when Mr. Willis entered his ex-wife's premises. Mrs. Willis lives at 2244 Clark Street. He hit her with a bat.
    B. Mr. Willis entered 2244 Clark Street, the premises of his ex-wife. He hit her with a bat, without permission and authority to do so. It caused Mrs. Willis to have head injuries.
    C. After Mr. Willis hit his ex-wife, Mrs. Willis, at 2244 Clark Street, the bat caused her to have head injuries. He had no permission nor authority do so so.
    D. Mr. Willis entered his ex-wife's premises at 2244 Clark Street without her permission or authority. He then struck Mrs. Willis with a bat, causing injuries to her head.

KEY (CORRECT ANSWERS)

1.	C	11.	B
2.	A	12.	D
3.	B	13.	C
4.	C	14.	D
5.	A	15.	A
6.	B	16.	D
7.	D	17.	C
8.	A	18.	B
9.	C	19.	A
10.	C	20.	B

21. D
22. C
23. D
24. D
25. D

REPORT WRITING

EXAMINATION SECTION

TEST 1

DIRECTIONS: Each question or incomplete statement is followed by several suggested answers or completions. Select the one that BEST answers the question or completes the statement. *PRINT THE LETTER OF THE CORRECT ANSWER IN THE SPACE AT THE RIGHT.*

Questions 1-10.

DIRECTIONS: Questions 1 through 10 are to be answered SOLELY on the basis of the following passage and Stolen Vehicle Report Form, which appears on the following page. The form contains 43 numbered boxes. Read the passage and look at the form before answering the questions.

Police Officers Walton and Wright, patrolling in their radio patrol car in the industrial area of the 29th Precinct, were dispatched to 523 Johnson Boulevard at 10:30 A.M. on October 30, 2020 by the Police Radio Dispatcher. The Dispatcher had received a telephone call from a Ms. Ann Graham at 10:28 A.M. that her friend's car was being stolen from in front of her house.

Officers Walton and Wright arrived at 523 Johnson Boulevard at 10:32 A.M. Ms. Graham was waiting outside and informed them that the car had already been stolen. She stated that her friend, Samantha Merlin, had gone on vacation to California three days before and had left her car in Ms. Graham's care. Ms. Graham had parked the car in front of her own house the night before.

Ms. Graham stated that she looked out of her window at 10:25 A.M. that day and saw a strange man breaking into the car using a wire coat hanger. The car's hood was raised. She ran to her telephone to call the police. When she returned to her window, she saw the man doing something under the hood and, within a minute, he drove the car away. She had been too frightened to try to stop him, and there was no one else on the street.

Ms. Graham described the car as a black 2002 Buick 2-door sedan, New York license plate number 113-ABT, Vehicle Identification Number 7641239877. She stated that her friend, Ms. Merlin, lives at 1905 Junis Road, her telephone number is 978-4123, she is unmarried, 30 years old, and will return from vacation on November 13. Until then, she can be reached by telephone at 213-804-9112. She is employed at the law firm of Adams and Adams, 360 Park Avenue, as an office manager.

Ms. Graham described the man who stole the car as white, in his early twenties, about 5'7", 155 lbs., and wearing blue pants, a black jacket, and an earring in his left ear. He had dark brown, short curly hair.

Ms. Graham gave her telephone number as 275-8722 and stated that she is divorced, employed as a securities analyst at F.G. Sutton and Company, 125 Wall Street, and is 32 years old. Her birth date is June 13, 1976. Her telephone number at work is 217-7273.

2 (#1)

STOLEN VEHICLE REPORT FORM

COMPLAINT INFORMATION	Complaint Number (1)	Precinct (2)	Date Complaint Reported (3)	Time Reported (4)	Place Complaint Taken (5)
VEHICLE DESCRIPTION	Year (6)	Make (7)	Color (8)		License Number (9)
	I.D. Number (10)	Type (11)		Location of Theft (122)	
OWNER INFORMATION	Name (13)	Address (14)		Home Telephone (15)	
	Age (16)	Marital Status (17)		Occupation (18)	
	Business Address (19)		Business Telephone (20)		
WITNESS INFORMATION	Name (21)	Address (22)		Home Telephone (23)	
	Age (24)	Marital Status (25)		Occupation (26)	
	Business Address (27)		Business Telephone (28)		
	Witness' Description of Incident (29)				
DESCRIPTION OF SUSPECT	Name (If Known) (30)	Age (31)	Race (32)	Sex (33)	Height (34)	Weight (35)	Hair (36)
	Eyes (37)	Clothing (38)		Distinctive Marks (39)	
	Other (40)				
OFFICER INFORMATION	Name (41)		Date (42)		
	Shield Number (43)				

1. Which one of the following should be entered in Box 3?
   A. June 13
   B. October 13
   C. October 30
   D. November 13

1.____

2. Which one of the following should be entered in Box 31? 2._____
   A. Late teens   B. Early twenties   C. 30   D. 32

3. Which one of the following should be entered in Box 12? 3._____
   In front of
   A. 1905 Junis Road   B. 523 Johnson Boulevard
   C. 125 Wall Street   D. 360 Park Avenue

4. Which one of the following should be entered in Box 8? 4._____
   A. Blue   B. Brown   C. Black   D. Red

5. Which one of the following should be entered in Box 11? 5._____
   A. 2-door sedan   B. 4-door sedan
   C. 4-door station wagon   D. 2-door sportscar

6. Which one of the following should be entered in Box 15? 6._____
   A. 804-9112   B. 217-7273   C. 275-8722   D. 978-4123

7. Which one of the following should be entered in Box 17? 7._____
   A. Married   B. Legally separated
   C. Single   D. Divorced

8. Which one of the following should be entered in Box 21? 8._____
   A. Samantha Merlin   B. Samantha Graham
   C. Ann Merlin   D. Ann Graham

9. Which one of the following should be entered in Box 26? 9._____
   A. Securities analyst   B. Housewife
   C. Office Manager   D. Secretary

10. Which one of the following should be entered in Box 40? 10._____
    A. Scar on left cheek   B. Earring in left ear
    C. Short curly brown hair D. Blue pants, black jacket

Questions 11-20.

DIRECTIONS: Questions 11 through 20 are to be answered SOLELY on the basis of the following story and Complaint Report Form.

Officers Fred Johnson and Carl Adams, patrolling in their radio car in the Riverfront section of Precinct #8, were dispatched to 124 Selwyn Lane at 3:23 P.M. on April 26 by the dispatcher. The dispatcher had received a telephone call at 3:20 P.M. from a Mrs. Green who said that her house had been burglarized and all of the contents of her house had been stolen.

Officers Johnson and Adams arrived at 124 Selwyn Lane at 3:28 P.M. Mrs. Green and two neighbors were waiting for them on the front steps. The Officers parked their patrol car in front of the house and locked the doors. Mrs. Green explained that she is a schoolteacher and her husband is a lawyer. They usually leave the house around 8:00 A.M. each morning. She is

4 (#1)

the first to arrive home since school lets out at 3:00 P.M. She tells the Officers that today, when she arrived home, she found the door to her house slightly open. She was frightened and went to her neighbor's house. Both women then returned to 124 Selwyn and, upon entering the house, found that the contents of the house had been removed. At that point, Mrs. Green called the Police Department.

While Officer Johnson took statements from Mrs. Green and Mrs. Walters, her neighbor, Officer Adams questioned other residents of the street. Most of the other residents were standing outside of the Green's house.

Mrs. Schneider, age 56, who lives 5 doors down at 138 Selwyn, told Officer Adams that she arrived home at 2:45 P.M. She then told Adams that she saw a large truck parked near 124 Selwyn and remembers wondering if anyone new was moving into the neighborhood. She remembers the truck was dented, painted bright blue with a white top, and it had New Jersey plates. Also she was able to describe one of the suspects. She saw him get into the truck before it pulled away. The man was white, about 6'2" tall, about 220 lbs., and thinning brown hair. He was wearing a pair of dirty white overalls and brown work boots. He appeared to walk with a limp. There was another man already in the truck, and Mrs. Schneider described him as a very short Black man wearing a white hat. Mrs. Schneider said the truck turned left on Second Street as it pulled away.

Mrs. Jones, Mrs. Dartnell, and Mrs. Leopold, when questioned by Officer Adams, said that they saw nothing. They were all at Mrs. Leopold's house playing cards and didn't come outside until they heard Mrs. Green screaming.

Officer Adams found that Mrs. Schneider's home phone number was 683-2291 and that she lives alone. Officer Johnson found that both Mrs. Green and her neighbor were 48 years of age and that the school's telephone number was 925-6394. Mrs. Walters' home telephone number is 683-7642, and she lives with her husband at 126 Selwyn Lane. Mr. Green's office number is 238-4296. It is located at 555 Fifth Avenue, Suite 816.

Officers Johnson and Adams then completed the complaint form. The complaint number assigned by the dispatcher was 479638G.

COMPLAINT REPORT

COMPLAINT INFORMATION	Complaint Number (1)	Precinct (2)	Date of Complaint (3)	Time of Complaint (4)	Place Complaint Taken (5)
INFORMATION ABOUT PERSON MAKING COMPLAINT	Name of Person Making Complaint (6) Last Name First Name Middle			Address of Person Making Complaint (7) Street City State	
	Age (8)	Marriage (9) Married ☐ Not-Married ☐		Occupation (If Any) (10)	
	Spouse's Occupation (If Any) (11)			Spouse's Business Address (12) Street City State	
WITNESS INFORMATION	Name of Witness (If Any) (13) Last Name First Name Middle			Address of Witness (If Any) (14) Street City State	
	Age (15)	Occupation (If Any) (16)			
	Spouse's Occupation (If Any) (17)			Spouse's Business Address (18) Street City State	
DESCRIPTION OF INCIDENT	Description (19)				

DESCRIPTION OF SUSPECTS (if Any)	Suspect #1	Name (20)	Age (21)	Race (22) *white*	Sex (23) *male*	Height (24)	Weight (25)	Hair (26)	Eyes (27)
	Suspect #2	Name (28)	Age (29)	Race (30) *black*	Sex (31) *male*	Height (32)	Weight (33)	Hair (34)	Eyes (35)
	Suspect #3	Name (36)	Age (37)	Race (38)	Sex (39)	Height (40)	Weight (41)	Hair (42)	Eyes (43)

	Special Suspect Description (44) Suspect Number _____	Description (45) *Walked with limp*
SUSPECT VEHICLE DESCRIPTION (If Any)	Year (46)	Make (47)	Color (48)	License Number 49)
OFFICER INFORMATION	Name (50)		Date (51)	
	Shield No. (52)			

11. Which one of the following should be entered in Box 4?   11.____
    A. 8:00 AM   B. 2:45 PM   C. 3:20 PM   D Not known

12. Which one of the following should be entered in Box 6?   12.____
    A. Mrs. Schneider   B. Mrs. Green
    C. Officer Johnson   D. Not known

13. Which one of the following should be entered in Box 7?   13.____
    A. 138 Selwyn Lane   B. 125 Selwyn Lane
    C. 124 Selwyn Lane   D. Not known

14. Which one of the following should be entered in Box 8? 14.____
    A. 48 B. 52 C. 46 D. Not known

15. Which one of the following should be entered in Box 10? 15.____
    A. Lawyer B. Widow C. Teacher D. Not known

16. Which one of the following should be entered in Box 11? 16.____
    A. Lawyer B. Widow C. Teacher D. Not known

17. Which one of the following should be entered in Box 13? 17.____
    A. Mrs. Green B. Mrs. Schneider
    C. Mrs. Leopold D. Not known

18. Which one of the following should be entered in Box 16? 18.____
    A. Lawyer B. Teacher C. Widow D. Not known

19. Which one of the following should be entered in Box 26? 19.____
    A. Black B. Brown C. Blonde D. Not known

20. Which one of the following should be entered in Box 44? 20.____
    A. 1 B. 2 C. 3 D. Not known

KEY (CORRECT ANSWERS)

1.	C	11.	C
2.	B	12.	B
3.	B	13.	C
4.	C	14.	A
5.	A	15.	C
6.	D	16.	A
7.	C	17.	B
8.	D	18.	D
9.	A	19.	B
10.	B	20.	A

TEST 2

DIRECTIONS: Each question or incomplete statement is followed by several suggested answers or completions. Select the one that BEST answers the question or completes the statement. *PRINT THE LETTER OF THE CORRECT ANSWER IN THE SPACE AT THE RIGHT.*

Questions 1-10.

DIRECTIONS: Questions 1 through 10 are to be answered SOLELY on the basis of the following story and Complaint Report Form.

Officers Hunt and Torry respond to a suspected burglary-in-process call at 285 E. Reed Street. They arrive there at 2:32 P.M. A man wearing gray slacks, white dress shirt, and red tie is standing in front of the store yelling, *Stop, robbers!* He is pointing east. Officer Hunt sees three men running about one hundred and fifty feet away. He immediately starts to chase after them. One suspect is 5'9" and weighs about 140 lbs. He has black hair in an Afro cut and is wearing tan pants with a blue work shirt. He is wearing white tennis shoes with blue stripes. He turns the corner and runs south on Elm Street. Another one is 6'2" and weighs about 200 lbs. He has long dark brown hair and is wearing a green headband, white jacket, and blue jeans. He is carrying a brown paper bag in his left hand. He also turns south on Elm. The third man is 5'9" and weighs about 180 lbs. He has long dark brown hair and is wearing a white cap. He is wearing blue jeans and a light blue jacket with a white stripe around it. He continues running east on Reed.

Officer Torry questions the man in the red tie and finds he is the manager of the Elite Jewelry Store and that he has just been robbed by the men running away. Torry radios in the information and continues his questioning. The manager, Mr. Oscar Freehold, says that he was showing a ruby and diamond necklace to Mrs. Mandt, a customer, when these men entered the store. One of them, the tallest one, pointed a gun at Freehold and grabbed the necklace. He put the necklace in the pocket of his white jacket. The other two men were shorter and the same height. The heaver one of the two opened the cash register and emptied the money into a brown paper bag.

The thinner short man opened a display case and put several sapphire and emerald rings in his pants pocket. He then took a knife from his pocket and held it on Mrs. Mandt. The tall one forced Mr. Freehold to open the safe. The tall one took jewels and money from the safe and put them in another brown paper bag. The three men ran out.

Officer Hunt chased the two suspects who turned south on Elm Street. At the next corner, they turned east on Maple. They ran one block to the corner of Beech, where the one with the Afro cut turned south. The other suspect got into a car and drove east on Maple. It was a dark blue 2018 Ford sedan with New York license number 677-HKL. As he drove east on Maple, he sideswiped a 2016 red Dodge and a 2019 tan Volvo.

Officer Hunt returns to the jewelry store and radios in the additional information. Officer Torry completes the Complaint Report.

2 (#2)

COMPLAINT REPORT					
COMPLAINT INFORMATION	Complaint Number (1)	Precinct (2)	Date of Complaint (3)	Time of Complaint (4)	Place Complaint Taken (5)
INFORMATION ABOUT PERSON MAKING COMPLAINT	Name of Person Making Complaint (6) Last Name First Name Middle			Address of Person Making Complaint (7) Street City State	
	Age (8)	Marriage (9) Married ☐ Not-Married ☐		Occupation (If Any) (10)	
	Spouse's Occupation (If Any) (11)			Spouse's Business Address (12) Street City State	
WITNESS INFORMATION	Name of Witness (If Any) (13) Last Name First Name Middle			Address of Witness (If Any) (14) Street City State	
	Age (15)	Occupation (If Any) (16)			
	Spouse's Occupation (If Any) (17)			Spouse's Business Address (18) Street City State	
DESCRIPTION OF INCIDENT	Description (19)				
DESCRIPTION OF SUSPECTS (if Any)	Suspect #1	Name (20)	Age (21)	Race (22)	Sex (23) *male*	Height (24) 5'9"	Weight (25) 140	Hair (26)	Eyes (27)
	Suspect #2	Name (28)	Age (29)	Race (30) *black*	Sex (31) *male*	Height (32) 6'2"	Weight (33) 200	Hair (34)	Eyes (35)
	Suspect #3	Name (36)	Age (37)	Race (38)	Sex (39) *male*	Height (40) 5'9"	Weight (41) 180	Hair (42)	Eyes (43)
	Special Suspect Description (44) Suspect Number _____			Description (45) *Walked with limp*	
SUSPECT VEHICLE DESCRIPTION (If Any)	Year (46)	Make (47)		Color (48)	License Number 49)
OFFICER INFORMATION	Name (50)			Date (51)	
	Shield No. (52)				

1. Which of the following should be entered in Box 6? 1.____
   - A. Officer Hunt
   - B. Mr. Oscar Freehold
   - C. Mrs. Mandt
   - D. Not known

2. Which of the following should be entered in Box 10? 2.____
   - A. Jewelry store manager
   - B. Police officer
   - C. Clerk
   - D. Not known

3. Which of the following should be entered in Box 13? 3.____
   - A. Mr. Oscar Freehold
   - B. Mrs. Mandt
   - C. Officer Hunt
   - D. Not known

4. Which of the following should be entered in Box 14? 4.____
   A. East Reed Street   B. East Elm Street
   C. South Beech Street   D. Not known

5. Which of the following should be entered in Box 26? 5.____
   A. Blonde   B. Brown   C. Black   D. Not known

6. Which of the following should be entered in Box 34? 6.____
   A. Blonde   B. Brown   C. Black   D. Not known

7. Which of the following should be entered in Box 42? 7.____
   A. Blonde   B. Brown   C. Black   D. Not known

8. Which of the following should be entered in Box 46? 8.____
   A. 2016   B. 2018   C. 2019   D. Not known

9. Which of the following should be entered in Box 48? 9.____
   A. Green   B. Tan   C. Blue   D. Not known

10. Which of the following should be entered in Box 50? 10.____
    A. Officer Hunt   B. Officer Freehold
    C. Officer Torry   D. Not known

Questions 11-20.

DIRECTIONS: Questions 11 through 20 are to be answered SOLELY on the basis of the following story and Arrest Form.

Officer John Smith, on foot patrol near a delicatessen, heard a man's cry for help. When he reached the man, Peter Laxalt Green, Green told him that he had just been robbed by a young white male who could be seen running down the street. The officer ran after the youth and saw him jump into a 2019 two-door white Buick, New York plate number 761-QCV. While the youth was trying to start the car, the officer caught up with him and arrested him in front of 49 Second Avenue, Brooklyn. The arrest took place ten minutes after the robbery occurred. The officer brought his prisoner to the 65th Precinct station house at 57 Second Avenue, Brooklyn. At the station house, thirty minutes after the robbery, it was determined that the prisoner's legal name was John Wright Doman and his nickname was *Beefy*. Mr. Doman lives at 914 East 140th Street, Brooklyn, Apartment 3G, telephone number 737-1392. He was born in Calgary, Canada, on February 3, 2005. He became a U.S. citizen on February 3, 2012. His Social Security number is 056-46-7056. Doman is not married. He is employed at the Bollero Wine Company, 213 Fourth Avenue, Brooklyn. An arrest report was prepared at the Precinct. The number assigned to the report was 17460.

At the station house, Mr. Green described the incident in detail. Mr. Green stated that at 11:55 P.M. on July 18, 2023, a young, heavy-set white male, 5'11" tall, weighing 220 pounds, with brown hair and blue eyes, entered Mr. Green's delicatessen, at 141 Second Avenue, Brooklyn, New York. Green, who lives in the apartment above the delicatessen, asked him if he could help him. The male replied, *Yes, you can*, and then immediately pulled out a knife. Mr.

4 (#2)

Green then noticed that the male had a red tattoo of an ax on his right arm. The male demanded that Mr. Green give him all the money from the cash register or else Mr. Green would get hurt. Mr. Green picked up a bottle that was on the counter and threw it at the male, striking him in the chest. The male fled from the delicatessen and headed south on Second Avenue. Mr. Green then ran out of the delicatessen and yelled for the police.

Mr. Green was born on March 17, 1969. His business phone number is 871-3113; his home phone number is 330-5286.

ARREST REPORT						
ARREST INFORMATION	Arrest Number (1)	Precinct (2)	Date of Arrest (3)	Time of Arrest (4)	Place of Arrest (5)	
DESCRIPTION OF INCIDENT	Date & Time (6)			Prisoner's Weapon (Description) (7)		
	Prisoner's Auto (color, year, make, model, license plate number, state) (8)					
	Location of Incident (be specific) (9)			Type of Business (10)		
DESCRIPTION OF PRISONER	Last Name First Name Middle (11)			Date of Birth (12)		
	Age (13)	Sex (14)	Race (15)	Eyes (16)	Hair (17)	Weight (18)	Height (19)
	Address City State			Apt. No. (21)	Home Phone Number (22)	
	Place of Birth (23)		Citizenship (24) Citizen ☐ Non-citizen ☐		Marital Status (25)	
	Social Security Number (26)		Where Employed (Company and Address) (27)			
	Nickname (28)	Scars, Tattoos (Describe fully and give location) (29)				
DESCRIPTION OF COMPLAINANT	Last Name First Name Middle (30)			Date of Birth (31)		
	Address City State (32)			Telephone Numbers Business: (33) Home: (34)		

11. Which of the following should be entered in Box 3? _____, 2018 11.____
 A. February 3   B. March 17   C. July 18   D. July 19

12. Which of the following should be entered in Box 4? 12.____
 A. 11:55 P.M.   B. 12:05 A.M.   C. 12:25 A.M.   D. 12:35 A.M.

13. Which of the following should be entered in Box 6? 13.____
    A. 7/18/23, 11:55 P.M.   B. 7/18/23, 11:55 A.M.
    C. 7/19/23, 11:55 P.M.   D. 7/19/23, 11:55 A.M.

14. Which of the following should be entered in Box 7? 14.____
    A. Ax   B. Gun   C. Bottle   D. Knife

15. Which of the following should be entered in Box 8? 15.____
    White _____ Buick, _____, New York
    A. 2019; two-door; 761-QCV   B. 2020; four-door; 762-QCV
    C. 2019; two-door; 761-VCQ   D. 2020; four-door; 167-QCV

16. Which of the following should be entered in Box 12? 16.____
    A. 3/17/69   B. 2/3/05   C. 7/18/05   D. 2/3/12

17. Which of the following should be entered in Box 27? 17.____
    Bollero _____, Brooklyn, N.Y.
    A. Beer Company, 213 Fourth Avenue
    B. Wine Company, 213 Fourth Avenue
    C. Beer & Wine Company, 213 Second Avenue
    D. Wine Company, 213 Fourth Street

18. Which of the following should be entered in Box 32? _____, Brooklyn. 18.____
    A. 49 Second Avenue   B. 57 Second Avenue
    C. 141 Second Avenue   D. 914 East 140th Street

19. Which of the following should be entered in Box 33? 19.____
    A. 330-1392   B. 330-5286   C. 737-1392   D. 871-3113

20. Which of the following should be entered in Box 28? 20.____
    A. Doman   B. Axe   C. Beefy   D. Maniac

KEY (CORRECT ANSWERS)

1.	B	11.	D
2.	A	12.	B
3.	B	13.	A
4.	D	14.	D
5.	C	15.	A
6.	B	16.	B
7.	B	17.	B
8.	B	18.	C
9.	C	19.	D
10.	C	20.	C

PREPARING WRITTEN MATERIAL

EXAMINATION SECTION

TEST 1

DIRECTIONS: Each question or incomplete statement is followed by several suggested answers or completions. Select the one that BEST answers the question or completes the statement. *PRINT THE LETTER OF THE CORRECT ANSWER IN THE SPACE AT THE RIGHT.*

1. The one of the following sentences which is LEAST acceptable from the viewpoint of correct usage is:
   A. The police thought the fugitive to be him.
   B. The criminals set a trap for whoever would fall into it.
   C. It is ten years ago since the fugitive fled from the city.
   D. The lecturer argued that criminals are usually cowards.
   E. The police removed four bucketfuls of earth from the scene of the crime.

1.____

2. The one of the following sentences which is LEAST acceptable from the viewpoint of correct usage is:
   A. The patrolman scrutinized the report with great care.
   B. Approaching the victim of the assault, two bruises were noticed by the patrolman.
   C. As soon as I had broken down the door, I stepped into the room.
   D. I observed the accused loitering near the building, which was closed at the time.
   E. The storekeeper complained that his neighbor was guilty of violating a local ordinance.

2.____

3. The one of the following sentences which is LEAST acceptable from the viewpoint of correct usage is:
   A. I realized immediately that he intended to assault the woman, so I disarmed him.
   B. It was apparent that Mr. Smith's explanation contained many inconsistencies.
   C. Despite the slippery condition of the street, he managed to stop the vehicle before injuring the child.
   D. Not a single one of them wish, despite the damage to property, to make a formal complaint.
   E. The body was found lying on the floor.

3.____

4. The one of the following sentences which contains NO error in usage is:
   A. After the robbers left, the proprietor stood tied in his chair for about two hours before help arrived.
   B. In the cellar I found the watchman's hat and coat.
   C. The persons living in adjacent apartments stated that they had heard no unusual noises.

4.____

D. Neither a knife or any firearms were found in the room.
E. Walking down the street, the shouting of the crowd indicated that something was wrong.

5. The one of the following sentences which contains NO error in usage is:
   A. The policeman lay a firm hand on the suspect's shoulder.
   B. It is true that neither strength nor agility are the most important requirement for a good patrolman.
   C. Good citizens constantly strive to do more than merely comply the restraints imposed by society.
   D. No decision was made as to whom the prize should be awarded.
   E. Twenty years is considered a severe sentence for a felony.

6. Which of the following sentences is NOT expressed in standard English usage?
   A. The victim reached a pay-phone booth and manages to call police headquarters.
   B. By the time the call was received, the assailant had left the scene.
   C. The victim has been a respected member of the community for the past eleven years.
   D. Although the lighting was bad and the shadows were deep, the storekeeper caught sight of the attacker.
   E. Additional street lights have since been installed, and the patrols have been strengthened.

7. Which of the following sentences is NOT expressed in standard English usage?
   A. The judge upheld the attorney's right to question the witness about the missing glove.
   B. To be absolutely fair to all parties is the jury's chief responsibility.
   C. Having finished the report, a loud noise in the next room startled the sergeant.
   D. The witness obviously enjoyed having played a part in the proceedings.
   E. The sergeant planned to assign the case to whoever arrived first.

8. In which of the following sentences is a word misused?
   A. As a matter of principle, the captain insisted that the suspect's partner be brought for questioning.
   B. The principle suspect had been detained at the station house for most of the day.
   C. The principal in the crime had no previous criminal record, but his closest associate had been convicted of felonies on two occasions.
   D. The interest payments had been made promptly, but the firm had been drawing upon the principal for these payments.
   E. The accused insisted that his high school principal would furnish him a character reference.

9. Which of the following statements is ambiguous? 9.____
   A. Mr. Sullivan explained why Mr. Johnson had been dismissed from his job.
   B. The storekeeper told the patrolman he had made a mistake.
   C. After waiting three hours, the patients in the doctor's office were sent home.
   D. The janitor's duties were to maintain the building in good shape and to answer tenants' complaints.
   E. The speed limit should, in my opinion, be raised to sixty miles an hour on that stretch of road.

10. In which of the following is the punctuation or capitalization faulty? 10.____
    A. The accident occurred at an intersection in the Kew Gardens section of Queens, near the bus stop.
    B. The sedan, not the convertible, was struck in the side.
    C. Before any of the patrolmen had left the police car received an important message from headquarters.
    D. The dog that had been stolen was returned to his master, John Dempsey, who lived in East Village.
    E. The letter had been sent to 12 Hillside Terrace, Rutland, Vermont 05702.

Questions 11-25.

DIRECTIONS: Questions 11 through 25 are to be answered in accordance with correct English usage; that is, standard English rather than nonstandard or substandard. Nonstandard and substandard English includes words or expressions usually classified as slang, dialect, illiterate, etc., which are not generally accepted as correct in current written communication. Standard English also requires clarity, proper punctuation and capitalization and appropriate use of words. Write the letter of the sentence NOT expressed in standard English usage in the space at the right.

11. A. There were three witnesses to the accident. 11.____
    B. At least three witnesses were found to testify for the plaintiff.
    C. Three of the witnesses who took the stand was uncertain about the defendant's competence to drive.
    D. Only three witnesses came forward to testify for the plaintiff.
    E. The three witnesses to the accident were pedestrians.

12. A. The driver had obviously drunk too many martinis before leaving for home. 12.____
    B. The boy who drowned had swum in these same waters many times before.
    C. The petty thief had stolen a bicycle from a private driveway before he was apprehended.
    D. The detectives had brung in the heroin shipment they intercepted.
    E. The passengers had never ridden in a converted bus before.

13. A. Between you and me, the new platoon plan sounds like a good idea.
    B. Money from an aunt's estate was left to his wife and he.
    C. He and I were assigned to the same patrol for the first time in two months.
    D. Either you or he should check the front door of that store.
    E. The captain himself was not sure of the witness's reliability.

    13.____

14. A. The alarm had scarcely begun to ring when the explosion occurred.
    B. Before the firemen arrived at the scene, the second story had been destroyed.
    C. Because of the dense smoke and heat, the firemen could hardly approach the now-blazing structure.
    D. According to the patrolman's report, there wasn't nobody in the store when the explosion occurred.
    E. The sergeant's suggestion was not at all unsound, but no one agreed with him.

    14.____

15. A. The driver and the passenger they were both found to be intoxicated.
    B. The driver and the passenger talked slowly and not too clearly.
    C. Neither the driver nor his passengers were able to give a coherent account of the accident.
    D. In a corner of the room sat the passenger, quietly dozing.
    E. the driver finally told a strange and unbelievable story, which the passenger contradicted.

    15.____

16. A. Under the circumstances I decided not to continue my examination of the premises.
    B. There are many difficulties now not comparable with those existing in 1960.
    C. Friends of the accused were heard to announce that the witness had better been away on the day of the trial.
    D. The two criminals escaped in the confusion that followed the explosion.
    E. The aged man was struck by the considerateness of the patrolman's offer.

    16.____

17. A. An assemblage of miscellaneous weapons lay on the table.
    B. Ample opportunities were given to the defendant to obtain counsel.
    C. The speaker often alluded to his past experience with youthful offenders in the armed forces.
    D. The sudden appearance of the truck aroused my suspicions.
    E. Her studying had a good affect on her grades in high school.

    17.____

18. A. He sat down in the theater and began to watch the movie.
    B. The girl had ridden horses since she was four years old.
    C. Application was made on behalf of the prosecutor to cite the witness for contempt.
    D. The bank robber, with his two accomplices, were caught in the act.
    E. His story is simply not credible.

    18.____

19. A. The angry boy said that he did not like those kind of friends. 19.____
    B. The merchant's financial condition was so precarious that he felt he must avail himself of any offer of assistance.
    C. He is apt to promise more than he can perform.
    D. Looking at the messy kitchen, the housewife felt like crying.
    E. A clerk was left in charge of the stolen property.

20. A. His wounds were aggravated by prolonged exposure to sub-freezing temperatures. 20.____
    B. The prosecutor remarked that the witness was not averse to changing his story each time he was interviewed.
    C. The crime pattern indicated that the burglars were adapt in the handling of explosives.
    D. His rigid adherence to a fixed plan brought him into renewed conflict with his subordinates.
    E. He had anticipated that the sentence would be delivered by noon.

21. A. The whole arraignment procedure is badly in need of revision. 21.____
    B. After his glasses were broken in the fight, he would of gone to the optometrist if he could.
    C. Neither Tom nor Jack brought his lunch to work.
    D. He stood aside until the quarrel was over.
    E. A statement in the psychiatrist's report disclosed that the probationer vowed to have his revenge.

22. A. His fiery and intemperate speech to the striking employees fatally affected any chance of a future reconciliation. 22.____
    B. The wording of the statute has been variously construed.
    C. The defendant's attorney, speaking in the courtroom, called the official a demagogue who contempuously disregarded the judge's orders.
    D. The baseball game is likely to be the most exciting one this year.
    E. The mother divided the cookies among her two children.

23. A. There was only a bed and a dresser in the dingy room. 23.____
    B. John was one of the few students that have protested the new rule.
    C. It cannot be argued that the child's testimony is negligible; it is, on the contrary, of the greatest importance.
    D. The basic criterion for clearance was so general that officials resolved any doubts in favor of dismissal.
    E. Having just returned from a long vacation, the officer found the city unbearably hot.

24. A. The librarian ought to give more help to small children. 24.____
    B. The small boy was criticized by the teacher because he often wrote careless.
    C. It was generally doubted whether the women would permit the use of her apartment for intelligence operations.
    D. The probationer acts differently every time the officer visits him.
    E. Each of the newly appointed officers has 12 years of service.

25. A. The North is the most industrialized region in the country. 25.____
    B. L. Patrick Gray 3d, the bureau's acting director, stated that, while "rehabilitation is fine" for some convicted criminals, "it is a useless gesture for those who resist every such effort."
    C. Careless driving, faulty mechanism, narrow or badly kept roads all play their part in causing accidents.
    D. The childrens' books were left in the bus.
    E. It was a matter of internal security; consequently, he felt no inclination to rescind his previous order.

KEY (CORRECT ANSWERS)

1.	C	11.	C
2.	B	12.	D
3.	D	13.	B
4.	C	14.	D
5.	E	15.	A
6.	A	16.	C
7.	C	17.	E
8.	B	18.	D
9.	B	19.	A
10.	C	20.	C

21. B
22. E
23. B
24. B
25. D

TEST 2

DIRECTIONS: Each question or incomplete statement is followed by several suggested answers or completions. Select the one that BEST answers the question or completes the statement. *PRINT THE LETTER OF THE CORRECT ANSWER IN THE SPACE AT THE RIGHT.*

Questions 1-6.

DIRECTIONS: Each of Questions 1 through 6 consists of a statement which contains a word (one of those underlined) that is either incorrectly used because it is not in keeping with the meaning the quotation is evidently intended to convey, or is misspelled. There is only one INCORRECT word in each quotation. Of the four underlined words, determine if the first one should be replaced by the word lettered A, the second replaced by the word lettered B, the third replaced by the word lettered C, or the fourth replaced by the word lettered D.

1. Whether one depends on fluorescent or artificial light or both, adequate standards should be maintained by means of systematic tests.
   A. natural   B. safeguards   C. established   D. routine

1.____

2. A police officer has to be prepared to assume his knowledge as a social scientist in the community.
   A. forced   B. role   C. philosopher   D. street

2.____

3. It is practically impossible to indicate whether a sentence is too long simply by measuring its length.
   A. almost   B. tell   C. very   D. guessing

3.____

4. Strong leaders are required to organize a community for delinquency prevention and for dissemination of organized crime and drug addiction.
   A. tactics   B. important   C. control   D. meetings

4.____

5. The demonstrators who were taken to the Criminal Courts building in Manhattan (because it was large enough to accommodate them), contended that the arrests were unwarranted.
   A. demonstraters   B. Manhatten
   C. accomodate   D. unwarranted

5.____

6. They were guaranteed a calm atmosphere, free from harassment, which would be conducive to quiet consideration of the indictments.
   A. guarenteed   B. atmspher
   C. harassment   D. inditements

6.____

Questions 7-11.

DIRECTIONS: Each of Questions 7 through 11 consists of a statement containing four words in capital letters. One of these words in capital letters is not in keeping with the meaning which the statement is evidently intended to carry. The four words in capital letters in each statement are reprinted after the statement. Print the capital letter preceding the one of the four words which does MOST to spoil the true meaning of the statement in the space at the right.

7. Retirement and pension systems are essential not only to provide employees with with a means of support in the future, but also to prevent longevity and CHARITABLE considerations from UPSETTING the PROMOTIONAL opportunities RETIRED members of the career service. 7.____
   A. charitable   B. upsetting   C. promotional   D. retired

8. Within each major DIVISION in a properly set up public or private organization, provision is made so that each NECESSARY activity is CARED for and lines of authority and responsibility are clear-cut and INFINITE. 8.____
   A. division   B. necessary   C. cared   D. infinite

9. In public service, the scale of salaries paid must be INCIDENTAL to the services rendered, with due CONSIDERATION for the attraction of the desired MANPOWER and for the maintenance of a standard of living COMMENSURATE with the work to be performed. 9.____
   A. incidental   B. consideration
   C. manpower   D. commensurate

10. An understanding of the AIMS of an organization by the staff will AID greatly in increasing the DEMAND of the correspondence work of the office, and will to a large extent DETERMINE the nature of the correspondence. 10.____
    A. aims   B. aid   C. demand   D. determine

11. BECAUSE the Civil Service Commission strongly feels that the MERIT system is a key factor in the MAINTENANCE of democratic government, it has adopted as one of its major DEFENSES the progressive democratization of its own procedures in dealing with candidates for positions in the public service. 11.____
    A. Because   B. merit   C. maintenance   D. defenses

Questions 12-14.

DIRECTIONS: Questions 12 through 14 consist of one sentence each. Each sentence contains an incorrectly used word. First, decide which is the incorrectly used word. Then, from among the options given, decide which word, when substituted for the incorrectly used word, makes the meaning of the sentence clear.
EXAMPLE:
The U.S. national income exhibits a pattern of long term deflection.
   A. reflection   B. subjection   C. rejoicing   D. growth

The word *deflection* in the sentence does not convey the meaning the sentence evidently intended to convey. The word *growth* (Answer D), when substituted for the word *deflection*, makes the meaning of the sentence clear. Accordingly, the answer to the question is D.

12. The study commissioned by the joint committee fell compassionately short of the mark and would have to be redone.
    A. successfully
    B. insignificantly
    C. experimentally
    D. woefully

13. He will not idly exploit any violation of the provisions of the order.
    A. tolerate
    B. refuse
    C. construe
    D. guard

14. The defendant refused to be virile and bitterly protested service.
    A. irked
    B. feasible
    C. docile
    D. credible

Questions 15-25.

DIRECTIONS: Questions 15 through 25 consist of short paragraphs. Each paragraph contains one word which is INCORRECTLY used because it is NOT in keeping with the meaning of the paragraph. Find the word in each paragraph which is INCORRECTLY used and then select as the answer the suggested word which should be substituted for the incorrectly used word.

SAMPLE QUESTION:
In determining who is to do the work in your unit, you will have to decide just who does what from day to day. One of your lowest responsibilities is to assign work so that everybody gets a fair share and that everyone can do his part well.
    A. new   B. old   C. important   D. performance

EXPLANATION:
The word which is NOT in keeping with the meaning of the paragraph is *lowest*. This is the INCORRECTLY used word. The suggested word *important* would be in keeping with the meaning of the paragraph and should be substituted for *lowest*. Therefore, the CORRECT answer is choice C.

15. If really good practice in the elimination of preventable injuries is to be achieved and held in any establishment, top management must refuse full and definite responsibility and must apply a good share of its attention to the task.
    A. accept
    B. avoidable
    C. duties
    D. problem

16. Recording the human face for identification is by no means the only service performed by the camera in the field of investigation. When the trial of any issue takes place, a word picture is sought to be distorted to the court of incidents, occurrences, or events which are in dispute.
    A. appeals
    B. description
    C. portrayed
    D. deranged

17. In the collection of physical evidence, it cannot be emphasized too strongly that a haphazard systematic search at the scene of the crime is vital. Nothing must be overlooked. Often the only leads in a case will come from the results of this search.
    A. important
    B. investigation
    C. proof
    D. thorough

17._____

18. If an investigator has reason to suspect that the witness is mentally stable, or a habitual drunkard, he should leave no stone unturned in his investigation to determine if the witness was under the influence of liquor or drugs, or was mentally unbalanced either at the time of the occurrence to which he testified or at the time of the trial.
    A. accused
    B. clue
    C. deranged
    D. question

18._____

19. The use of records is a valuable step in crime investigation and is the main reason every department should maintain accurate reports. Crimes are not committed through the use of departmental records alone but from the use of all records, of almost every type, wherever they may be found and whenever they give any incidental information regarding the criminal.
    A. accidental
    B. necessary
    C. reported
    D. solved

19._____

20. In the years since passage of the Harrison Narcotic Act of 1914, making the possession of opium amphetamines illegal in most circumstances, drug use has become a subject of considerable scientific interest and investigation. There is at present a voluminous literature on drug use of various kinds.
    A. ingestion
    B. derivatives
    C. addiction
    D. opiates

20._____

21. Of course, the fact that criminal laws are extremely patterned in definition does not mean that the majority of persons who violate them are dealt with as criminals. Quite the contrary, for a great many forbidden acts are voluntarily engaged in within situations of privacy and go unobserved and unreported.
    A. symbolic
    B. casual
    C. scientific
    D. broad-gauged

21._____

22. The most punitive way to study punishment is to focus attention on the pattern of punitive action: to study how a penalty is applied, too study what is done to or taken from an offender.
    A. characteristic
    B. degrading
    C. objective
    D. distinguished

22._____

23. The most common forms of punishment in times past have been death, physical torture, mutilation, branding, public humiliation, fines, forfeits of property, banishment, transportation, and imprisonment. Although this list is by no means differentiated, practically every form of punishment has had several variations and applications.
    A. specific
    B. simple
    C. exhaustive
    D. characteristic

23._____

24. There is another important line of inference between ordinary and professional criminals, and that is the source from which they are recruited. The professional criminal seems to be drawn from legitimate employment and, in many instances, from parallel vocations or pursuits. 24.____
    A. demarcation B. justification C. superiority D. reference

25. He took the position that the success of the program was insidious on getting additional revenue. 25.____
    A. reputed B. contingent C. failure D. indeterminate

KEY (CORRECT ANSWERS)

1.	A		11.	D
2.	B		12.	D
3.	B		13.	A
4.	C		14.	C
5.	D		15.	A
6.	C		16.	C
7.	D		17.	D
8.	D		18.	C
9.	A		19.	D
10.	C		20.	B

21.	D
22.	C
23.	C
24.	A
25.	B

TEST 3

DIRECTIONS: Each question or incomplete statement is followed by several suggested answers or completions. Select the one that BEST answers the question or completes the statement. *PRINT THE LETTER OF THE CORRECT ANSWER IN THE SPACE AT THE RIGHT.*

Questions 1-5.

DIRECTIONS: Questions 1 through 5 are to be answered on the basis of the following.

You are a supervising officer in an investigative unit. Earlier in the day, you directed Detectives Tom Dixon and Sal Mayo to investigate a reported assault and robbery in a liquor store within your area of jurisdiction.

Detective Dixon has submitted to you a preliminary investigative report containing the following information:

- At 1630 hours on 2/20, arrived at Joe's Liquor Store at 350 SW Avenue with Detective Mayo to investigate A & R.
- At store interviewed Rob Ladd, store manager, who stated that he and Joe Brown (store owner) had been stuck up about ten minutes prior to our arrival.
- Ladd described the robbers as male whites in their late teens or early twenties. Further stated that one of the robbers displayed what appeared to be an automatic pistol as he entered the store, and said, *Give us the money or we'll kill you.* Ladd stated that Brown then reached under the counter where he kept a loaded .38 caliber pistol. Several shots followed, and Ladd threw himself to the floor.
- The robbers fled, and Ladd didn't know if any money had been taken.
- At this point, Ladd realized that Brown was unconscious on the floor and bleeding from a head wound.
- Ambulance called by Ladd, and Brown was removed by same to General Hospital.
- Personally interviewed John White, 382 Dartmouth Place, who stated he was inside store at the time of occurrence. White states that he hid behind a wine display upon hearing someone say, *Give us the money.* He then heard shots and saw two young men run from the store to a yellow car parked at the curb. White was unable to further describe auto. States the taller of the two men drove the car away while the other sat on passenger side in front.
- Recovered three spent .38 caliber bullets from premises and delivered them to Crime Lab.
- To General Hospital at 1800 hours but unable to interview Brown, who was under sedation and suffering from shock and a laceration of the head.
- Alarm #12487 transmitted for car and occupants.
- Case Active.

Based solely on the contents of the preliminary investigation submitted by Detective Dixon, select one sentence from the following groups of sentences which is MOST accurate and is grammatically correct.

1. A. Both robbers were armed.
    B. Each of the robbers were described as a male white.
    C. Neither robber was armed.
    D. Mr. Ladd stated that one of the robbers was armed.

    1.____

2. A. Mr. Brown fired three shots from his revolver.
    B. Mr. Brown was shot in the head by one of the robbers.
    C. Mr. Brown suffered a gunshot wound of the head during the course of the robbery.
    D. Mr. Brown was taken to General Hospital by ambulance.

    2.____

3. A. Shots were fired after one of the robbers said, *Give us the money or we'll kill you.*
    B. After one of the robbers demanded the money from Mr. Brown, he fired a shot.
    C. The preliminary investigation indicated that although Mr. Brown did not have a license for the gun, he was justified in using deadly physical force.
    D. Mr. Brown was interviewed at General Hospital.

    3.____

4. A. Each of the witnesses were customers in the store at the time of occurrence.
    B. Neither of the witnesses interviewed was the owner of the liquor store.
    C. Neither of the witnesses interviewed were the owner of the store.
    D. Neither of the witnesses was employed by Mr. Brown.

    4.____

5. A. Mr. Brown arrived at General Hospital at about 5:00 P.M.
    B. Neither of the robbers was injured during the robbery.
    C. The robbery occurred at 3:30 P.M. on February 10.
    D. One of the witnesses called the ambulance.

    5.____

Questions 6-10.

DIRECTIONS: Each of Questions 6 through 10 consists of information given in outline form and four sentences labeled A, B, C, and D. For each question, choose the one sentence which CORRECTLY expresses the information given in outline form and which also displays PROPER English usage.

6. Client's Name: Joanna Jones
    Number of Children: 3
    Client's Income: None
    Client's Marital Status: Single

    6.____

    A. Joanna Jones is an unmarried client with three children who have no income.
    B. Joanna Jones, who is single and has no income, a client she has three children.
    C. Joanna Jones, whose three children are clients, is single and has no income.
    D. Joanna Jones, who has three children, is an unmarried client with no income.

7. Client's Name: Bertha Smith
   Number of Children: 2
   Client's Rent: $1050 per month
   Number of Rooms: 4

   A. Bertha Smith, a client, pays $1050 per month for her four rooms with two children.
   B. Client Bertha Smith has two children and pays $1050 per month for four rooms.
   C. Client Bertha Smith is paying $1050 per month for two children with four rooms.
   D. For four rooms and two children client Bertha Smith pays $1050 per month.

7.____

8. Name of Employee: Cynthia Dawes
   Number of Cases Assigned: 9
   Date Cases were Assigned: 12/16
   Number of Assigned Cases Completed: 8

   A. On December 16, employee Cynthia Dawes was assigned nine cases; she has completed eight of these cases.
   B. Cynthia Dawes, employee on December 16, assigned nine cases, completed eight.
   C. Being employed on December 16, Cynthia Dawes completed eight of nine assigned cases.
   D. Employee Cynthia Dawes, she was assigned nine cases and completed eight, on December 16.

8.____

9. Place of Audit: Broadway Center
   Names of Auditors: Paul Cahn, Raymond Perez
   Date of Audit: 11/20
   Number of Cases Audited: 41

   A. On November 20, at the Broadway Center 41 cases was audited by auditors Paul Cahn and Raymond Perez.
   B. Auditors Raymond Perez and Paul Cahn has audited 41 cases at the Broadway Center on November 20.
   C. At the Broadway Center, on November 20, auditors Paul Cahn and Raymond Perez audited 41 cases.
   D. Auditors Paul Cahn and Raymond Perez at the Broadway Center, on November 20, is auditing 41 cases.

9.____

10. Name of Client: Barbra Levine
    Client's Monthly Income: $2100
    Client's Monthly Expenses: $4520

    A. Barbra Levine is a client, her monthly income is $2100 and her monthly expenses is $4520.
    B. Barbra Levine's monthly income is $2100 and she is a client, with whose monthly expenses are $4520.

10.____

4 (#3)

C. Barbra Levine is a client whose monthly income is $2100 and whose monthly expenses are $4520.
D. Barbra Levine, a client, is with a monthly income which is $2100 and monthly expenses which are $4520.

Questions 11-13.

DIRECTIONS: Questions 11 through 13 involve several statements of fact presented in a very simple way. These statements of fact are followed by 4 choices which attempt to incorporate all of the facts into one logical statement which is properly constructed and grammatically correct.

11. I. Mr. Brown was sweeping the sidewalk in front of his house.
    II. He was sweeping it because it was dirty.
    III. He swept the refuse into the street.
    IV. Police Officer gave him a ticket.

    Which one of the following BEST presents the information given above?
    A. Because his sidewalk was dirty, Mr. Brown received a ticket from Officer Green when he swept the refuse into the street.
    B. Police Officer Green gave Mr. Brown a ticket because his sidewalk was dirty and he swept the refuse into the street.
    C. Police Officer Green gave Mr. Brown a ticket for sweeping refuse into the street because his sidewalk was dirty.
    D. Mr. Brown, who was sweeping refuse from his dirty sidewalk into the street, was given a ticket by Police Officer Green.

11.____

12. I. Sergeant Smith radioed for help.
    II. The sergeant did so because the crowd was getting larger.
    III. It was 10:00 A.M. when he made his call.
    IV. Sergeant Smith was not in uniform at the time of occurrence.

    Which one of the following BEST presents the information given above?
    A. Sergeant Smith, although not on duty at the time, radioed for help at 10 o'clock because the crowd was getting uglier.
    B. Although not in uniform, Sergeant Smith called for help at 10:00 A.M. because the crowd was getting uglier.
    C. Sergeant Smith radioed for help at 10:00 A.M. because the crowd was getting larger.
    D. Although he was not in uniform, Sergeant Smith radioed for help at 10:00 A.M. because the crowd was getting larger.

12.____

13. I. The payroll office is open on Fridays.
    II. Paychecks are distributed from 9:00 A.M. to 12 Noon.
    III. The office is open on Fridays because that's the only day the payroll staff is available.
    IV. It is open for the specified hours in order to permit employees to cash checks at the bank during lunch hour.

13.____

The choice below which MOST clearly and accurately presents the above idea is:
- A. Because the payroll office is open on Fridays from 9:00 A.M. to 12 Noon, employees can cash their checks when the payroll staff is available.
- B. Because the payroll staff is only available on Fridays until noon, employees can cash their checks during their lunch hour.
- C. Because the payroll staff is available only on Fridays, the office is open from 9:00 A.M. to 12 Noon to allow employees to cash their checks.
- D. Because of payroll staff availability, the payroll office is open on Fridays. It is open from 9:00 A.M. to 12 Noon so that distributed paychecks can be cashed at the bank while employees are on their lunch hour.

Questions 14-16.

DIRECTIONS: In each of Questions 14 through 6, the four sentences are from a paragraph in a report. They are not in the right order. Which of the following arrangements is the BEST one?

14. I. An executive may answer a letter by writing his reply on the face of the letter itself instead of having a return letter typed.
    II. This procedure is efficient because it saves the executive's time, the typist's time, and saves office file space.
    III. Copying machines are used in small offices as well as large offices to save time and money in making brief replies to business letters.
    IV. A copy is made on a copy machine to go into the company files, while the original is mailed back to the sender.

    The CORRECT answer is:
    A. I, II, IV, III   B. I, IV, II, III   C. III, I, IV, II   D. III, IV, II, I

14.____

15. I. Most organizations favor one of the types but always include the others to a lesser degree.
    II. However, we can detect a definite trend toward greater use of symbolic control.
    III. We suggest that our local police agencies are today primarily utilizing material control.
    IV. Control can be classified into three types: physical, material, and symbolic.

    The CORRECT answer is:
    A. IV, II, III, I   B. II, I, IV, III   C. III, IV, II, I   D. IV, I, III, II

15.____

16. I. They can and do take advantage of ancient political and geographical boundaries, which often give them sanctuary from effective policy activity.
    II. This country is essentially a country of small police forces, each operating independently within the limits of its jurisdiction.
    III. The boundaries that define and limit police operations do not hinder the movement of criminals, of course.
    IV. The machinery of law enforcement in America is fragmented, complicated, and frequently overlapping.

16.____

The CORRECT answer is:
A. III, I, IV   B. II, IV, I, III   C. IV, II, III, I   D. IV, III, II, I

17. Examine the following sentence, and then choose from below the words which should be inserted in the blank spaces to produce the best sentence.
The unit has exceeded _____ goals and the employees are satisfied with _____ accomplishments.
   A. their, it's   B. it's; it's   C. its, there   D. its, their

17.____

18. Examine the following sentence, and then choose from below the words which should be inserted in the blank spaces to produce the best sentence.
Research indicates that employees who _____ no opportunity for close social relationships often find their work unsatisfying, and this _____ of satisfaction often reflects itself in low production.
   A. have; lack   B. have; excess   C. has; lack   D. has; excess

18.____

19. Words in a sentence must be arranged properly to make sure that the intended meaning of the sentence is clear.
The sentence below that does NOT make sense because a clause has been separated from the word on which its meaning depends is:
   A. To be a good writer, clarity is necessary.
   B. To be a good writer, you must write clearly.
   C. You must write clearly to be a good writer.
   D. Clarity is necessary to good writing.

19.____

Questions 20-21.

DIRECTIONS: Each of Questions 20 and 21 consists of a statement which contains a word (one of those underlined) that is either incorrectly used because it is not in keeping with the meaning the quotation is evidently intended to convey, or is misspelled. There is only one INCORRECT word in each quotation. Of the four underlined words, determine if the first one should be replaced by the word lettered A, the second one replaced by the word lettered B, the third one replaced by the word lettered C, or the fourth one replaced by the word lettered D.

20. The alleged killer was occasionally permitted to excercise in the corridor.
   A. alledged   B. ocasionally   C. permited   D. exercise

20.____

21. Defense counsel stated, in affect, that their conduct was permissible under the First Amendment.
   A. council   B. effect   C. there   D. permissable

21.____

Question 22.

DIRECTIONS: Question 22 consists of one sentence. This sentence contains an incorrectly used word. First, decide which is the incorrectly used word. Then, from among the options given, decide which word, when substituted for the incorrectly used word, makes the meaning of the sentence clear.

22. As today's violence has no single cause, so its causes have no single scheme. 22.____
    A. deference B. cure C. flaw D. relevance

23. In the sentence, *A man in a light-grey suit waited thirty-five minutes in the ante-room for the all-important document*, the word IMPROPERLY hyphenated is 23.____
    A. light-grey   B. thirty-five
    C. ante-room   D. all-important

24. In the sentence, *The candidate wants to file his application for preference before it is too late*, the word *before* is used as a(n) 24.____
    A. preposition   B. subordinating conjunction
    C. pronoun   D. adverb

25. In the sentence, *The perpetrators ran from the scene*, the word *from* is a 25.____
    A. preposition B. pronoun C. verb D. conjunction

KEY (CORRECT ANSWERS)

1.	D	11.	D
2.	D	12.	D
3.	A	13.	D
4.	B	14.	C
5.	D	15.	D
6.	D	16.	C
7.	B	17.	D
8.	A	18.	A
9.	C	19.	A
10.	C	20.	D

21.	B
22.	B
23.	C
24.	B
25.	A

PREPARING WRITTEN MATERIAL

PARAGRAPH REARRANGEMENT
COMMENTARY

The sentences that follow are in scrambled order. You are to rearrange them in proper order and indicate the letter choice containing the correct answer at the space at the right.

Each group of sentences in this section is actually a paragraph presented in scrambled order. Each sentence in the group has a place in that paragraph; no sentence is to be left out. You are to read each group of sentences and decide upon the best order in which to put the sentences so as to form a well-organized paragraph.

The questions in this section measure the ability to solve a problem when all the facts relevant to its solution are not given.

More specifically, certain positions of responsibility and authority require the employee to discover connection between events sometimes, apparently, unrelated. In order to do this, the employee will find it necessary to correctly infer that unspecified events have probably occurred or are likely to occur. This ability becomes especially important when action must be taken on incomplete information.

Accordingly, these questions require competitors to choose among several suggested alternatives, each of which presents a different sequential arrangement of the events. Competitors must choose the MOST logical of the suggested sequences.

In order to do so, they may be required to draw on general knowledge to infer missing concepts or events that are essential to sequencing the given events. Competitors should be careful to infer only what is essential to the sequence. The plausibility of the wrong alternatives will always require the inclusion of unlikely events or of additional chains of events which are NOT essential to sequencing the given events.

It's very important to remember that you are looking for the best of the four possible choices, and that the best choice of all may not even be one of the answers you're given to choose from.

There is no one right way to solve these problems. Many people have found it helpful to first write out the order of the sentences, as they would have arranged them, on their scrap paper before looking at the possible answers. If their optimum answer is there, this can save them some time. If it isn't, this method can still give insight into solving the problem. Others find it most helpful to just go through each of the possible choices, contrasting each as they go along. You should use whatever method feels comfortable and works for you.

While most of these types of questions are not that difficult, we've added a higher percentage of the difficult type, just to give you more practice. Usually there are only one or two questions on this section that contain such subtle distinctions that you're unable to answer confidently. And you then may find yourself stuck deciding between two possible choices, neither of which you're sure about.

EXAMINATION SECTION
TEST 1

DIRECTIONS: The sentences that follow are in scrambled order. You are to rearrange them in proper order and indicate the letter choice containing the CORRECT answer. *PRINT THE LETTER OF THE CORRECT ANSWER IN THE SPACE AT THE RIGHT.*

1. Fire Marshal Adams has arrested a man for pulling a false alarm. He has recorded the following items of information about the incident in his notebook for use in his subsequent report: 1.____
    I. I was on surveillance at a frequently pulled false alarm box located at Edison Street and Harvard Road.
    II. At 1605 hours, I observed the white male, with long brown hair and a mustache, wearing black pants and a red shirt, pull the fire alarm box.
    III. I interviewed the officer of the first due ladder company, Lt. Morgan - L-37, who informed me that a search of the area disclosed no cause for an alarm to be transmitted.
    IV. A man wearing a red shirt, black pants, with long brown hair and a mustache came out of Ryan's Pub, located at Edison Street and Harvard Road, and walked directly to the alarm box.
    V. I stopped the man about five blocks away at 33rd Street and Harvard Road and asked him why he pulled the fire alarm box, and he replied, *Because I felt like it.*

    The MOST logical order for the above sentences to appear in the report is

    A. I, IV, II, III, V
    B. I, II, III, IV, V
    C. I, IV, III, II, V
    D. I, IV, V, II, III

2. A fire marshal is preparing a report regarding Tom Jones, who was a witness to an arson fire at his apartment building. Following are five sentences which will be included in the report: 2.____
    I. On July 16, I responded to the fire building, address 2020 Elm Street, to interview Tom Jones.
    II. Tom Jones described the *super* (name unknown) as a middle-aged male with beard, six feet tall, wearing a blue jumpsuit.
    III. Tom Jones stated that he saw the *super* of the building next door set the fire.
    IV. After being advised of his constitutional rights at the 44th Precinct detective's squad room, the *super* confessed.
    V. I interviewed the *super* and took him to the precinct for further investigation.

    The MOST logical order for the above sentences to appear in the report is

    A. I, II, III, V, IV
    B. I, II, III, IV, V
    C. I, III, II, IV, V
    D. I, III, II, V, IV

3. A fire marshal is preparing a report on a shooting incident which will include the following five sentences:
    I. I ran around the corner and observed a man pointing a gun at another man.
    II. I informed the man I was a police officer and that he should drop his gun.
    III. I was on the corner of 4th Avenue and 43rd Street when I heard a gunshot coming from around the corner.
    IV. The man turned around and pointed his gun at me.
    V. I fired once, shooting him in the chest and causing him to fall to the ground.
   The MOST logical order for the above sentences to appear in the report is

   A. I, III, IV, II, V   B. IV, V, II, I, III
   C. III, I, II, IV, V   D. III, I, V, II, IV

4. Fire Marshal Smith is writing a report. The report will include the following five sentences:
    I. I asked the woman for a description of the man and his location in the building.
    II. When I said, *Don't move, Five Marshal,* the man dropped the can containing a flammable liquid.
    III. I transmitted on my handie-talkie for fire companies to respond.
    IV. A woman approached our car and said there was a man pouring a liquid, which she thought to be gasoline, on a staircase at 123 East Street.
    V. Upon entering that location, I observed a man spilling a liquid on the floor.
   The MOST logical order for the above sentences to appear on the interview sheet is

   A. IV, I, V, II, III   B. I, IV, III, V, II
   C. V, II, IV, I, III   D. IV, III, I, V, II

5. Fire Marshal Fox is completing an interview report for a fire in the kitchen of an apartment at 1700 Clayton Road. The following five sentences will be included in the interview report:
    I. This is the first fire in which Mrs. Brown has ever been involved.
    II. A neighbor smelled the food burning and called the Fire Department.
    III. Mrs. Brown has been a tenant in Apt. 4C for 7 years.
    IV. Mrs. Brown was very tired and laid down to rest and fell asleep.
    V. Mrs. Brown was cooking beef stew in the kitchen after coming home from work.
   The MOST logical order for the above sentences to appear in the report is

   A. II, III, I, IV, V   B. III, V, IV, II, I
   C. I, III, II, V, IV   D. III, V, I, IV, II

6. A fire marshal is completing a report of an arson fire. The report will contain the following five statements made by a witness:
    I. I heard the sound of breaking glass; and when I looked out my window, I saw orange flames coming from the building across the street.
    II. I saw two young men on bicycles rapidly riding away, one with long blond hair, the other had long brown hair.
    III. He made a threat to get even when he was being evicted.
    IV. The young man with long blond hair was evicted from the fire building last week.
    V. The two young men rode in the direction of Flowers Avenue.
   The MOST logical order for the above statements to appear in the report is

A. I, II, V, IV, III	B. I, II, IV, V, III
C. III, I, V, II, IV	D. III, I, II, IV, V

7. A fire marshal is preparing a report regarding an eleven-year-old who was burned in a fire at the Midtown School for Boys. The report will include the following five sentences:

    I. The child described the fire-setter as a male with glasses, five feet tall, wearing a blue uniform.
    II. On December 12, I responded to Hill Top Hospital to interview a child who was burned in a fire at the Midtown School for Boys.
    III. The male perpetrator made a full confession in front of the Assistant District Attorney at the precinct.
    IV. I responded to the school, after interviewing the boy, and found a security guard who fit the description.
    V. I interviewed the security guard and took him to the precinct for further questioning.

    The MOST logical order for the above sentences to appear in the fire report is

A. I, IV, V, II, III	B. IV, III, II, I, V
C. II, I, IV, V, III	D. II, IV, I, V, III

8. A fire marshal is preparing a report concerning a fire in an auto body shop. The report will contain the following five sentences:

    I. The shop owner stated that he argued with a customer about the cost of a repair job.
    II. The shop owner will be the complainant in the arson case.
    III. While on surveillance, my partner and I saw the fire and called it in over the Department radio.
    IV. The customer paid the bill and left saying, *I'll fix you for charging so much.*
    V. According to witnesses, the customer returned to the shop and threw a Molotov cocktail on the floor.

    The MOST logical order for the above sentences to appear in the report is

A. I, IV, V, II, III	B. III, I, IV, V, II
C. V, I, IV, III, II	D. III, V, I, IV, II

9. Security Officer Mace is completing an entry in her memo-book. The entry has the following five sentences:

    I. I observed the defendant removing a radio from a facility vehicle.
    II. I placed the defendant under arrest and escorted him to the patrolroom.
    III. I was patrolling the facility parking lot.
    IV. I asked the defendant to show identification. V. I determined that the defendant was not authorized to remove the radio.

    The MOST logical order for these sentences to be entered in Officer Mace's memo-book is

A. I, III, II, IV, V	B. II, V, IV, I, III
C. III, I, IV, V, II	D. IV, V, II, I, III

10. Security Officer Riley is completing an entry in his memo-book. The entry has the following five sentences:
    I. Anna Jones admitted that she stole Mary Green's wallet.
    II. I approached the women and asked them who they were and why they were arguing.
    III. I arrested Anna Jones for stealing Mary Green's wallet.
    IV. They identified themselves and Mary Green accused Anna Jones of stealing her wallet.
    V. I was in the lobby area when I observed two women arguing about a wallet.
    The MOST logical order for these sentences to be entered in Officer Riley's memo-book is

    A. II, IV, I, III, V
    B. III, I, IV, V, II
    C. IV, I, V, II, III
    D. V, II, IV, I, III

11. Assume that Security Officer John Ryan is completing an entry in his memobook. The entry has the following five sentences:
    I. I then cleared the immediate area of visitors and staff.
    II. I noticed smoke coming from a broom closet outside Room A71.
    III. Sergeant Mueller arrived with other officers to assist in clearing the area.
    IV. Upon investigation, I determined the smoke was due to burning material in the broom closet.
    V. I pulled the corridor fire alarm and notified Sergeant Mueller of the fire.
    The MOST logical order for these sentences to be entered in Officer Ryan's memo-book is

    A. II, III, IV, V, I
    B. II, IV, V, I, III
    C. IV, I, II, III, V
    D. V, III, II, I, IV

12. Security Officer Hernandez is completing an entry in his memobook. The entry has the following five sentences:
    I. I asked him to leave the premises immediately.
    II. A visitor complained that there was a strange man loitering in Clinic B hallway.
    III. I went to investigate and saw a man dressed in rags sitting on the floor of the hallway.
    IV. As he walked out, he started yelling that he had no place to go.
    V. I asked to see identification, but he said that he did not have any.
    The MOST logical order for these sentences to be entered in Officer Hernandez's memobook is

    A. II, III, V, I, IV
    B. III, I, II, IV, V
    C. IV, I, V, II, III
    D. III, I, V, II, IV

13. Officer Hogan is completing an entry in his memobook. The entry has the following five sentences:
    I. When the fighting had stopped, I transmitted a message requesting medical assistance for Mr. Perkins.
    II. Special Officer Manning assisted me in stopping the fight,
    III. When I arrived at the scene, I saw a client, Adam Finley, strike a facility employee, Peter Perkins.
    IV. As I attempted to break up the fight, Special Officer Manning came on the scene.
    V. I received a radio message from Sergeant Valez to investigate a possible fight in progress in the waiting room.

    The MOST logical order for these sentences to be entered in Officer Hogan's memobook is

    A. II, I, IV, V, III
    B. III, V, II, IV, I
    C. IV, V, III, I, II
    D. V, III, IV, II, I

14. Police Officer White is preparing a crime report concerning the burglary of Mr. Smith's home. The report will contain the following five sentences:
    I. Upon entering the house, Mr. Smith noticed that the mortgage money, which had been left on the kitchen table, had been taken.
    II. An investigation by the reporting Officer determined that the burglar had left the house through the first floor rear door.
    III. Further investigation revealed that there were no witnesses to the burglary.
    IV. In addition, several pieces of jewelry were missing from a first floor bedroom.
    V. After arriving at home, Mr. Smith discovered that someone had broken into the house by jimmying the front door.

    The MOST logical order for the above sentences to appear in the report is

    A. V, IV, II, III, I
    B. V, I, III, IV, II
    C. V, I, IV, II, III
    D. V, IV, II, I, III

15. Police Officer Jenner responds to the scene of a burglary at 2106 La Vista Boulevard. He is approached by an elderly man named Richard Jenkins, whose account of the incident includes the following five sentences:
    I. I saw that the lock on my apartment door had been smashed and the door was open.
    II. My apartment was a shambles; my belongings were everywhere and my television set was missing.
    III. As I walked down the hallway toward the bedroom, I heard someone opening a window.
    IV. I left work at 5:30 P.M. and took the bus home.
    V. At that time, I called the police.

    The MOST logical order for the above sentences to appear in the report is

    A. I, V, IV, II, III
    B. IV, I, II, III, V
    C. I, V, II, III, IV
    D. IV, III, II, V, I

16. Police Officer LaJolla is writing an Incident Report in which back-up assistance was required. The report will contain the following five sentences:
    I. The radio dispatcher asked what my location was and he then dispatched patrol cars for back-up assistance.
    II. At approximately 9:30 P.M., while I was walking my assigned footpost, a gunman fired three shots at me.
    III. I quickly turned around and saw a White male, approximately 5'10", with black hair, wearing blue jeans, a yellow T-shirt, and white sneakers, running across the avenue carrying a handgun.
    IV. When the back-up officers arrived, we searched the area but could not find the suspect.
    V. I advised the radio dispatcher that a gunman had just fired a gun at me, and then I gave the dispatcher a description of the man.

    The MOST logical order for the above sentences to appear in the report is

    A. III, V, II, IV, I
    B. II, III, V, I, IV
    C. III, II, IV, I, V
    D. II, V, I, III, IV

17. Police Officer Engle is completing a Complaint Report of a burglary which occurred at Monty's Bar. The following five sentences will be included in the Complaint Report:
    I. The owner said that approximately $600 was taken, along with eight bottles of expensive brandy.
    II. The burglar apparently gained entry to the bar through the window and exited through the front door.
    III. When Mr. Barrett returned to reopen the bar at 1:00 P.M., he found the front door open and items thrown all over the bar.
    IV. Mr. Barrett, the owner of Monty's Bar, said he closed the bar at 4:00 M. and locked all the doors.
    V. After interviewing the owner, I conducted a search of the bar and found that a window in the back of the bar was broken.

    The MOST logical order for the above sentences to appear in the report is

    A. II, IV, III, V, I
    B. IV, III, I, V, II
    C. IV, II, III, I, V
    D. II, V, IV, III, I

18. Police Officer Revson is writing a report concerning a vehicle pursuit. His report will include the following five sentences:
    I. I followed the vehicle for several blocks and then motioned to the driver to pull the car over to the curb and stop.
    II. I informed the radio dispatcher that I was in a high-speed pursuit.
    III. When the driver ignored me, I turned on my siren and the driver increased his speed.
    IV. The vehicle hit a tree, and I was able to arrest the driver.
    V. While on patrol in Car #4135, I observed a motorist driving suspiciously.

    The MOST logical order for the above sentences to appear in the report is

    A. V, I, III, II, IV
    B. II, V, III, I, IV
    C. V, I, II, IV, III
    D. II, I, V, IV, III

19. Crime Reports are completed by Police Officers. One section of a report contains the following five sentences: 19._____
    I. The man, seeing that the woman had the watch, pushed Mr. Lugano to the ground.
    II. Frank Lugano was walking into the Flame Diner on Queens Boulevard when he was jostled by a man in front of him.
    III. A few minutes later, Mr. Lugano told a police officer on foot patrol about a man and a woman taking his watch.
    IV. As soon as he was jostled, a woman reached toward Mr. Lugano's wrist and removed his expensive watch.
    V. The man and woman, after taking Mr. Lugano's watch, ran around the corner.

    The MOST logical order for the above sentences to appear in the report is

    A. II, IV, I, III, V   B. II, IV, I, V, III
    C. IV, I, III, II, V   D. IV, II, I, V, III

20. Detective Adams completed a Crime Report which includes the following five sentences: 20._____
    I. I arrived at the scene of the crime at 10:20 A.M. and began to question Mr. Sands about the security devices he had installed.
    II. Several clearly identifiable fingerprints were found.
    III. A Fingerprint Unit specialist arrived at the scene and immediately began to dust for fingerprints.
    IV. After questioning Mr. Sands, I called the Fingerprint Unit.
    V. On Friday morning at 10 A.M., Mr. Sands, the owner of the High Fashion Fur Store on Fifth Avenue, called the precinct to report that his safe had been broken into.

    The MOST logical order for the above sentences to appear in the Crime Report is

    A. I, V, IV, III, II   B. I, V, III, IV, II
    C. V, I, IV, II, III   D. V, I, IV, III, II

KEY (CORRECT ANSWERS)

1. A	11. B
2. D	12. A
3. C	13. D
4. A	14. C
5. B	15. B
6. A	16. B
7. C	17. B
8. B	18. A
9. C	19. B
10. D	20. D

TEST 2

DIRECTIONS: The sentences that follow are in scrambled order. You are to rearrange them in proper order and indicate the letter choice containing the CORRECT answer. *PRINT THE LETTER OF THE CORRECT ANSWER IN THE SPACE AT THE RIGHT.*

1. Police Officer Ling is preparing a Complaint Report of a missing person. His report will contain the following five sentences:
    I. I was greeted by Mrs. Miah Ali, who stated her daughter Lisa, age 17, did not return from school.
    II. I questioned Mrs. Ali as to what time her daughter left for school and what type of clothing she was wearing.
    III. I notified the Patrol Sergeant, searched the building and area, and prepared a Missing Person Complaint Report.
    IV. I received a call from the radio dispatcher to respond to 9 Maple Street, Apartment 1H, on a missing person complaint.
    V. Mrs. Ali informed me that Lisa was wearing a grey suit and black shoes, and departed for school at 7:30 A.M.

    The MOST logical order for the above sentences to appear in the report is

    A. IV, I, V, II, III
    B. I, IV, V, III, II
    C. IV, I, II, V, III
    D. III, I, IV, II, V

    1.___

2. Police Officer Dunn is preparing a Complaint Report which will include the following five sentences:
    I. Mrs. Field screamed and fought with the man.
    II. A man wearing a blue ski mask grabbed Mrs. Field's purse.
    III. Mrs. Field was shopping on 34th Street and Broadway at 1 o'clock in the afternoon.
    IV. The man then ran around the corner.
    V. The man was white, five feet six inches tall with a medium build.

    The MOST logical order for the above sentences to appear in the report is

    A. I, V, II, IV, III
    B. III, II, I, IV, V
    C. III, IV, V, I, II
    D. V, IV, III, I, II

    2.___

3. Police Officer Davis is preparing a written report concerning child abuse. The report will include the following five sentences:
    I. I responded to the scene and was met by an adult and a child who was approximately four years old.
    II. I was notified by an unidentified pedestrian of a possible case of child abuse at 325 Belair Terrace.
    III. The adult told me that the child fell and that the police were not needed.
    IV. I felt that this might be a case of child abuse, and I requested that a Sergeant respond to the scene.
    V. The child was bleeding from the head and had several bruises on the face.

    The MOST logical order for the above sentences to appear in the report is

    A. II, I, V, III, IV
    B. I, II, IV, III, V
    C. I, III, IV, II, V
    D. II, IV, I, V, III

    3.___

4. The following five sentences will be part of a memobook entry concerning found property:

    I. Mr. Gustav said that while cleaning the lobby he found six credit cards and a passport.
    II. The credit cards and passport were issued to Manuel Gomez.
    III. I went to the precinct to give the property to the Desk Officer.
    IV. I prepared a receipt listing the property, gave the receipt to Mr. Gustav, and had him sign my memobook.
    V. While on foot patrol, I was approached by Mr. Gustav, the superintendent of 50-12 Maiden Parkway.

The MOST logical order for the above sentences to appear in the memobook is

    A. V, I, II, IV, III   B. I, II, IV, III, V
    C. V, I, III, IV, II   D. I, IV, III, II, V

5. Police Officer Thomas is making a memobook entry that will include the following five sentences:

    I. My partner obtained a brief description of the suspects and the direction they were heading when they left the store.
    II. Edward Lemkin was asked to come with us to search the immediate area.
    III. I transmitted this information over the radio.
    IV. At the corner of 72nd Street and Broadway, our patrol car was stopped by Edward Lemkin, the owner of PJ Records.
    V. He told us that a group of teenagers stole some merchandise from his record store.

The MOST logical order for the above sentences to appear in the report is

    A. V, IV, I, III, II   B. IV, V, I, III, II
    C. V, I, III, II, IV   D. IV, I, III, II, V

6. Police Officer Caldwell is completing a Complaint Report. The report will include the following five sentences:

    I. When I yelled, *Don't move, Police,* the taller man dropped the bat and ran.
    II. I asked the girl for a description of the two men.
    III. I called for an ambulance.
    IV. A young girl approached me and stated that a man with a baseball bat was beating another man in front of 1700 Grande Street.
    V. Upon approaching the location, I observed the taller man hitting the other man with the bat.

The MOST logical order for the above sentences to appear in the report is

    A. IV, V, I, II, III   B. V, IV, II, III, I
    C. V, I, III, IV, II   D. IV, II, V, I, III

7. Police Officer Moore is writing a memobook entry concerning a summons he issued. The entry will contain the following five sentences:
   I. As I was walking down the platform, I heard music coming from a radio that a man was holding on his shoulder.
   II. I asked the man for some identification.
   III. I was walking in the subway when a passenger complained about a man playing a radio loudly at the opposite end of the station.
   IV. I then gave the man a summons for playing the radio. V. As soon as the man saw me approaching, he turned the radio off.

   The MOST logical order for the above sentences to appear in the memobook entry is

   A. III, V, II, I, IV
   B. I, II, V, IV, III
   C. III, I, V, II, IV
   D. I, V, II, IV, III

8. Police Officer Kashawahara is completing an Incident Report regarding fleeing suspects he had pursued earlier. The report will include the following five sentences:
   I. I saw two males attempting to break into a store through the front window.
   II. On Myrtle Avenue, they ran into an alley between two abandoned buildings.
   III. I yelled to them, *Hey, what are you guys doing by that window?*
   IV. At that time, I lost sight of the suspects and I returned to the station house.
   V. They started to run south on Wycoff Avenue heading towards Myrtle Avenue.

   The MOST logical order for the above sentences to appear in the report is

   A. I, V, II, IV, III
   B. III, V, II, IV, I
   C. I, III, V, II, IV
   D. III, I, V, II, IV

9. Police Officer Bloom is completing an entry in his memo-book regarding a confession made by a perpetrator. The entry will include the following five sentences:
   I. I went towards the dresser and took $400 in cash and a jewelry box with rings, watches, and other items in it.
   II. There in the bedroom, lying on the bed, a woman was sleeping.
   III. It was about 1:00 A.M. when I entered the apartment through an opened rear window.
   IV. I spun around, punched her in the face with my free hand, and then jumped out the window into the street.
   V. I walked back to the window carrying the money and the jewelry box and was about to go out when all of a sudden I heard the woman scream.

   The MOST logical order for the above sentences to appear in the memobook entry is

   A. I, III, II, V, IV
   B. I, V, IV, III, II
   C. III, II, I, V, IV
   D. III, V, IV, I, II

10. Police Officer Webster is preparing an Arrest Report which will include the following five sentences:
    I. I noticed that the robber had a knife placed at the victim's neck.
    II. I told the robber to drop the knife.
    III. While on patrol, I observed a robbery which was in progress.
    IV. I grabbed the robber, placed him in handcuffs, and took him to the precinct.
    V. The robber dropped the knife and tried to flee.

    The MOST logical order for the above sentences to appear in the report is

    A. I, II, V, IV, III
    B. III, I, II, V, IV
    C. III, II, IV, I, V
    D. I, III, IV, V, II

11. Police Officer Lee is preparing a report regarding someone who apparently attempted to commit suicide with a gun. The report will include the following five sentences:
    I. At the location, the woman pointed to the open door of Apartment 7L.
    II. I called for an ambulance to respond.
    III. The male had a gun in his hand and a large head wound.
    IV. A call was received from the radio dispatcher regarding a woman who heard a gunshot at 936 45th Avenue.
    V. Upon entering Apartment 7L, I saw the body of a male on the kitchen floor.

    The MOST logical order for the above sentences to appear in the report is

    A. IV, I, V, III, II
    B. I, III, V, IV, II
    C. I, V, III, II, IV
    D. IV, V, III, II, I

12. Police Officer Modrak is completing a memobook entry which will include the following five sentences:
    I. The victim, a male in his thirties, told me that the robbery occurred a few minutes ago.
    II. My partner and I jumped out of the patrol car and arrested the suspect.
    III. We responded to an armed robbery in progress at Billings Avenue and 59th Street.
    IV. On Chester Avenue and 68th Street, the victim spotted and identified the suspect.
    V. I told the victim to get into the patrol car and that we would drive him around the area.

    The MOST logical order for the above sentences to appear in the memobook is

    A. III, I, V, IV, II
    B. I, III, V, II, IV
    C. I, IV, III, V, II
    D. III, V, I, II, IV

13. Police Officer Rodriguez is preparing a report concerning an incident in which she used her revolver. Her report will include the following five sentences:
    I. Upon seeing my revolver, the robber dropped his gun to the ground.
    II. At about 10:55 P.M., I was informed by a passerby that several people were being robbed at gunpoint on 174th Street and Walton Avenue.
    III. I was assigned to patrol on 174th Street and Ghent Avenue during the evening shift.
    IV. I saw a man holding a gun on three people, took out my revolver, and shouted, *Police, don't move!*
    V. After calling for assistance, I went to 174th Street and Walton Avenue and took cover behind a car.

    The MOST logical order for the above sentences to appear in the report is

    A. II, III, IV, V, I
    B. IV, V, I, III, II
    C. III, II, V, IV, I
    D. II, IV, I, V, III

14. Police Officer Davis is completing an Activity Log entry which will include the following five sentences:
    I. A radio car was dispatched and the male was taken to Greenville Hospital.
    II. Several people saw him and called the police.
    III. A naked man was running down the street waving his arms above his head and screaming, *Insects are all over me!*
    IV. I arrived on the scene and requested an ambulance.
    V. The dispatcher informed me that no ambulances were available.

    The MOST logical order for the above sentences to appear in the Activity Log is

    A. III, IV, V, I, II
    B. II, III, V, I, IV
    C. III, II, IV, V, I
    D. II, IV, III, V, I

15. Police Officer Peake is completing an entry in his Activity Log. The entry contains the following five sentences:
    I. He went to his parked car only to find he was blocked in.
    II. The owner of the vehicle refused to move the van until he had finished his lunch.
    III. Approximately 30 minutes later, I arrived on the scene and ordered the owner of the van to remove the vehicle.
    IV. Mr. O'Neil had an appointment and was in a hurry to keep it.
    V. Mr. O'Neil entered a nearby delicatessen and asked if anyone in there drove a dark blue van, license plate number BUS 265.

    The MOST logical order for the above sentences to appear in the Activity Log is

    A. II, III, I, IV, V
    B. IV, I, V, II, III
    C. V, IV, I, III, II
    D. II, I, III, IV, V

16. Police Officer Harrison is preparing a report regarding a 10-year-old who was sexually abused at school. The report will include the following five sentences:
    I. The child described the perpetrator as a white male with a mustache, six feet tall, wearing a green uniform.
    II. On September 10, I responded to General Hospital to interview a child who was sexually abused.
    III. He later confessed at the station house.
    IV. After I interviewed the child, I responded to the school and found a janitor who fit the description.
    V. I interviewed the janitor and took him to the station house for further investigation.

    The MOST logical order for the above sentences to appear in the report is

    A. II, IV, I, V, III
    B. I, IV, V, II, III
    C. II, I, IV, V, III
    D. V, III, II, I, IV

17. Police Officer Madden is completing a report of a theft. The report will include the following five sentences:
    I. I followed behind the suspect for two blocks.
    II. I saw a man pass by the radio car carrying a shopping bag.
    III. I looked back in the direction he had just come from and noticed that the top of a parking meter was missing.
    IV. As he saw me, he started to walk faster, and I noticed a red piece of metal with the word *violation* drop out of the shopping bag.
    V. When I saw a parking meter in the shopping bag, I apprehended the suspect and placed him under arrest.

    The MOST logical order for the above sentences to appear in the report is

    A. I, IV, II, III, V
    B. II, I, IV, V, III
    C. II, IV, III, I, V
    D. III, II, IV, I, V

18. Police Officer McCaslin is preparing a report of disorderly conduct which will include the following five sentences:
    I. Police Officer Kenny and I were on patrol in a radio car when we received a dispatch to go to the Hard Rock Disco on Third Avenue.
    II. We arrived at the scene and found three men arguing loudly and obviously intoxicated.
    III. The dispatcher had received a call from a bartender regarding a dispute.
    IV. Two of the men left the disco shortly before we did.
    V. We calmed the men down after managing to separate them.

    The MOST logical order for the above sentences to appear in the report is

    A. I, II, V, III, IV
    B. III, I, IV, II, V
    C. II, I, III, IV, V
    D. I, III, II, V, IV

19. Police Officer Langhorne is completing a report of a murder. The report will contain the following five statements made by a witness:
    I. The noise created by the roar of a motorcycle caused me to look out of my window.
    II. I ran out of the house and realized the man was dead, which is when I called the police.
    III. I saw a man driving at high speed down the dead-end street on a motorcycle, closely followed by a green BMW.
    IV. The motorcyclist then parked the bike and approached the car, which was occupied by two males.
    V. Two shots were fired and the cyclist fell to the ground; then the car made a u-turn and sped down the street.

    The MOST logical order for the above sentences to appear in the report is

    A. I, II, IV, III, V
    B. V, II, I, IV, III
    C. I, III, IV, V, II
    D. III, IV, I, II, V

20. Police Officer Murphy is preparing a report of a person who was assaulted. The report will include the following five sentences:
    I. I responded to the scene, but Mr. Jones had already fled.
    II. She was bleeding profusely from a cut above her right eye.
    III. Mr. and Mrs. Jones apparently were fighting in the street when Mr. Jones punched his wife in the face.
    IV. I then applied pressure to the cut to control the bleeding.
    V. I called the dispatcher on the radio to send an ambulance to respond to the scene.

    The MOST logical order for the above sentences to appear in the report is

    A. III, II, IV, I, V
    B. III, I, II, IV, V
    C. I, V, II, III, IV
    D. II, V, IV, III, I

KEY (CORRECT ANSWERS)

1.	C	11.	A
2.	B	12.	A
3.	A	13.	C
4.	A	14.	C
5.	B	15.	B
6.	D	16.	C
7.	C	17.	C
8.	C	18.	D
9.	C	19.	C
10.	B	20.	B

READING COMPREHENSION
UNDERSTANDING AND INTERPRETING WRITTEN MATERIAL
EXAMINATION SECTION
TEST 1

DIRECTIONS: Each question or incomplete statement is followed by several suggested answers or completions. Select the one that BEST answers the question or completes the statement. *PRINT THE LETTER OF THE CORRECT ANSWER IN THE SPACE AT THE RIGHT.*

Questions 1-3.

DIRECTIONS: Questions 1 through 3 are to be answered SOLELY on the basis of the following passage.

When police officers search for a stolen car, they first check for the color of the car, then for make, model, year, body damage, and finally license number. The first five can be detected from almost any angle, while the recognition of the license number is often not immediately apparent. The serial number and motor number, though less likely to be changed than the easily substituted license number, cannot be observed in initial detection of the stolen car.

1. According to the above passage, the one of the following features which is LEAST readily observed in checking for a stolen car in moving traffic is
   A. license number
   B. serial number
   C. model
   D. make
   E. color

   1.____

2. The feature of a car that cannot be determined from most angles of observation is the
   A. make
   B. model
   C. year
   D. license number
   E. color

   2.____

3. Of the following, the feature of a stolen car that is MOST likely to be altered by a car thief shortly after the car is stolen is the
   A. license number
   B. motor number
   C. color
   D. model
   E. minor body damage

   3.____

Questions 4-5.

DIRECTIONS: Questions 4 and 5 are to be answered SOLELY on the basis of the following passage.

The racketeer is primarily concerned with business affairs, legitimate or otherwise, and preferably those which are close to the margin of legitimacy. He gets his best opportunities from business organizations which meet the need of large sections of the public for goods or services which are defined as illegitimate by the same public, such as prostitution, gambling, illicit drugs or liquor. In contrast to the thief, the racketeer and the establishments he controls deliver goods and services for money received.

4. From the above passage, it can be deduced that suppression of racketeers is difficult because
   A. victims of racketeers are not guilty of violating the law
   B. racketeers are generally engaged in fully legitimate enterprises
   C. many people want services which are not obtainable through legitimate sources
   D. the racketeers are well organized
   E. laws prohibiting gambling and prostitution are unenforceable

5. According to the above passage, racketeering, unlike theft, involves
   A. objects of value
   B. payment for goods received
   C. organized gangs
   D. public approval
   E. unlawful activities

Questions 6-8.

DIRECTIONS: Questions 6 through 8 are to be answered SOLELY on the basis of the following passage.

A number of crimes, such as robbery, assault, rape, certain forms of theft and burglary, are high visibility crimes in that it is apparent to all concerned that they are criminal acts prior to or at the time they are committed. In contrast to these, check forgeries, especially those committed by first offenders, have low visibility. There is little in the criminal act or in the interaction between the check passer and the person cashing the check to identify it as a crime. Closely related to this special quality of the forgery crime is the fact that, while it is formally defined and treated as a felonious or infamous crime, it is formally held by the legally untrained public to be a relatively harmless form of crime.

6. According to the above passage, crimes of *high visibility*
   A. are immediately recognized as crimes by the victim
   B. take place in public view
   C. always involve violence or the threat of violence
   D. usually are committed after dark
   E. can be observed from a distance

7. According to the above passage,
   A. the public regards check forgery as a minor crime
   B. the law regards check forgery as a minor crime
   C. the law distinguishes between check forgery and other forgery
   D. it is easier to spot inexperienced check forgers than other criminals
   E. it is more difficult to identify check forgers than other criminals

8. As used in the above passage, an *infamous* crime is
   A. a crime attracting great attention from the public
   B. more serious than a felony
   C. less serious than a felony
   D. more or less than a felony depending upon the surrounding circumstances
   E. the same as a felony

Questions 9-11.

DIRECTIONS: Questions 9 through 11 are to be answered SOLELY on the basis of the following passage.

Criminal science is largely the science of identification. Progress in this field has been marked and sometimes very spectacular because new techniques, instruments, and facts flow continuously from the scientists. But the crime laboratories are undermanned, trade secrets still prevail, and inaccurate conclusions are often the results. However, modern gadgets cannot substitute for the skilled intelligent investigator; he must be their master.

9. According to the above passage, criminal science 9._____
   A. excludes the field of investigation
   B. is primarily interested in establishing identity
   C. is based on the equipment used in crime laboratories
   D. uses techniques different from those used in other sciences
   E. is essentially secret in nature

10. Advances in criminal science have been, according to the above passage, 10._____
    A. extremely limited   B. slow but steady
    C. unusually reliable   D. outstanding
    E. infrequently worthwhile

11. A problem that has NOT been overcome completely in crime work is, according 11._____
    to the above passage,
    A. unskilled investigators
    B. the expense of new equipment and techniques
    C. an insufficient number of personnel in crime laboratories
    D. inaccurate equipment used in laboratories
    E. conclusions of the public about the value of this field

Questions 12-14.

DIRECTIONS: Questions 12 through 14 are to be answered SOLELY on the basis of the following passage.

The New York City Police Department will accept for investigation no report of a person missing from his residence, if such residence is located outside of New York City. The person reporting same will be advised to report such fact to the police department of the locality where the missing person lives, which will, if necessary, communicate officially with the New York City Police Department. However, a report will be accepted of a person who is missing from a temporary residence in New York City, but the person making the report will be instructed to make a report also to the police department of the locality where the missing person lives.

12. According to the above passage, a report to the New York City Police Depart- 12._____
    ment of a missing person whose permanent residence is outside of New York
    City will
    A. always be investigated provided that a report is also made to his local
       police authorities

B. never be investigated unless requested officially by his local police authorities
C. be investigated in cases of temporary New York City residence, but a report should always be made to his local police authorities
D. be investigated if the person making the report is a New York City resident
E. always be investigated and a report will be made to the local police authorities by the New York City Police Department

13. Of the following, the MOST likely reason for the procedure described in the above passage is that 13.____
    A. non-residents are not entitled to free police service from New York City
    B. local police authorities would resent interference in their jurisdiction
    C. local police authorities sometimes try to unload their problems on the New York City Police
    D. local police authorities may be better able to conduct an investigation
    E. few persons are erroneously reported as missing

14. Mr. Smith, who lives in Jersey City, and Mr. Jones, who lives in Newark, arrange to meet in New York City, but Mr. Jones doesn't keep the appointment. Mr. Smith telephones Mr. Jones several times the next day and gets no answer. Mr. Smith believes that something has happened to Mr. Jones. According to the above passage, Mr. Smith should apply to the police authorities of 14.____
    A. Jersey City
    B. Newark
    C. Newark and New York City
    D. Jersey City and New York City
    E. Newark, Jersey City, and New York City

Questions 15-17.

DIRECTIONS: Questions 15 through 17 are to be answered SOLELY on the basis of the following passage.

Some early psychologists believed that the basic characteristic of the criminal type was inferiority of intelligence, if not outright feeblemindedness. They were misled by the fact that they had measurements for all kinds of criminals, but, until World War I gave them a draft army sample, they had no information on a comparable group of non-criminal adults. As soon as acceptable measurements could be taken of criminals and a comparable group of non-criminals, concern with feeblemindedness or with low intelligence as a type took on less and less significance in research in criminology.

15. According to the above passage, some early psychologists were in error because they didn't 15.____
    A. distinguish among the various types of criminals
    B. devise a suitable method of measuring intelligence
    C. measure the intelligence of non-criminals as a basis for comparison

D. distinguish between feeblemindedness and inferiority of intelligence
E. clearly define the term *intelligence*

16. The above passage implies that studies of the intelligence of criminals and non-criminals
    A. are useless because it is impossible to obtain comparable groups
    B. are not meaningful because only the less intelligent criminals are detected
    C. indicate that criminals are more intelligent than non-criminals
    D. indicate that criminals are less intelligent than non-criminals
    E. do not indicate that there are any differences between the two groups

16._____

17. According to the above passage, studies of the World War I draft gave psychologists vital information concerning
    A. adaptability to army life of criminals and non-criminals
    B. criminal tendencies among draftees
    C. the intelligence scores of large numbers of men
    D. differences between intelligence scores of draftees and volunteers
    E. the behavior of men under abnormal conditions

17._____

Questions 18-20.

DIRECTIONS: Questions 18 through 20 are to be answered SOLELY on the basis of the following passage.

    The use of a roadblock is simply an adaptation to police practices of the military concept of encirclement. Successful operation of a roadblock plan depends almost entirely on the amount of advance study and planning given to such operations. A thorough and detailed examination of the roads and terrain under the jurisdiction of a given policy agency should be made with the locations of the roadblocks pinpointed in advance. The first principle to be borne in mind in the location of each roadblock is the time element. Its location must be at a point beyond which the fugitive could not have possibly traveled in the time elapsed from the commission of the crime to the arrival of the officers at the roadblock.

18. According to the above passage,
    A. military operations have made extensive use of roadblocks
    B. the military concept of encirclement is an adaptation of police use of roadblocks
    C. the technique of encirclement has been widely used by military forces
    D. a roadblock is generally more effective than encirclement
    E. police use of roadblocks is based on the idea of military encirclement

18._____

19. According to the above passage,
    A. the factor of time is the sole consideration in the location of a roadblock
    B. the maximum speed possible in the method of escape is of major importance in roadblock location
    C. the time of arrival of officers at the site of a proposed roadblock is of little importance

19._____

D. if the method of escape is not known, it should be assumed that the escape is by automobile
E. a roadblock should be sited as close to the scene of the crime as the terrain will permit

20. According to the above passage, 20._____
    A. advance study and planning are of minor importance in the success of roadblock operations
    B. a thorough and detailed examination of all roads within a radius of fifty miles should precede the determination of a roadblock location
    C. consideration of terrain features are important in planning the location of roadblocks
    D. the pinpointing of roadblocks should be performed before any advance study is made
    E. a roadblock operation can seldom be successfully undertaken by a single police agency

KEY (CORRECT ANSWERS)

1.	B	11.	C
2.	D	12.	C
3.	A	13.	D
4.	C	14.	B
5.	B	15.	C
6.	A	16.	E
7.	A	17.	C
8.	E	18.	E
9.	B	19.	B
10.	D	20.	C

TEST 2

DIRECTIONS: Each question or incomplete statement is followed by several suggested answers or completions. Select the one that BEST answers the question or completes the statement. *PRINT THE LETTER OF THE CORRECT ANSWER IN THE SPACE AT THE RIGHT.*

Questions 1-3.

DIRECTIONS: Questions 1 through 3 are to be answered SOLELY on the basis of the following passage.

Modern police science may be said to have three phases. The first phase embraces the identification of living and dead persons. The second embraces the field work carried out by specially trained detectives at the scene of the crime. The third embraces methods used in the police laboratory to examine and analyze clues and traces discovered in the course of the investigation. While modern police science has had a striking influence on detective work and will surely further enhance its effectiveness, the time-honored methods and practical detective work will always be important. The time-honored methods, that is knowledge of methods used by criminals, patience, tact, industry, thoroughness, and imagination, will always be requisites for successful detective work.

1. According to the above passage, we may expect modern police science to   1.____
   A. help detective work more and more
   B. become more and more scientific
   C. depend less and less on the time-honored methods
   D. bring together the many different approaches to detective work
   E. play a less important role in detective work

2. According to the above passage, a knowledge of the procedures used by   2.____
   criminals is
   A. solely an element of the modern police science approach to detective work
   B. related to the identification of persons
   C. not related to detective field work
   D. related to methods used in the police laboratory
   E. an element of the traditional approach to detective work

3. Modern police science and practical detective work, according to the above   3.____
   passage,
   A. when used together can only lead to confusion
   B. are based distinctly different theories of detective work
   C. have had strikingly different influence on detective work
   D. should both be used for successful detective work
   E. lead usually to similar results

Questions 4-7.

DIRECTIONS: Questions 4 through 7 are to be answered SOLELY on the basis of the following passage.

A member of the force shall render reasonable aid to a sick or injured person. He shall summon an ambulance, if necessary, by telephoning the communications bureau of the borough, who shall notify the precinct concerned. If possible, he shall wait in full view of the arriving ambulance and take necessary action to direct the responding doctor or attendant to the patient, without delay. If the ambulance does not arrive in twenty minutes, he shall send in a second call. However, if the sick person is in his or her own home, a member of the force, before summoning an ambulance, will ascertain whether such person is willing to be taken to a hospital for treatment.

4. According to the above passage, if a patrolman wants to get an ambulance for a sick person, he should telephone
    A. the precinct concerned
    B. only if the sick person is in his home
    C. the nearest hospital
    D. only if the sick person is not in his home
    E. the borough communications bureau

5. According to the above passage, if a patrolman telephones for an ambulance and none arrives within twenty minutes, he should
    A. ask the injured person if he is willing to be taken to a hospital
    B. call the borough communications bureau
    C. call the precinct concerned
    D. attempt to give the injured person such assistance as he may need
    E. call the nearest hospital

6. A patrolman is called to help a woman who has fallen in her own home and has apparently broken her leg.
   According to the above passage, he should
    A. ask her if she wants to go to a hospital
    B. try to set her leg if it is necessary
    C. call for an ambulance at once
    D. attempt to get a doctor as quickly as possible
    E. not attempt to help the woman in any way before competent medical aid arrives

7. A man falls from a window into the backyard of an apartment house. Assume that you are a patrolman and that you are called to assist this man.
   According to the above passage, after you have called for an ambulance and comforted the injured man as much as you can, you should
    A. wait in front of the house for the ambulance
    B. ask the injured man if he wishes to go to the hospital for treatment
    C. remain with the injured man until the ambulance arrives
    D. send a bystander to direct the nearest doctor to the patient
    E. not ask the man to explain how the accident happened

Questions 8-10.

DIRECTIONS: Questions 8 through 10 are to be answered SOLELY on the basis of the following passage.

What is required is a program that will protect our citizens and their property from criminal and antisocial acts, will effectively restrain and reform juvenile delinquents, and will prevent the further development of antisocial behavior. Discipline and punishment of offenders must necessarily play an important part in any such program. Serious offenders cannot be mollycoddled merely because they are under twenty-one. Restraint and punishment necessarily follow serious antisocial acts. But punishment, if it is to be effective, must be a planned part of a more comprehensive program of treating delinquency.

8. The one of the following goals NOT included among those listed above is to
    A. stop young people from defacing public property
    B. keep homes from being broken into
    C. develop an intra-city boys' baseball league
    D. change juvenile delinquents into useful citizens
    E. prevent young people from developing antisocial behavior patterns

8.____

9. According to the above passage, punishment is
    A. not satisfactory in any program dealing with juvenile delinquents
    B. the most effective means by which young vandals and hooligans can be reformed
    C. not used sufficiently when dealing with serious offenders who are under twenty-one
    D. of value in reducing juvenile delinquency only if it is part of a complete program
    E. most effective when it does not relate to specific antisocial acts

9.____

10. With respect to serious offenders who are under twenty-one, the above passage suggests that they
    A. be mollycoddled
    B. be dealt with as part of a comprehensive program to punish mature criminals
    C. should be punished
    D. be prevented, by brute force if necessary, from performing antisocial acts
    E. be treated as delinquent children who require more love than punishment

10.____

Questions 11-14.

DIRECTIONS: Questions 11 through 14 are to be answered SOLELY on the basis of the following passage.

In all cases of homicide, members of the Police Department who investigate will make every effort to obtain statements from dying persons. Such statements are of the greatest importance to the District Attorney. In many cases, there may be a failure to solve the crime if they are not taken. The principle element to be considered in taking the declaration of a dying person is his mental attitude. In order to be admissible in evidence, the person must have no hope of recovery. The patient will be fully interrogated on that point before a statement is taken.

11. In cases of homicide, according to the above passage, members of the police force will
    A. try to change the mental attitude of the dying person
    B. attempt to obtain a statement from the dying person
    C. not give the information they obtain directly to the District Attorney
    D. be careful not to injure the dying person unnecessarily
    E. prevent unauthorized persons from taking dying declarations

12. The mental attitude of the person making the dying statement is of great importance because it can determine, according to the above passage, whether the
    A. victim should be interrogated in the presence of witnesses
    B. victim will be willing to make a statement of any kind
    C. victim has been forced to make the statement
    D. statement will tell the District Attorney who committed the crime
    E. statement can be used as evidence

13. District Attorneys find that statements of a dying person are important, according to the above passage, because
    A. it may be that the victim will recover and refuse to testify
    B. they are important elements in determining the mental attitude of the victim
    C. they present a point of view
    D. it may be impossible to punish the criminal without such a statement
    E. dead men tell no tales

14. A well-known gangster is found dying from a bullet wound. The patrolman first on the scene, in the presence of witnesses, tells the man that he is going to die and asks, *Who shot you?* The gangster says, *Jones shot me, but he hasn't killed me. I'll live to get him.* He then falls back dead.
    According to the above passage, this statement is
    A. *admissible* in evidence; the man was obviously speaking the truth
    B. *not admissible* in evidence; the man obviously did not believe that he was dying
    C. *admissible* in evidence; there were witnesses to the statement
    D. *not admissible* in evidence; the victim did not sign any statement and the evidence is merely hearsay
    E. *admissible* in evidence; there was no time to interrogate the victim

Questions 15-17.

DIRECTIONS: Questions 15 through 17 are to be answered SOLELY on the basis of the following passage.

The factors contributing to crime and delinquency are varied and complex. The home and its immediate environment have been found to be crucial in determining the behavior patterns of the individual, and criminality can frequently be traced to faulty family relationships and a bad neighborhood. But in the search for a clearer understanding of the underlying causes of delinquent and criminal behavior, the total environment must be taken into consideration.

15. According to the above passage, family relationships   15._____
    A. tend to become faulty in bad neighborhoods
    B. are important in determining the actions of honest people as well as criminals
    C. are the only important element in the understanding of causes of delinquency
    D. are determined by the total environment
    E. of criminals are understandable only in terms of the behavior patterns of the individuals concerned

16. According to the above passage, the causes of crime and delinquency are   16._____
    A. not simple   B. not meaningless
    C. meaningless   D. simple
    E. always understandable

17. According to the above passage, faulty family relationships frequently are   17._____
    A. responsible for varied and complex results
    B. caused by differences
    C. caused when one or both parents have a criminal behavior pattern
    D. independent of the total environment
    E. the cause of criminal acts

Questions 18-20.

DIRECTIONS: Questions 18 through 20 are to be answered SOLELY on the basis of the following passage.

A change in the specific problems which confront the police and in the methods for dealing with them has taken place in the last few decades. The automobile is a two-way symbol of this change in policing. It menaces every city with a complicated traffic problem and has speeded up the process of committing a crime and making a getaway, but at the same time has increased the effectiveness of police operations. However, the major concern of police departments continues to be the antisocial or criminal actions and behavior of human beings.

18. On the basis of the above passage, it can be stated that for the most part in   18._____
    the past few decades, the specific problems of a police force
    A. have changed but the general problems have not
    B. as well as the general problems have changed
    C. have remained the same but the general problems have changed
    D. as well as the general problems have remained the same
    E. have caused changes in the general problems

19. According to the above passage, advances in science and industry have, in general, made the police   19.____
    A. operations less effective from the overall point of view
    B. operations more effective from the overall point of view
    C. abandon older methods of solving police problems
    D. concern themselves more with the antisocial acts of human beings
    E. concern themselves less with the antisocial acts of human beings

20. The automobile is a *two-way symbol*, according to the above passage, because its use   20.____
    A. has speeded up getting to, and away from, the scene of a crime
    B. both helps and hurts police operations
    C. introduces a new antisocial act—traffic violation—and does away with criminals like horse thieves
    D. both increases and decreases speed by introducing traffic problems
    E. helps people get to the city but prevents them from moving once they are there

KEY (CORRECT ANSWERS)

1.	A	11.	B
2.	E	12.	E
3.	D	13.	D
4.	E	14.	B
5.	B	15.	B
6.	A	16.	A
7.	A	17.	E
8.	C	18.	A
9.	D	19.	B
10.	C	20.	B

READING COMPREHENSION
UNDERSTANDING AND INTERPRETING WRITTEN MATERIAL

EXAMINATION SECTION
TEST 1

DIRECTIONS: Each question or incomplete statement is followed by several suggested answers or completions. Select the one that BEST answers the question or completes the statement. *PRINT THE LETTER OF THE CORRECT ANSWER IN THE SPACE AT THE RIGHT.*

Questions 1-5.

DIRECTIONS: Questions 1 through 5 are based on the following passage. You are to answer the questions which follow based SOLELY upon the information in the passage.

More than 700 dolphins and whales piled up on France's Atlantic coast last February and March. Most were common dolphins, but the toll also included striped and bottlenose dolphins — even a few harbor porpoises and fin, beaked, pilot, and minke whales. Many victims had ropes around their tails or had heads or tails cut off; some had been partly butchered for food. To scientists the cause is obvious: These marine mammals were seen as waste, *byaatah,* to the fishermen who snared them in their nets while seeking commercial fish.

Mid-water trawlers are responsible for this, not drift nets, says Anne Collet, a French biologist who examined the carcasses. The European Union has banned large drift nets. Two other European treaties call for bycatch reduction by vessels using huge trawls for hake and other species. But the Bay of Biscay falls beyond the treaties, a painfully obvious loophole.

1. What killed the dolphins and whales at the Bay of Biscay? 1.____

   A. The propellers of recreational motorboats
   B. Fishermen using drift nets to catch commercial fish
   C. Fishermen seeking commercial fish
   D. Fishermen seeking their tails and heads as trophies

2. What is *bycatch*? 2.____

   A. Animals accidentally caught in the same nets used to catch other types of fish
   B. Animals which typically gather close to certain types of fish, allowing fishermen to hunt more than one species at a time
   C. Those parts of animals and fish discarded by fishermen after the catch
   D. Those fish which exceed the fisherman's specified limit and must be thrown back

3. The dolphins and whales were killed around the Bay of Biscay because the 3.____

   A. treaties which protect these species of dolphins and whales do not reach the Bay of Biscay
   B. bodies of the animals were dumped at the Bay of Biscay, but scientists do not know where they were killed
   C. treaties which limit the use of drift nets do not reach the Bay of Biscay
   D. treaties which limit the use of trawls do not reach the Bay of Biscay

4. Where is the Bay of Biscay located?

   A. France's Pacific coast
   B. France's Atlantic coast
   C. The European Union's Atlantic coast
   D. The French Riviera

4.___

5. What types of fish are mid-water trawlers usually used for?

   A. Common, striped, and bottlenose dolphins
   B. Common dolphins, harbor porpoises, and pilot whales
   C. Hake and pilot, minke, fin, and beaked whales
   D. Hake and other species

5.___

Questions 6-10.

DIRECTIONS: Questions 6 through 10 are based on the following passage. You are to answer the questions which follow based SOLELY upon the information in the passage.

Malaria once infected 9 out of 10 people in North Borneo, now known as Brunei. In 1955, the World Health Organization (WHO) began spraying the island with dieldrin (a DDT relative) to kill malaria-carrying mosquitoes. The program was so successful that the dread disease was virtually eliminated.

Other, unexpected things began to happen, however. The dieldrin also killed other insects, including flies and cockroaches living in houses. At first, the islanders applauded this turn of events, but then small lizards that also lived in the houses died after gorging themselves on dieldrin-contaminated insects. Next, cats began dying after feeding on the lizards. Then, in the absence of cats, rats flourished and overran the villages. Now that the people were threatened by sylvatic plague carried by rat fleas, WHO parachuted healthy cats onto the island to help control the rats.

Then the villagers' roofs began to fall in. The dieldrin had killed wasps and other insects that fed on a type of caterpillar that either avoided or was not affected by the insecticide. With most of its predators eliminated, the caterpillar population exploded, munching its way through its favorite food: the leaves used in thatched roofs.

Ultimately, this episode ended happily: Both malaria and the unexpected effects of the spraying program were brought under control. Nevertheless, the chain of unforeseen events emphasizes the unpredictability of interfering in an ecosystem.

6. The World Health Organization (WHO) began spraying dieldrin on North Borneo in order to

   A. kill the bacteria which causes malaria
   B. kill the mosquitoes that carry malaria
   C. disrupt the foodchain so that malaria-carrying mosquitoes would die
   D. kill the mosquitoes, flies, and cockroaches that carry malaria

6.___

7. Which of the following did the dieldrin kill? 7.____

   A. Mosquitoes
   B. Rats
   C. Caterpillars
   D. All of the above

8. The villagers' roofs caved in because the dieldrin killed 8.____

   A. mosquitoes, flies, rats, and cats
   B. the trees whose leaves are used in thatched roofs
   C. the caterpillar that eats the leaves used in thatched roofs
   D. the predators of the caterpillar that eats the leaves used in thatched roofs

9. Which of the following was NOT a side effect of spraying dieldrin on Borneo? 9.____

   A. Malaria was virtually eliminated.
   B. The rat population exploded.
   C. The cat population exploded.
   D. The caterpillar population exploded.

10. Why did the World Health Organization (WHO) deliver healthy cats to Borneo without trying to replenish the other animals and insects which had been wiped out by the dieldrin? The 10.____

    A. presence of a healthy cat population was all that was required to restore the balanced ecosystem
    B. rats that cats preyed upon carried an illness threatening to humans
    C. other insects and animals killed by the dieldrin were nuisances and the villagers were happy to be free of them
    D. villagers' had become attached to cats as domestic pets

Questions 11-15.

DIRECTIONS: Questions 11 through 15 are based on the following passage. You are to answer the questions which follow based SOLELY upon the information in the passage.

Historically, towns and cities grew as a natural byproduct of people choosing to live in certain areas for agricultural, business, or recreational reasons. Beginning in the 1920s, private and governmental planners began to think about how an ideal town would be planned. These communities would be completely built before houses were offered for sale. This concept of preplanning, designing, and building an ideal town was not fully developed until the 1960s. By 1976, about forty-three towns could be classified as planned *new towns*.

One example of a new town is Reston, Virginia, located about 40 kilometers west of Washington, D.C. Reston began to accept residents in 1964 and has a projected population of eighty thousand. Because developers tried to preserve the great natural beauty of the area and the high quality of architectural design of its buildings, Reston has attracted much attention. Reston also has innovative programs in education, government, transportation, and recreation. For example, the stores in Reston are within easy walking distance of the residential parts of the community, and there are many open spaces for family activities. Because Reston is not dependent upon the automobile, noise and air pollution have been greatly reduced. Recent research indicates that the residents of Reston have rated their community much higher than residents of less well-planned suburbs.

11. When did the concept of first building a town and then offering houses for sale fully develop?

   A. 1920s B. 1950s C. 1960s D. 1970s

12. The goal of planners who develop and build ideal towns and suburbs is to

   A. eliminate the tendency of towns and cities to naturally develop around business or recreational centers
   B. control population growth
   C. regulate the resources devoted to housing and recreation
   D. cut down on suburban sprawl by developing communities where residents are not dependent on cars to maintain a high quality of living

13. Which of the following goals did developers have in mind when planning the community of Reston?
   I. Preservation of natural beauty
   II. Communal living spaces
   III. Communal recreational spaces
   IV. High standards of architectural design

   The CORRECT answer is:

   A. I, II, III, IV
   B. I, III, IV
   C. II, III, IV
   D. I, II, IV

14. The fact that stores in Reston are within easy walking distance of the residential parts of the community is an example of innovation in

   A. transportation B. recreation
   C. education   D. all of the above

15. What are the environmental advantages to towns like Reston?

   A. Uniform architecture
   B. Individual recreational spaces cut down on the overuse of resources
   C. Decreased noise and air pollution
   D. Ability to control the number and type of residents

Questions 16-20.

DIRECTIONS: Questions 16 through 20 are based on the following passage. You are to answer the questions which follow based SOLELY upon the information in the passage.

Lead is one of the most common toxic (harmful or poisonous) metals in the intercity environment. It is found, to some extent, in all parts of the urban environment (e.g., air, soil, and older pipes and paint) and in all biological systems, including people. There is no apparent biologic need for lead, but it is sufficiently concentrated in the blood and bones of children living in inner cities to cause health and behavior problems. In some populations over 20% of the children have levels of lead concentrated in their blood above that believed safe. Lead affects nearly every system of the body. Acute lead toxicity may be characterized by a variety of symptoms, including anemia, mental retardation, palsy, coma, seizures, apathy, uncoordination, subtle loss of recently acquired skills, and bizarre behavior. Lead toxicity is particularly a problem for young children who tend to be exposed to higher concentrations in some urban areas and apparently are more susceptible to lead poisoning than are adults. Following exposure to lead and having acute toxic response, some children manifest aggressive, difficult to manage behavior.

The occurrence of lead toxicity or lead poisoning has cultural, political, and sociological implications. Over 2,000 years ago, the Roman Empire produced and used tremendous amounts of lead for a period of several hundred years. Production rates were as high as 55,000 metric tons per year. Romans had a wide variety of uses for lead, including pots in which grapes were crushed and processed into a syrup for making wine, cups, and goblets from which the wine was drunk, as a base for cosmetics and medicines, and finally for the wealthy class of people who had running water in their homes, lead was used to make the pipes that carried the water. It has been argued by some historians that gradual lead poisoning among the upper class in Rome was partly responsible for Rome's eventual fall.

16. In which parts of the urban environment can lead be found?
    I. Air
    II. Water
    III. Adults
    IV. Children
    The CORRECT answer is:

    A. I, II, III
    B. I, III, IV
    C. II, III, IV
    D. All of the above

17. Lead toxicity has the most powerful effect on which of the following?

    A. Mentally retarded children
    B. Young children
    C. Anemic women
    D. Children who suffer from seizures

18. Romans used lead in which of the following?

    A. Cosmetics   B. Paint   C. Wine   D. Clothes

19. Humans require a certain level of lead in the bloodstream in order to avoid which of the following?

    A. Anemia
    B. Uncoordination
    C. Seizures
    D. Scientists have found no biological need for lead among humans

20. Which of the following would most directly support the theory that lead poisoning was partially responsible for the fall of Rome?

    A. Evidence of bizarre behavior among ancient Roman leaders
    B. Evidence of lead in the drinking water of ancient Rome
    C. Studies analyzing the lead content of bones of ancient Romans which detect increased levels of lead
    D. Evidence of lead in the environment of ancient Rome

Questions 21-25.

DIRECTIONS: Questions 21 through 25 are based on the following passage. You are to answer the questions which follow based SOLELY upon the information in the passage.

The city of Venice, Italy has been known to be slowly sinking, but for a long time no one knew the cause or a solution. Floods were becoming more and more common, especially during the winter storms when the winds drove waters from the Adriatic Sea into the city's streets. Famous for its canals and architectural beauty, Venice was in danger of being destroyed by the very lagoon that had sustained its commerce for more than a thousand years. Then the reason that the city was sinking was discovered: groundwater in the region was being pumped out and used; the depletion of the water table, over time, caused the soil to compress under the weight of the city above it. The wells that influenced Venice, which were located on the Italian mainland as well as on the islands that make up Venice, supplied water to nearly industrial and domestic users.

Once the cause was discovered, the wells were capped .and other sources of water were found; as a result the city has stopped sinking. This is an example of the application of scientific research on the environment to achieve a solution helpful to a major city.

21. What causes the winter floods in Venice? 21.____

    A. The disintegration of the canals that used to protect the city from the floods
    B. Storms that drive waters from the wells into the streets
    C. The flawed canal system for which the city is famous
    D. Storms that drive waters from the Adriatic Sea into the streets

22. Venice was sinking because of depletion of the 22.____

    A. lagoon upon which the city was founded
    B. wells used to flood the lagoons
    C. water table beneath the city
    D. soil beneath the city

23. What was the water beneath Venice used for? 23.____

    A. Wastewater
    B. To supply water to the famous canals
    C. To supply drinking water to Venetians
    D. To supply local industrial users

24. How was the problem remedied? 24.____

    A. City leaders regulated use of the wells and found other sources of water.
    B. The wells were capped.
    C. Flood water was diverted back to the Adriatic Sea.
    D. The wells were used to supply water to nearby industrial and domestic users.

25. How were scientists able to restore Venice to its proper (and previous) elevation? 25.____
    A. Venice was not restored to its previous elevation
    B. By diverting water back into the soil beneath Venice
    C. By capping the wells and finding other sources of water
    D. By restoring the water table

KEY (CORRECT ANSWERS)

1. C
2. A
3. D
4. B
5. D

6. B
7. A
8. D
9. C
10. B

11. C
12. D
13. B
14. A
15. C

16. D
17. B
18. A
19. D
20. C

21. D
22. C
23. D
24. B
25. A

TEST 2

DIRECTIONS: Each question or incomplete statement is followed by several suggested answers or completions. Select the one that BEST answers the question or completes the statement. *PRINT THE LETTER OF THE CORRECT ANSWER IN THE SPACE AT THE RIGHT.*

Questions 1-5.

DIRECTIONS: Questions 1 through 5 are based on the following passage. You are to answer the questions which follow based SOLELY upon the information in the passage.

China, with one-fifth of the world's population, is the most populous country in the world. Between 1980 and 1995, China's population grew by 200 million people — about three-fourths of the population of the United States — to reach 1.2 billion. Although its growth rate is expected to slow somewhat in the coming decades, population experts predict that there will be 1.5 billion Chinese by 2025. But can China's food production continue to keep pace with its growing population? Should China develop a food deficit, it may need to import more grain from other countries than those countries can spare from their own needs.

To give some idea of the potential impact of China on the world's food supply, consider the following examples. All of the grain produced by Norway would be needed to supply two more beers to each person in China. If the Chinese were to eat as much fish as the Japanese do, China would consume the entire world fish catch. Food for all the chickens required for China to reach its goal of 200 eggs per person per year by 2010 will equal all the grain exported by Canada — the world's second largest grain exporter. Increased demand by China for world grain supplies could result in dramatic increases in food prices and precipitate famines in other areas of the world.

1. China's population increased between 1980 and 1995 by

    A. 200 million people
    B. 1.2 billion people
    C. 1.5 billion people
    D. one-fifth of the world's population

2. If China developed a food deficit, which of the following would most negatively affect the world's supply of food?

    A. Famines resulting from the increased price of grain
    B. Domestic increase in the production of grain to meet the needs of the Chinese people
    C. International increase in the production of grain to meet China's need
    D. Importing more grain from other countries than those countries could spare

3. Which of the following was a goal the Chinese government hoped to reach by 2010?

    A. Importing Canada's entire supply of grain
    B. Supplying 200 eggs annually to every citizen
    C. A population of 1.5 billion people
    D. Supplying enough fish to each citizen to match Japan's consumption

1.____

2.____

3.____

4. Which of the following countries exports the most grain? 4._____

   A. China   B. Norway   C. Canada   D. Japan

5. Which of the following groups contains 200 million people? 5._____

   A. The current population of the United States
   B. Three-quarters of the population of the United States
   C. China's current population
   D. Three-quarters of the population of China

Questions 6-10.

DIRECTIONS: Questions 6 through 10 are based on the following passage. You are to answer the questions which follow based SOLELY upon the information in the passage.

On Tuesday, 16 June 1987, the last dusky seaside sparrow *(Ammo-dramus maratimus nigrescens)* died in captivity at Walt Disney World's Discovery Island Zoological Park in Orlando, Florida. The bird was a male that was probably about twelve years old. Originally, this subspecies and several other subspecies were found in the coastal salt marshes on the Atlantic coast of Florida. (A subspecies is a distinct population of a species that has several characteristics that distinguish it from other populations.) One other subspecies, the Smyrna seaside sparrow *(Ammodramus maratimus pelonata)*, is believed to have become extinct several years ago, and a third subspecies, the Cape Sable seaside sparrow *(Ammodramus maratimus mirabilis)*, was listed as an endangered species in 1967. Before the deaths of the last remaining dusky seaside sparrows, a few males were crossed with another subspecies, Scott's seaside sparrow *(Ammodramus maratimus peninsulae)*. Thus, the hybrid offspring between these two subspecies contain some of the genes that made the dusky seaside sparrow unique.

The endangerment and extinction of these different birds was a direct result of the land development and drainage that destroyed the salt-marsh habitat to which they were adapted. The development of Cape Canaveral as a major center for the U.S. space program also resulted in the modification of much of the birds' original habitat and was a partial cause of their extinction.

6. Which of the following subspecies is NOT yet extinct? 6._____

   A. Dusky seaside sparrow
   B. Cape Sable seaside sparrow
   C. Smyrna seaside sparrow
   D. All of the listed subspecies are extinct

7. A subspecies is a population 7._____

   A. within a species that has been crossed with another population within the same species in order to avoid extinction
   B. within a subspecies that has distinguishing characteristics
   C. that has distinguishing characteristics
   D. within a species that has distinguishing characteristics

8. What was the dusky seaside sparrow's natural habitat? 8.____

   A. Coastal salt marshes of Florida
   B. Man-made parks and zoos such as Discovery Land
   C. Flat, desert-like plains around Cape Canaveral
   D. Areas of land development

9. A hybrid is an animal that 9.____

   A. cannot reproduce
   B. is extinct
   C. is the result of a cross between two subspecies
   D. is the result of a cross between two species

10. What caused the extinction of the dusky seaside sparrow? 10.____

    A. An overabundance of predators caused by human influence and development
    B. Destruction of its natural habitat by human development
    C. Inability to reproduce in captivity
    D. All of the above

Questions 11-15.

DIRECTIONS: Questions 11 through 15 are based on the following passage. You are to answer the questions which follow based SOLELY upon the information in the passage.

For more than 600 years only Adelie penguins lived along the chilly shores of the Western Antarctic Peninsula in the Palmer region. Ornithologist and paleontologist Steven Emslie of the University of North Carolina, Wilmington, found Adelie bones in nests near Palmer Station dating from as early as the 14th century.

But two other penguin species have moved in, apparently as the result of a 50-year warming trend that has seen winter temperatures rise seven to nine degrees F and lessened the amount of ice around the peninsula. *Adelies require the edges of pack ice for foraging,* Emslie says. As the ice shrinks, he believes, their numbers decline. Chinstrap penguins, which forage in the open ocean and aren't affected by ice breakup, began to arrive in the 1950s. Gentoos, normally a subantarctic species, first appeared here in 1975. The two newcomers now form a major portion of the region's penguin population.

11. When did new penguin species begin arriving in the Palmer region? 11.____

    A. 1400s   B. 1950s   C. 1975   D. 1990s

12. Which of the following penguin species are NOT affected by ice breakup? 12.____

    A. Adelie   B. Gentoos   C. Chinstrap   D. Emslie

13. What has caused the new penguin species to move into the Palmer region? 13.____

    A. A warming trend
    B. An increase in the amount of pack ice around the peninsula
    C. An increase in the availability of food
    D. All of the above

14. Adelie penguins have lived in the Palmer region since 14.____

    A. the 14th century
    B. the early 1900s
    C. the 1950s
    D. 1975

15. What effect does the decrease in the amount of pack ice have on Adelie penguins? 15.____

    A. Decreased ability to fight off predators
    B. Increased ability to fight off predators
    C. Increased ability to forage for food
    D. Decreased ability to forage for food

Questions 16-20.

DIRECTIONS: Questions 16 through 20 are based on the following passage. You are to answer the questions which follow based SOLELY upon the information in the passage.

The price of a liter of gasoline is determined by two major factors: (1) the cost of purchasing and processing crude oil into gasoline, and (2) various taxes. Most of the differences in gasoline prices between countries are a result of the differences in taxes and reflect differences in government policy toward motor vehicle transportation.

A major objective of governments is to collect money to build and repair roads, and governments often charge the user by taxing the fuel used by the car or truck. Governments can also discourage the use of automobiles by increasing the cost of fuel. An increase in fuel costs also creates a demand for increased fuel efficiency in all forms of motor transport.

Many European countries raise more money from fuel taxes than they spend on building and repairing roads, while the United States raises approximately 60 percent of the moneys needed for roads from fuel taxes. The relatively low cost of fuel in the United States encourages more travel and increases road repair costs. The cost of taxes to the United States consumer is about 20 percent of the cost of fuel, while in Japan and many European countries, the percentage is 60 to 75 percent.

16. Which of the following is likely to result from an increase in the cost of fuel? 16.____

    A. *Decreased* fuel efficiency
    B. *Increased* fuel efficiency
    C. *Increased* travel
    D. *Increased* road repair costs

17. Which of the following affects the price of gasoline? 17.____

    A. Cost of purchasing crude oil
    B. Cost of processing crude oil
    C. Taxes
    D. All of the above

18. Most governments tax car and truck fuel in order to 18.____

    A. finance the costs of repairing roads
    B. discourage motor travel as much as possible

C. finance various social welfare programs
D. finance public transportation systems

19. Differences in _____ accounts for the differences in gasoline prices between countries. 19.____

   A. the cost of purchasing a car
   B. the amount of crude oil each country exports
   C. government taxes
   D. the number of automobiles imported by individual countries

20. Which of the following is most likely to discourage travel? 20.____

   A. *Decrease* in fuel tax
   B. *Increase* in fuel tax
   C. *Decrease* in fuel efficiency
   D. *Increase* in road repair

Questions 21-25.

DIRECTIONS: Questions 21 through 25 are based on the following passage. You are to answer the questions which follow based SOLELY upon the information in the passage.

Wyoming rancher Jack Turnell is one of a new breed of cowpuncher who gets along with environmentalists. He talks about riparian ecology and biodiversity as fluently as he talks about cattle. *I guess I have learned how to bridge the gap between the environmentalists, the bureaucracies, and the ranching industry.*

Turnell grazes cattle on his 32,000-hectare (80,000 acre) ranch south of Cody, Wyoming, and on 16,000 hectares (40,000 acres) of Forest Service land on which he has grazing rights. For the first decade after he took over the ranch, he punched cows the conventional way. Since then, he's made some changes.

Turnell disagrees with the proposals by environmentalists to raise grazing fees and remove sheep and cattle from public rangeland. He believes that if ranchers are kicked off the public range, ranches like his will be sold to developers and chopped up into vacation sites, irreversibly destroying the range for wildlife and livestock alike.

At the same time, he believes that ranches can be operated in more ecologically sustainable ways. To demonstrate this, Turnell began systematically rotating his cows away from the riparian areas, gave up most uses of fertilizers and pesticides, and crossed his Hereford and Angus cows with a French breed that tends to congregate less around water. Most of his ranching decisions are made in consultation with range and wildlife scientists, and changes in range condition are carefully monitored with photographs.

The results have been impressive. Riparian areas on the ranch and Forest Service land are lined with willows and other plant life, providing lush habitat for an expanding population of wildlife, including pronghorn antelope, deer, moose, elk, bear, and mountain lions. And this *eco-rancher* now makes more money because the higher-quality grass puts more meat on his cattle. He frequently talks to other ranchers about sustainable range management; some of them probably think he has been chewing locoweed.

21. The fact that Turnell's decision-making process involves range and wildlife scientists is an example of   21.____

    A. successful government oversight
    B. enforced government regulation
    C. conventional ranching
    D. successful sustainable ranching

22. What is the environmental drawback to removing grazing animals from government range land?   22.____

    A. The loss of ranches which rely on public ranges to real-estate developers
    B. The loss of public range land to real-estate developers
    C. Under-use of public range land
    D. Increased vulnerability to forest fires due to under-use

23. Which of the following is a result of Turnell's decision to rotate his cattle?   23.____

    A. The production of cattle which tend to congregate less around water
    B. Increased bio-diversity which attracts and supports several animal species
    C. The production of beefier, more profitable cattle
    D. All of the above

24. Which of the following is an example of sustainable ranching?   24.____

    A. The use of pesticides to control disease
    B. Non-use of, and non-reliance on, public grazing lands
    C. Rotation of cattle away from riparian areas
    D. Independent decision-making

25. Which of the following is an effect of the increased diversity of plant life on the grazing land that Turnell uses?   25.____

    A. Production of leaner cattle
    B. Production of larger, meatier cattle
    C. Production of more abundant but less nutritious grasses
    D. Less reliance on pesticides

KEY (CORRECT ANSWERS)

1.	A	11.	B
2.	D	12.	C
3.	B	13.	A
4.	C	14.	A
5.	B	15.	D
6.	B	16.	B
7.	D	17.	D
8.	A	18.	A
9.	C	19.	C
10.	B	20.	B

21. D
22. A
23. B
24. C
25. B

ARITHMETICAL REASONING

EXAMINATION SECTION
TEST 1

DIRECTIONS: Each question or incomplete statement is followed by several suggested answers or completions. Select the one that BEST answers the question or completes the statement. *PRINT THE LETTER OF THE CORRECT ANSWER IN THE SPACE AT THE RIGHT.*

1. Two patrol cars hurry to the scene of an accident from different directions. The first proceeds at the rate of 45 miles per hour and arrives in four minutes. Although the second car travels over a route which is three-fourths of a mile longer, it arrives at the scene only a half minute later.
   The speed of the second car, expressed in miles per hour, is

   A. 50   B. 55   C. 60   D. 65

   1.____

2. A motorcycle policeman issued 72 traffic summonses in January, 60 in February, and 83 in March.
   In order to average 75 summonses per month for the four months of January, February, March, and April, during
   April he will have to issue _____ summonses.

   A. 80   B. 85   C. 90   D. 95

   2.____

3. In a unit of the Police Department to which 40 patrolmen are assigned, the sick report during the year was as follows:
   - 1 was absent 8 days
   - 4 were absent 5 days each
   - 8 were absent 4 days each
   - 5 were absent 3 days each
   - 10 were absent 2 days each
   - 5 were absent 1 day each

   The average number of days on sick report for all the members of this unit is MOST NEARLY

   A. 1/2   B. 1   C. 2 1/2   D. 3

   3.____

4. For a certain police department, the average officer is entitled to two days off per week, gets 18 vacation days per year, takes 11 days for sick leave per year, and spends approximately 4 days per year (on the average) on training assignments. A certain shift commander has 20 men assigned to his shift for field patrol.
   Which one of the following is MOST NEARLY the average number of man-days per week that the shift commander has available to him for assignment?
   _____ man-days.

   A. 62.5   B. 75.0   C. 84.0   D. 87.5

   4.____

5. A car speeds through the toll entrance of a 2 1/4 mile long bridge without paying the toll and reaches the other end of the bridge 1 minute and 30 seconds later.
   The car was traveling MOST NEARLY at a rate of _____ miles per hour.

   A. 60   B. 70   C. 80   D. 90

   5.____

6. During one week, 21,500 vehicles passed through the toll booths of a certain bridge. Of these, 550 were buses, 2,230 were trucks, and the rest were passenger cars. The toll charges were $1.00 for a passenger car, $2.00 for a truck, and $4.00 for a bus.
The TOTAL income for the week was

   A. $23,100   B. $25,380   C. $29,300   D. $31,300

7. A bullet fired from a revolver travels 100 feet the first second, and each succeeding second it travels a distance 10% less than during the immediately preceding second. The number of feet the bullet will have traveled at the end of the fourth second is MOST NEARLY

   A. 272   B. 320   C. 344   D. 360

8. An officer receives a uniform allowance of $250 a year in a lump sum. Of this amount, he spends $90 for a winter jacket and 40% of the remainder for two pairs of trousers. The officer now wishes to buy a winter overcoat which costs $120.
The percentage of the purchase price of the overcoat by which he will be short is

   A. 20%   B. 25%   C. 48%   D. 60%

9. It has been suggested that small light cars be used for certain kinds of police work. These light vehicles can run 30 miles per gallon of gasoline as contrasted with standard cars which run only 15 miles per gallon. Assume gasoline costs the city $3.75 per gallon During 9,000 miles of travel, use of the small light car in preference to the standard car would result in a saving in gasoline costs of MOST NEARLY

   A. $1,125   B. $15,000   C. $1,875   D. $2,250

10. Out of a total of 34,750 felony complaints in 2007, 14,200 involved burglary. In 2006, there was a total of 32,300 felony complaints of which 12,800 were burglary.
Of the increase in felonies from 2006 to 2007, the increase in burglaries comprised APPROXIMATELY

   A. 27%   B. 37%   C. 47%   D. 57%

11. A certain city department has two offices which issue permits, one office handling twice as many applicants as the other. The smaller office grants permits to 40% of its applicants. The larger office handling twice as many applicants grants permits to 60% of its applicants. If there were 900 applicants at both offices together on a given day, the total number of permits granted by both offices would be MOST NEARLY

   A. 420   B. 450   C. 480   D. 510

12. You are making a report on the number of incoming calls handled by two different switchboards. Over a five-day period, the total count of incoming calls per day for both switchboards together was 2,773. The average number of incoming calls per day for Switchboard A was 301.
You cannot find one day's tally for Switchboard B, but the total for the other four days for Switchboard B comes to 1,032.
Determine from this how many incoming calls must have been reported on the missing tally for Switchboard B?

   A. 236   B. 258   C. 408   D. 1,440

13. Assume that one-page notices for distribution may be reproduced by photocopy or by stencil. The cost for photocopying is 5 1/2 cents per copy. It can also be reproduced by the stencil method for an initial preparation cost of $1.38 plus a per-copy cost of one cent. Strictly according to cost, which of the following is the LOWEST number of copies at which it would be more economical to choose the stencil method instead of photocopying?

    A. 15   B. 30   C. 45   D. 138

14. An employee completed 75% of a clerical assignment in four days.
    How much of it did he complete in the last two days if he finished 3/8 of it in the first two days?

    A. 1/4   B. 3/8   C. 5/8   D. 3/4

15. Seven hundred people are to be scheduled for interviews. If 58% of these 700 people have already been scheduled, how many MORE must be scheduled?

    A. 138   B. 294   C. 406   D. 410

16. In recent years, an average of 35% of the violations reported in any given month have been corrected by the time of a follow-up inspection one month later. Last month, 240 violations were reported, and this month's follow-up inspections show that 93 of them have been corrected.
    How many MORE violations have been corrected than would have been expected, based on the average rate?

    A. 5   B. 9   C. 33   D. 58

17. Suppose that, on a scaled drawing of an office floor plan, 1/2 inch equals 2 feet. An office that is actually 12 feet wide and 17 feet long has which of the following dimensions on this scaled drawing?
    _____ inches wide and _____ inches long.

    A. 3; 4.25   B. 6; 8.5   C. 12; 17   D. 24; 34

Questions 18-21.

In questions 18–21, assume that all arrests fall into two mutually exclusive categories, felonies and misdemeanors. Last week 620 arrests were made in Precinct A, of which 403 were for felonies.

18. The percent of all arrests made in Precinct A last week which were for felonies was _____ percent.

    A. 55   B. 60   C. 65   D. 70

19. If 3/5 of all persons arrested for felonies and 1/4 of all persons arrested for misdemeanors were carrying weapons, then the number of arrests involving persons carrying weapons in Precinct A last week was MOST NEARLY

    A. 135   B. 295   C. 415   D. 525

20. If five times as many men as women were arrested for felonies, and half as many women as men were arrested for misdemeanors, then the number of women arrested in Precinct A last week was APPROXIMATELY

    A. 90   B. 120   C. 140   D. 210

21. If the ratio of arrests made on weekends (Friday through Sunday) to arrests made on weekdays (Monday through Thursday) is 2:1, then the number of arrests made in Precinct A last weekend was approximately

    A. 308   B. 340   C. 372   D. 413

22. The police precincts covering the county receive calls at the average rate of two per minute during the 8 A.M. to 4 P.M. tour, but this rate increases by 50 percent during the 4 P.M. to 12 Midnight tour. However, the initial rate decreases by 50 percent during the 12 Midnight to 8 A.M. tour.
    The number of calls received by the precincts covering the county on this basis in one 24-hour day is

    A. 960   B. 1,440   C. 2,880   D. 3,360

23. If an administrative aide is expected to handle 15 calls per hour and Precinct C averages 840 calls during the 4 P.M. to 12 Midnight tour, then the number of aides needed in Precinct C to handle calls during this tour is

    A. 4   B. 5   C. 6   D. 7

24. If in a group of ten administrative aides four type 40 words per minute, one types 45, two type 50, two type 60, and one types 65, then the average speed in the group is _____ words per minute.

    A. 49   B. 50   C. 51   D. 52

25. An administrative aide works from Midnight to 8 A.M. on a certain day and then is off for 64 hours.
    He is due back at work at

    A. 8 A.M.   B. 12 Noon
    C. 4 P.M.   D. 12 Midnight

KEY (CORRECT ANSWERS)

1.	A	11.	C
2.	B	12.	A
3.	C	13.	C
4.	D	14.	B
5.	D	15.	B
6.	B	16.	B
7.	C	17.	A
8.	A	18.	C
9.	A	19.	B
10.	D	20.	C

21.	D
22.	C
23.	D
24.	A
25.	D

SOLUTIONS TO PROBLEMS

1. The distance the 1st car travels = (45)(4/60) = 3 miles. The 2nd car travels 3 3/4 miles in 4 1/2 min. Thus, its speed, in mph, = (3 3/4)(60/4 1/2) = 50

2. Let x = summonses issued in April. Then, (72+60+83+x)/4 = 75 Solving, x = 85

3. Note that 7 patrolmen had 0 absences. Average number of sick days per member = [(1)(8)+(4)(5)+(8)(4)+(5)(3)+(10)(2)+(5)(1)+(7)(0)] ÷ 40 = 100 ÷ 40 = 2 1/2

4. $(7-2-\frac{18}{52}-\frac{11}{52}-\frac{4}{52})(20) \approx 87.3$ man-days, closest to 87.5

5. The car travels 2 1/4 miles in 1 1/2 min. This is equivalent to (2 1/4)(60/1 1/2) = 90 mph.

6. There were 21,500 - 550 - 2230 = 18,720 cars. Total income = (18,720)($1) + ($2)(2230) + ($4)(550) = $25,380

7. Distance = 100 + (100)(.90) + (100)(.90)(.90) + (100)(.90)(.90)(.90) = 343.9 ≈ 344 ft.

8. $250 - $90 = $160, and ($160)(.40) = $64. After buying the jacket and trousers, he has $250 - $90 - $64 = $96 left.
   He will be short of the overcoat's price by ($120-$96) ÷ $120 = 20%

9. 9000 ÷ 30 = 300 gallons, 9000 ÷ 15 = 600 gallons. The savings = (600-300)($3.75) = $1,125

10. (14,200-12,800) ÷ (34,750-32,300) ≈ 57%

11. The 1st office handles 600 applicants while the 2nd office handles 300 applicants. The total number of permits = (.60)(600) + (.40X300) = 480

12. 2773 - (5)(301) - 1032 = 236 calls

13. Let x = number of copies where the two methods are equal in cost. Then, .055x = $1.38 + .01x. Solving, x = 30 2/3. Thus, 31 copies would be the lowest number so that the stencil method is more economical. (For 31 copies, stencil method costs $1.69, whereas the photocopying method costs $1.705.)

14. $.75 - \frac{3}{8} = \frac{3}{4} - \frac{3}{8} = \frac{3}{8}$

15. (100%-58%)(700) = (.42X700) = 294

16. 93 - (.35)(240) = 9

17. (12/2)(1/2") = 3" and (17/2)(1/2") = 4.25"

18. 403/620 = 65% for felonies

19. (3/5)(403) + (1/4)(217) = 296.05, closest to 295

20. Let x = number of women arrested for felonies and let y = number of women arrested for misdemeanors. Then, x + 5x = 403 and y + 2y = 217. Solving, x = 67.1$\overline{6}$ and y = 72.$\overline{3}$. Thus, x + y = 140

21. Let x = arrest on weekends, 1/2x = those during week. 3/2x = 620, so x ≈ 413

22. (2)(480 min.) + (3)(480 min.) + (1)(480 min.) = 2880 calls

23. 4 PM to Midnight = 8 hrs. Then, one aide can handle (15)(8) = 120 calls during this shift. Thus, 840 ÷ 120 = 7 aides are needed.

24. Average speed in wpm = [(4)(40)+(1)(45)+(2)(50)+(2)(60)+(1)(65)] ÷ 10 = 49

25. 8 AM + 64 hrs. = 8 AM + 2 days + 16 hrs., which would be 12 Midnight

TEST 2

DIRECTIONS: Each question or incomplete statement is followed by several suggested answers or completions. Select the one that BEST answers the question or completes the statement. *PRINT THE LETTER OF THE CORRECT ANSWER IN THE SPACE AT THE RIGHT.*

1. If a security officer gets $10.82 per hour and $16.26 per hour for overtime work, his GROSS salary for a week in which he works 5 hours over his regular 40 hours is   1.___

    A. $433.60   B. $487.80   C. $514.10   D. $650.40

2. It takes 2 minutes 45 seconds for a security officer to travel to his first clock station, 3 minutes to get to the second, 2 minutes to get to the third, 5 1/2 minutes to get to the fourth, and 4 minutes 15 seconds to get from the fourth back to the starting point. Neglecting the time spent at each clock station, the TOTAL time needed to make one round tour is _____ minutes _____ seconds.   2.___

    A. 16; 45   B. 17; 15   C. 17; 30   D. 18; 0

3. The log book of a security officer stationed at an entry gate shows 47 entries in two hours.
   At this rate, the number of entries in eight hours is   3.___

    A. 108   B. 168   C. 188   D. 376

4. A truck driver leaving Authority property has a requisition form showing 14 cartons of pencils, 12 cartons of pens, 27 cartons of envelopes, and 39 cartons of writing pads.
   If an actual count of the cartons on the truck shows only 77 cartons, the number of cartons missing is   4.___

    A. 15   B. 14   C. 12   D. 5

5. If a certain aide takes one hour to type 2 accident reports or 6 missing persons reports, then the length of time he will require to finish 7 accident reports and 15 missing persons reports is _____ hours _____ minutes.   5.___

    A. 6; 0   B. 6; 30   C. 8; 0   D. 8; 40

6. If one administrative aide can alphabetize 320 reports per hour and another can do 280 per hour, then the number of reports that both could alphabetize during an 8-hour tour is   6.___

    A. 4,800   B. 5,200   C. 5,400   D. 5,700

7. If 1,000 candidates applied for administrative aide, and out of those applying 7/8 appear for the written test, and out of those who take the written test 66 2/3 percent pass it, and out of those who pass the written test 85 percent pass the medical exam, then the number of candidates still eligible to become administrative aides will be about   7.___

    A. 245   B. 495   C. 585   D. 745

8. If the number of murders in the city in 2005 was 415, and the number of murders has increased by 8 percent each year since that year, then in 2008 we would expect the number of murders to be about   8.___

    A. 484   B. 523   C. 548   D. 565

9. If a person reported missing on April 15 was found murdered on July 4, how many days was he missing? (Include April 15 but NOT July 4 in the total.)

   A. 76 B. 80 C. 82 D. 84

10. Suppose that a pile of 96 file cards measures one inch in height and that it takes you half an hour to file these cards away.
    If you are given three piles of cards which measure 2 1/2 inches high, 1 3/4 inches high, and 3 3/8 inches high, respectively, the time it would take to file the cards is MOST NEARLY _____ hours and _____ minutes.

    A. 2; 30 B. 3; 50 C. 6; 45 D. 8; 15

11. Suppose that police expenses in the city in a certain year amounted to 7.5% of total expenses.
    In indicating this percentage on a *pie* or circular chart, which is 360°, the size of the angle between the two radiuses would be MOST NEARLY

    A. 3.7° B. 7.5° C. 27° D. 54°

12. Suppose that in police precinct A, where there are 4,180 children, 627 children entered a contest sponsored by the Police Community Relations Bureau. In precinct B, where there were 7,840 children, 1,960 children entered the contest.
    The total percentage of all children in both precincts who entered the contest amounted to MOST NEARLY

    A. 19.5% B. 20% C. 21.5% D. 22.5%

13. If Circle A represents Police Administrative Aides (PAA's) who scored above 85 on a PAA test and Circle B represents PAA's who scored above 85 on a Senior PAA test, then the diagram shown at the right means that

    A. no PAA who scored above 85 on a PAA test scored above 85 on the Senior PAA test
    B. the majority of PAA's who scored above 85 on a PAA test scored above 85 on the Senior PAA test
    C. there were some PAA's who did not take the Senior PAA test
    D. some PAA's who scored above 85 on a PAA test scored above 85 on the Senior PAA test

14. Suppose that in 1844 the city had a population of 550,000 and a police force of 200, and that in 1992 the city had a population of 8,000,000 and a police force of 32,000.
    If the ratio of police to population in 1992 is compared with the same ratio in 1844, what is the resulting relationship of the 1992 ratio to the 1844 ratio?

    A. 160:11 B. 160:1 C. 16:1 D. 11:1

15. A squad of patrolmen assigned to enforce a new parking regulation in a particular area issued tag summonses on a particular day as follows: four patrolmen issued 16 summonses each, three issued 19 each, one issued 22, seven issued 25 each, eleven issued 28 each, ten issued 30 each, two issued 36 each, one issued 41; and three issued 45 each.
    The average number of summonses issued by a member of this squad was MOST NEARLY

    A. 6.2   B. 17.2   C. 21.0   D. 27.9

16. A water storage tank is 75 feet long and 30 feet wide and has a depth of 6 1/2 feet. Each cubic foot of the tank holds 9 1/2 gallons.
    The TOTAL capacity of the tank is _____ gallons.

    A. 73,125 1/2   B. 131,625   C. 138,937 1/2   D. 146,250

17. The prices of admission to a PAL entertainment were $1.25 each for adults and $.50 for children. The turnstile at the entrance showed that 358 persons entered, and the gate receipts were $313.25.
    The number of children who attended was

    A. 170   B. 175   C. 179   D. 183

18. A patrol car travels six times as fast as a bicycle.
    If the patrol car goes 168 miles in two hours less time than the bicycle requires to go 42 miles, their respective rates of speed are _____ miles per hour.

    A. 36 and 6   B. 42 and 7   C. 63 and 10 1/2   D. 126 and 21

19. A man received an inheritance of $8,000 and wanted to invest it so that it would produce an annual income sufficient to pay his rent of $40 a month.
    In order to do this, he will have to receive interest or dividends at the rate of _____% per annum.

    A. 3   B. 4   C. 5 3/4   D. 6

20. If the price of a bus ticket varies DIRECTLY as the mileage involved and a ticket to travel 135 miles costs $29.70, a ticket for a 30-mile trip will cost

    A. $15.20   B. $13.40   C. $6.60   D. $2.20

21. A man owed a debt of $580. After a first payment of $10, he agreed to pay the balance by monthly payments in which each payment after this first would be $2 more than that of the preceding month.
    If no interest charge is made, he will have to make, including the first payment, a total of _____ monthly payments.

    A. 16   B. 20   C. 24   D. 28

22. The written test of a civil service examination has a weight of 30, the oral test a weight of 20, experience a weight of 20, and the physical test a weight of 30.
    A candidate received ratings of 76 on the written test, 84 on the oral, and 80 for experience.
    In order to attain an average of 85 on the examination, his rating on the physical test must be

    A. 86   B. 90   C. 94   D. 98

23. A family has an income of $320 per week. It spends 22% of this amount for rent, 36% for food, 16% for clothing, and 12% for additional household expenses. After meeting these expenses, 50% of the balance is deposited in the bank.
The amount deposited weekly is

    A. $22.40 B. $36.60 C. $44.80 D. $52.00

23._____

24. Upon retirement last July, a patrolman bought a farm of 64 acres for $1800 per acre. He made a downpayment of $61,200 and agreed to pay the balance in installments of $750 a month commencing on August 1, 1993. Disregarding interest, he will make his LAST payment on

    A. July 1999   B. August 2001
    C. January 2003   D. April 2006

24._____

25. 40% of those who commit a particular crime are subsequently arrested and convicted; 75% of these convicted receive sentences of 10 years or more.
Assuming that those arrested for the first time serve less than 10 years, the percentage of those committing this crime who receive sentences of ten years or more is MOST NEARLY

    A. 20% B. 30% C. 40% D. 50%

25._____

KEY (CORRECT ANSWERS)

1.	C	11.	C
2.	C	12.	C
3.	C	13.	D
4.	A	14.	D
5.	A	15.	D
6.	A	16.	C
7.	B	17.	C
8.	B	18.	B
9.	B	19.	D
10.	B	20.	C

21. B
22. D
23. A
24. A
25. B

SOLUTIONS TO PROBLEMS

1. Gross salary = (40)($10.82) + (5)($16.26) = $514.10

2. 2 min. 45 sec. + 3 min. + 2 min. + 5 min. 30 sec. + 4 min. 15 sec. = 16 min. 90 sec. = 17 min. 30 sec.

3. (47)(8/2) = 188 entries

4. 14 + 12 + 27 + 39 - 77 = 15 cartons missing

5. (1 hr.)(7/2) + (1 hr.)(15/6) = 6 hrs. 0 min.

6. 8)(320+280) = 4800 reports

7. Number of eligibles = $(1000)(\frac{7}{8})(\frac{2}{3})(\frac{85}{100}) \approx 495$ (Actual answer is 495.8$\bar{3}$)

8. Number of murders in 2008 = $(415)(1.08)^3 \approx 523$

9. Number of days in April, May, June, July = 16, 31, 30, 3 Total is 80 days

10. Total inches = 7 5/8 . Then, (7 5/8)(1/2 hr.) = 3 3/16 hrs. $\approx$ 3 hrs. 50 min.

11. (360°)(.075) = 27°

12. (627+1960)7(4180+7840) = 2587/12,020 $\approx$ 21.5%

13. Since the circles overlap, some PAA's scored above 85 on both a PAA test and a Senior PAA test.

14. 32,000/8,000,000 = .004; 200/550,000 = 1/2750 Then, $.004; \frac{1}{2750} = (\frac{1}{25})(\frac{2750}{1}) = 11:1$

15. [(4)(16)+(3)(19)+(1)(22)+(7)(25)+(11)(28)+(10)(30)+(2)(36) +(1)(41)+(3)(45)] $\div$ 42 $\approx$ 27.9

16. Total capacity = (9 1/2)(75)(30)(6 1/2) = 138,937 1/2 gallons

17. Let x = number of children, 358-x = number of adults. Then, $.50x + ($1.25)(358-x) = $313.25. Simplifying, -.75x + $447.50 = $313.25. Solving, x = 179

18. Let x = rate of patrol car (in mph), 1/6x = rate of bike (in mph). Then, 168/x + 2 = 42/1/6x. Simplifying, 168 + 2x = 252. Solving, x = 42 and 1/6x = 7

19. ($40)(12) = $480. Then, $480/$8000 = 6%

20. Cost = (30/135)($29.70) = $6.60

21. This is an arithmetic series $10 + $12 + $14 + ... The formula for a sum of n terms is S = n/2[2a+(n-1)d], where a = 1st term, d = difference between terms. Thus, $580 = n/2[20+(n-1)($2)] . Simplifying, $580 = n(n+4). Then, n^2 + 9n - 580 = 0. This becomes (n+29)(n-20) = 0. Ignoring the negative answer, n = 20

22. Let x = rating on physical test. Then, (76)(.30)+(84)(.20)+ (80)(.20) + (x)(.30) = 85. Solving, x = 98

23. 100% - 22% - 36% - 16% - 12% = 14%. This means that (1/2)(.14)($320) = $22.40 is deposited in the bank.

24. (64)($1800) = $115,200. Then, $115,200 - $61,200 = $54,000 to be paid off in installments of $750 per month. So, $54,000 ÷ $750 = 72 months = 6 yrs. If August 1993 is his first payment, July 1999 is his last payment.

25. (.40)(.75) = .30 = 30%

TEST 3

DIRECTIONS: Each question or incomplete statement is followed by several suggested answers or completions. Select the one that BEST answers the question or completes the statement. *PRINT THE LETTER OF THE CORRECT ANSWER IN THE SPACE AT THE RIGHT.*

1. During the first nine months of 2008, an officer spent an average of $270 a month. In October and November, he spent an average of $315 a month. In December, he spent $385.
   His average monthly spending during the year was MOST NEARLY

   A. $254   B. $287   C. $323   D. $3,000

   1.____

2. In 2005, there were 8,270 arrests in a certain city. In 2006, the number of arrests increased by 12 1/2%. In 2007, the number of arrests decreased 5% from the 2006 figures. The number of arrests in 2007 was MOST NEARLY

   A. 8,840   B. 9,770   C. 6,870   D. 7,600

   2.____

3. Assume that parking space is to be provided for 25% of the tenants in a new housing development. The project will have five 6-story buildings, having seven tenants on each floor, and eight 11-story buildings, having eight tenants on each floor.
   The number of parking spaces needed is MOST NEARLY

   A. 215   B. 230   C. 700   D. 895

   3.____

4. A stolen vehicle traveling at 60 miles per hour passes by a police car, which is standing still with the engine running. The police car immediately starts out in pursuit, and one minute later, having covered a distance of half a mile, it reaches a speed of 90 miles per hour and continues at this speed.
   In how many minutes after the stolen vehicle passes the police car will the police car overtake it? ____ minutes.

   A. 1   B. 1 1/2   C. 2   D. 3

   4.____

5. A police officer found his 42-hour work week was divided as follows: 1/6 of his time in investigating incidents on his patrol post, 1/2 of his time patrolling his post, and 1/8 of his time in special traffic duty. The rest of his time was devoted to assignments at precinct headquarters.
   The percentage of his work week which was spent at precinct headquarters is MOST NEARLY

   A. 10%   B. 15%   C. 20%   D. 25%

   5.____

6. During the year, the Department of Sanitation towed away 8,430 cars which were abandoned or illegally parked on city streets.
   If the value of the abandoned cars was $10,382,000 and that of the illegally parked cars was $62,348,000, then the average value of one of the towed away cars was MOST NEARLY

   A. $4,000   B. $7,200   C. $8,600   D. $11,000

   6.____

7. Two percent of all school children are problem children. Some 80% of these problem children become delinquents, and about 80% of the delinquent children become criminals. If the school population is 1,000,000 children, the number of this group who will eventually become criminals, according to this analysis, is

   A. 12,800 B. 1,280 C. 640 D. 128

8. A patrol car began a trip with 12 gallons of gasoline in the tank and ended with 7 1/2 gallons. The car traveled 17.3 miles for each gallon of gasoline. During the trip, gasoline was bought for $27.84 at a cost of $3.48 per gallon.
   The total number of miles traveled during this trip was MOST NEARLY

   A. 79 B. 196 C. 216 D. 229

9. A radio motor patrol car has to travel a distance of 15 miles in an emergency.
   If it does the first two-thirds of the distance at 40 mph and the last third at 60 mph, the total number of minutes required for the entire run is MOST NEARLY

   A. 15 B. 20 C. 22 1/2 D. 25

10. A patrol car had 11 1/2 gallons of gasoline at the beginning of a trip of 196 miles and 5 1/2 gallons at the end of the trip. During the trip, gasoline was bought for $21.70 at a cost of $4.65 per gallon.
    The average number of miles driven per gallon of gasoline is MOST NEARLY

    A. 14 B. 14.5 C. 15 D. 15.5

11. There are 15 patrolmen assigned to a certain operation. One-third earn $21,000 per year, three earn $22,050 per year, one earns $24,675 per year, and the rest earn $27,905 per year.
    The average annual salary of these patrolmen is MOST NEARLY

    A. $23,750 B. $24,000 C. $24,250 D. $24,500

12. In 1991, the cost of patrol car maintenance and repair was $2,500 more than in 1990, representing an increase of 10%.
    The cost of patrol car maintenance and repair in 1991 was MOST NEARLY

    A. $2,750 B. $22,500 C. $25,000 D. $27,500

13. A police precinct has an assigned strength of 180 men. Of this number, 25% are not available for duty due to illness, vacations, and other reasons. Of those who are available for duty, 1/3 are assigned outside of the precinct for special emergency duty.
    The ACTUAL available strength of the precinct in terms of men immediately available for precinct duty is

    A. 45 B. 60 C. 90 D. 135

14. Five police officers are taking target practice. The number of rounds fired by each and the percentage of perfect shots is as follows:

Officer	Rounds Fired	Perfect Shots
R	80	30%
S	70	40%
T	75	60%
U	92	25%
V	96	66-2/3%

    The average number of perfect shots fired by them is MOST NEARLY
    A. A. 30 B. 36 C. 42 D. 80

15. A dozen 5-gallon cans of paint weigh 494 pounds. Each can, when empty, weighs 3 pounds.
    The weight of one gallon of paint is MOST NEARLY ____ lbs.

    A. 5   B. 6 1/2   C. 7 1/2   D. 8

16. Assume that a parking space for six cars is to be outlined with white paint. The total area to be outlined is 24 feet by 40 feet, and the space for each car, also marked off by white lines, is to be 8 feet by 20 feet. The total length of white lines to be painted is MOST NEARLY ____ feet.

    A. 64   B. 128   C. 184   D. 232

17. A police car is ordered to report to the scene of a crime 5 miles away.
    If the car travels at an average rate of 40 miles per hour, the length of time it will take to reach its destination is MOST NEARLY ____ minutes.

    A. 3   B. 7   C. 10   D. 13

18. A block has metered parking for 19 cars from 7 A.M. to 9 P.M. at a charge of 10 cents per hour.
    Assuming that each car that is parked remains for a full hour and that on an average, for each hour of parking, there is a vacancy of five minutes for each meter, the amount of revenue from the meters for a day will be MOST NEARLY

    A. $10   B. $15   C. $20   D. $25

19. The standard formula for the stopping distance of a car with all four wheels locked is:

    $$S = \frac{V \times V}{30W}$$

    where S is the stopping distance in feet, V the speed of the car in miles per hour at the moment the brakes are applied, and W is a number which depends on the friction between the tires and the road.
    If the speed of a car is 50 miles per hour and W is equal to 5/3, the stopping distance will be MOST NEARLY ____ feet.

    A. 30   B. 40   C. 50   D. 60

20. The radiator of a police car contains 20 quarts of a mixture consisting of 80% water and 20% anti-freeze compound. Assume that you have been ordered to draw off some of the mixture and add pure anti-freeze compound until the mixture is 75% water and 25% anti-freeze compound.
    The number of quarts of the mixture which should be removed is MOST NEARLY

    A. 2   B. 3   C. 4   D. 5

KEY (CORRECT ANSWERS)

1.	B	11.	C
2.	A	12.	D
3.	B	13.	C
4.	C	14.	B
5.	C	15.	C
6.	C	16.	D
7.	A	17.	B
8.	C	18.	D
9.	B	19.	C
10.	C	20.	A

SOLUTIONS TO PROBLEMS

1. Average = [($270)(9)+($315)(2)+($385)(1)] ÷ 12 ≈ $287

2. Number of arrests in 2007 = (8270)(1.125)(.95) ≈ 8839, closest to 8840

3. Number of parking spaces = (.25)[(5)(6)(7)+(8)(11)(8)] = (.25)(914) = 228.5 ≈ 230

4. After 1 min., the stolen car has traveled 1 mile, while the police car has traveled 1/2 mile. Let x = additional minutes needed for the police car to catch up to the stolen vehicle. Using (rate)(time) = distance and the fact that the police car will travel 1/2 extra mile, (1 mi./min.)(x) = (1 1/2 mi./min.)(x) - 1/2. Solving, x = 1. Total time = 2 min.

5. $1 - \frac{1}{6} - \frac{1}{2} - \frac{1}{8} = \frac{5}{24} \approx 20\%$

6. ($10,382,000+$62,348,000)/8430 ≈ $8628, which is closest to $8600

7. (1,000,000)(.02)(.80)(.80) = 12,800

8. Total miles = (17.3)(12-7 1/2) + (17.3)($27.84/$3.48) = 77.85 + 138.4 ≈ 216

9. Total min. = (10)(60/40) + (5)(60/60) = 20

10. Total miles = 196. Number of gallons used = (11 1/2-5 1/2) + ($21.70/$4.65) = 13. Avg. mil/gallon = 196 ÷ 13 ≈ 15

11. Average annual salary = [(5)($21,000)+(3)($22,050)+(1)($24,675) +(6)($27,905)] ÷ 15 = $24,217, closest to $24,250

12. Cost in 1991 = $2500 + $2500/.10 = $27,500

13. Number of men actually available for precinct duty = (180)(.75X2/3) = 90

14. Avg. number of perfect shots = [(80)(.30)+(70)(.40)+(75)(.60) +(92)(.25)+(96)(2/3)] ÷ 5 = 36.8, closest to 36

15. Each full can weighs 494 ÷ 12 = 41 1/6 lbs. The weight of 5 gallons = 41 1/6 - 3 = 38 1/6 lbs. So, one gallon of paint weighs 38 1/6 ÷ 5 = 7.63, closest to 7 1/2 lbs.

16. Length of vertical lines = (3)(24') = 72 ft.
    Length of horizontal lines = (4)(40) = 160 ft.
    Total length of white lines = 232 ft.

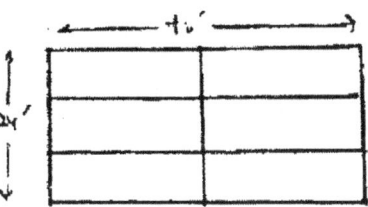

17. 40 mi/hr = 2/3 mi/min. Thus, a distance of 5 miles requires $5 \div \frac{2}{3} = 7\frac{1}{2} \approx 7$ min.

18. Each meter will produce revenue from 13 cars, due to the 5 min. vacancy between cars leaving and parking. Amount of revenue for all meters = (19)(13)(.10) = $24.70 ≈ $25

19. S = (50)(50)/(30)(5/3) = 50 ft.

20. Let x = amount of mixture removed and also amount of anti-freeze added back in. When x quarts of the mixture are removed, 20-x quarts are left, of which 4-.20x is antifreeze. After adding back x quarts of antifreeze, we have 4-.20x+x quarts of antifreeze and 20 quarts of mixture. Then, (4+.80x)/20 = .25. Solving, x = 1.25, closest to 2 quarts.

www.ingramcontent.com/pod-product-compliance
Lightning Source LLC
Chambersburg PA
CBHW080932020526
44116CB00033B/2323